VIRTUAL FREEDOM

VIRTUAL FREEDOM

*Net Neutrality and Free Speech
in the Internet Age*

Dawn C. Nunziato

STANFORD LAW BOOKS
An Imprint of Stanford University Press
Stanford, California

Stanford University Press
Stanford, California
©2009 by the Board of Trustees of the
Leland Stanford Junior University
All rights reserved.

Printed in the United States of America

Library of Congress Cataloging-in-Publication Data

Nunziato, Dawn C.
  Virtual freedom : net neutrality and free speech in the Internet age / Dawn C.
Nunziato.
     p. cm.
  Includes bibliographical references and index.
  ISBN 978-0-8047-5574-0 (cloth : alk. paper)—ISBN 978-0-8047-6385-1
(pbk.   )
  1. Freedom of speech—United States. 2. Internet—Censorship—United States.
3. Internet—Law and legislation—United States. I. Title.
  KF4772.N86 2009
  342.7308'53—dc22   2009012532

Designed by Bruce Lundquist
Typeset by Classic Typography in 10/14 Minion

To my wonderful children, Allie and Zach—
may you always be free to express yourselves
to my husband, Jon, my favorite author—for leading the way
and to my parents, Frances and Joseph—for always believing in me

"[W]e could be witnessing the beginning of the end of the Internet as we know it."
—Michael J. Copps, FCC commissioner, "The Beginning of the End of the Internet?" New America Foundation, Washington, D.C., October 9, 2003

"The potential for abuse of this private power over a central avenue of communication cannot be overlooked. . . ."
—*Turner Broadcasting System, Inc.* v. *F.C.C.*, 512 U.S. 622, 657 (1994)

"When we balance the constitutional rights of owners of property against those of the people to enjoy [First Amendment freedoms], . . . we remain mindful of the fact that the latter occupy a preferred position."
—*Marsh* v. *Alabama*, 326 U.S. 501, 509 (1946)

Contents

Acknowledgments

I WAS FORTUNATE TO HAVE THE SUPPORT OF MANY COLLEAGUES and family members in writing this book. I am grateful to my dean, Fred Lawrence, for his encouragement and generous financial support, as well as for his careful reading of and thoughtful comments on many drafts; to Professor Jerome Barron for his inspiration, advice, and guidance; to the participants of The George Washington University Law School Works in Progress Series, Vanderbilt Law School's The Internet Meets the First Amendment Conference, University of North Carolina Law School's Cyberspeech Symposium, and American University Washington College of Law's Distinguished Faculty Colloquium, especially Tony Varona; to Jonathan Lowy for his expert advice, constant encouragement, and editorial assistance; to Todd Peterson, for his patience and his insightful comments on many drafts, especially on Chapters 5 and 7; to Ellen Goodman, for her careful reading and expert commentary and critique; to Padmaja Balakrishnan, for tireless and outstanding secretarial support; to Brian Day, Megan Matthews, Michelle Rosenthal, Aaron Johnson, Bryan Mechell, Jeremy McGinley, and Jordan Segal for excellent research assistance; to Leonard Klein and Matthew Braun for superb library research assistance; and to Frances and Joseph Nunziato, for their advice on many versions of the book cover. Finally, I am indebted to the supportive and diligent editors at Stanford University Press, especially Kate Wahl and Joa Suorez, and to David Horne of Classic Typography, for expert editorial assistance.

Introduction

THE INTERNET PROVIDES THE GREATEST FORUM FOR COMMUNICATION and expression that the world has ever seen. At the same time, however, it ultimately is subject to the control of a handful of dominant, private entities that are unregulated under the First Amendment in their duty to facilitate communication and expression. That paradox lies at the center of this book.

More than at any time in our history, a small number of private entities enjoy unfettered control over what speech to facilitate—and what speech to restrict or disfavor—within our most important medium for expression. Although the Internet is generally seen as a forum for free expression, in reality speech on the Internet is subject to censorship and discrimination at a variety of chokepoints. Internet speech conduits—such as broadband service providers—are now responsible for facilitating a vast amount of expression. Unlike telephone companies or the postal service—which have long been legally required not to discriminate against the content they are charged with carrying—these Internet speech conduits are not similarly regulated. While many individuals may be content to entrust to the market their ability to communicate, recent developments suggest that such trust is misplaced and may very well lead to the "end of the Internet as we know it."

U.S.-based Internet speech conduits have recently invested extensive resources into developing methods to censor expression at the behest of speech-restrictive regimes such as China.[1] With such methods in hand, Internet speech conduits are increasingly poised to restrict speech by United States' Internet users, in order to advance their commercial, political, or other interests. In a recent incident, Comcast—one of the nation's dominant broadband providers—secretly restricted its subscribers from using legal file-sharing applications and prevented its email subscribers from receiving communications from two public interest groups critical of President George W. Bush. Comcast blocked emails from AfterDowningStreet, an organization that sought to lobby Congress to impeach the president for his conduct in bringing about the war with Iraq, and from the antiwar organization MeetWithCindy, established by antiwar activist Cindy Sheehan. Similarly, DSL provider AT&T censored the anti-Bush lyrics of Pearl Jam lead singer Eddie Vedder during a live cablecast of a concert. Google for its part has restricted speech that is critical of its role in censoring speech in overseas markets, as well as a host of other political expression. Speech on political and protest issues is traditionally accorded the highest degree of protection within our constitutional scheme, but because such speech restrictions as these occur at the hands of "private" conduits, they are not considered First Amendment violations under the prevailing understanding of the free speech guarantee. Nor are broadband providers regulated as "common carriers," as a result of a recent policy shift by the FCC.

How is it that we find ourselves at this juncture in free speech jurisprudence? And what, if anything, should be done about it? Over the past two decades, the U.S. government divested itself of ownership and control of the Internet's infrastructure and ceded ownership and control to a handful of private entities. At the time it did so, those private speech conduits were still regulated as common carriers and legally required to facilitate, and not to discriminate against, speech. Providers of narrowband and DSL Internet access were considered telecommunications providers subject to common carriage duties and were prohibited from discriminating against content. Since 2002, however, the FCC has embarked on a path of gradually removing such obligations from Internet speech conduits. And in its decision in *Brand X* in 2005, the United States Supreme Court approved of this course of action. Our free speech rights on the Internet are quietly slipping away.

Since 2005, individuals concerned about the future of the Internet have sought to remedy these (and related) problems of unfettered control by those few powers who serve as gatekeepers for the Internet's content. They have proposed "net neutrality" legislation and have sought to convince the FCC to impose meaningful constraints on such power. Although proposed net neutrality regulation is aimed at limiting conduits' power in a variety of ways, my focus is on constraining their power to discriminate against Internet speech on the basis of its content, which is essential to protecting individuals' free speech rights within our liberal democracy.

A few decades ago, the fact that conduits for speech were privately owned would not necessarily have insulated them from First Amendment obligations. In a number of early decisions, the Supreme Court adopted an *affirmative* conception of the free speech guarantee and imposed obligations on public *and powerful private* conduits of speech to facilitate individuals' right to speak without discrimination. In recent years, however, the Court has unwisely trended toward a *negative* conception of the First Amendment, in which individuals' free speech rights apply only against government censorship, and private speech conduits are left unrestricted in their ability to regulate expression.

This book is intended to serve as a wakeup call and a call to action for those who are concerned about our free speech rights as U.S. citizens in this unprecedented forum for expression. Courts and policymakers—and members of the public—should embrace an affirmative conception of the First Amendment for the Internet age. The prevailing negative conception of the First Amendment fails to recognize and protect the important role that the state should serve in regulating these dominant private conduits of expression in order to facilitate the conditions necessary for democratic self-government. Simply put, entrusting all speech decisions to a market dominated by a few powerful speech regulators disserves democracy and the freedom of speech that democracy requires. Those of us who are concerned with the role that free speech plays in facilitating liberal democracy must rethink the appropriate conception of the First Amendment in the context of the media landscape of today—and tomorrow. Decisions regarding what speech is allowed—and what speech is censored—should not be committed solely to the dictates of the dominant private entities that control expression on the Internet. A fundamental rethinking of the meaning of the First Amendment's protections, and of free speech values in general, is therefore in order.

VIRTUAL FREEDOM

1 Speech and Censorship on the Internet

ACCORDING TO THE CONVENTIONAL WISDOM, THE INTERNET is a forum for free expression of unprecedented scope and importance. And much about the conventional wisdom is accurate. Since the limitations on the permissible uses of the Internet were lifted and the Internet was opened up as a forum for expression of all kinds,[1] members of the public from every corner of the world have flocked to it to express themselves and to access the expression of others.[2] The Internet enables individuals to use all manner and forms of expression—text, images, voice, audio, and video—to communicate with one another on a global scale. As one federal district court explained in reviewing an early Internet First Amendment challenge, "It is no exaggeration to conclude that the Internet has achieved, and continues to achieve, the most participatory marketplace of mass speech that this country—and indeed the world—has yet seen."[3]

The conventional wisdom accurately maintains that the Internet serves as an important forum for expression in large part because of the unprecedented ease of entry into this forum for expression. Yet such expression is ultimately controlled by—and may be facilitated or frustrated by—a small handful of powerful conduits, that is, the broadband providers, Internet backbone providers, email providers, and search engines that make it all happen. Within the United States market for Internet expression, a small number of broadband providers have the power ultimately to control which expression is facilitated and which is not. In recent years, the regulation of the Internet has evolved so as to grant these private entities unfettered control over individuals' expression, to the point at which the potential for private conduits to censor speech in this medium is unprecedented. Although initially conceived—

by both courts and commentators[4]—as a speech utopia, the Internet is now in danger of becoming a dystopia for expression because of this concentration of power and private regulation and control. We would do well to heed the Supreme Court's admonition from a decade ago involving regulation of other private conduits of speech:

> The potential for abuse of private power over a central avenue of communication cannot be overlooked. . . . Each medium of expression must be assessed for First Amendment purposes by standards suited to it, for each may present its own problems. The First Amendment's command that government not impede the freedom of speech does not disable the government from taking steps to ensure that private interests not restrict, through physical control of a critical pathway of communication, the free flow of information and ideas.[5]

Assessing the features of the Internet as a communications medium demonstrates that—as within the cable television medium to which the Court refers above—private Internet speech conduits such as broadband providers indeed exercise substantial "control of critical pathways of communication" and enjoy the power to threaten "the free flow of information and ideas"— power that should be held in check under a proper understanding of the First Amendment.[6]

Censorship by private broadband providers is growing. Most Internet users are unaware of the restrictions on speech imposed by their Internet service providers, and may be surprised to learn that such censorship does not violate the First Amendment or communications laws (as currently interpreted by the courts). The majority of courts, which have adopted a negative conception of the First Amendment, have been unwilling to find First Amendment violations in restrictions of speech implemented by broadband providers or other private regulators of Internet expression. Similarly, policymakers within the Federal Communications Commission (FCC) have shifted toward a negative conception of the First Amendment, in which communications conduits such as broadband providers are unregulated in their obligation to facilitate the speech flowing through their pipes. Furthermore, Congress in 1996 explicitly encouraged Internet service providers (ISPs) to restrict access to content that the providers consider objectionable and expressly insulated the providers from liability for doing so[7]—even though such restrictions of speech would constitute First Amendment violations if they were undertaken by public conduits of speech. The result is that the small handful of private entities that exercise control over the pipelines for Internet expression now essentially enjoy free rein to censor such expression—and are increasingly doing just that.

It wasn't always so. In the early years of the Internet, conduits for Internet speech were governed by regulations that prohibited them from discriminating against content or applications (and were not insulated from liability for restricting such expression). A decade ago, the FCC regulated the telephone companies that provided dial-up Internet access as "common carriers" and prohibited them from discriminating against—in the form of blocking, censoring, or degrading—Internet content or applications. Just as the telephone companies, from the early days of communications regulation, have been subject to common carriage obligations under the Communications Act of 1934[8] requiring them to facilitate the transmission of all (legal) conversations, so too were they required under the common carriage doctrine to facilitate the transmission of all (legal) Internet content. Indeed, the Internet developed and flourished as "the most participatory form of mass speech yet developed"[9] under this regime in which nondiscrimination obligations were imposed on Internet speech conduits. Under this nondiscrimination regime, Internet users could post, transmit, and access any and all (legal) content of their choosing. As FCC commissioner Michael Copps described the state of affairs prior to the widespread deployment of broadband Internet access:

> In the dial-up world, [each Internet user] has jurisdiction over the applications that prevail, and what power that is! No network owner telling you where to go and what to do. You run the show. This freedom—this openness—has always been at the heart of what the Internet community and its original innovators have celebrated. Anyone can access the Internet . . . and read or say what they want. No one can corner control of the Internet for their purposes.[10]

All that began to change in 2002, when the FCC concluded that one class of broadband providers cable broadband providers—were not subject to common carriage nondiscrimination requirements under the Communications Act. Although the lower federal courts rejected the FCC's interpretation, the United States Supreme Court in 2005 upheld the FCC's decision to deregulate cable broadband providers in the *Brand X* case.[11] Upon receiving the green light to remove common carriage nondiscrimination obligations from broadband providers, the FCC moved quickly to do so. Today, no broadband providers are subject to the requirement historically imposed on telecommunications conduits—to facilitate all legal content without discrimination.

Nor have the FCC or the courts ever imposed nondiscrimination obligations on any Internet email provider. While the postal service has an obligation to deliver all legal content,[12] and the telephone companies have the obligation to facilitate all legal conversations,[13] email providers have no obligation to deliver email without discrimination. Even though email has completely outpaced snail mail in terms of the amount of content delivered daily, email providers are under no legal obligation to deliver content and have increasingly exercised their power to censor content, frequently in ways that are not transparent to the sender or intended recipient.[14] Furthermore, neither the FCC nor the courts has imposed any duties on dominant search engines such as Google to serve up requested content in a neutral, nondiscriminatory manner—despite the representations of such search engines that they will serve as purely neutral conduits for the billions of pages of content available on the Internet.

These decisions by policymakers and courts to allow the market to decide whether and what speech to censor are especially unwise in light of the characteristics of the marketplace for Internet speech. The market for residential broadband Internet access is essentially dominated by the cable-DSL duopoly, and these providers have an incentive to censor or degrade applications and content that conflict with their financial, political, or other interests. Because broadband providers offer their own content and applications, they have the financial incentive to restrict or impede competing content and applications from other providers. Broadband providers have the ability, have the incentive, and—under the current regime—appear to enjoy the legal right to engage in a variety of types of discrimination against the content and applications that they are charged with carrying. And most, if not all, broadband providers explicitly claim the right in their terms of service to censor whatever speech they choose. AT&T, for example, claims the right in its "sole discretion to refuse, block, move, or remove any content that is available via the service."[15] (So don't say you weren't on notice.)

Since 2005, when the Supreme Court placed its imprimatur on the FCC's decision to remove common carriage nondiscrimination obligations from broadband providers, individuals and groups concerned about the future of free speech on the Internet have sought to reimpose nondiscrimination obligations on Internet conduits in the form of "net neutrality" regulation. With the specter of such legislation hanging over them, one would expect that broadband providers would seek to minimize such acts of censorship, as public scrutiny is trained on them more than ever before. Notwithstanding such scrutiny, however, in the post–*Brand X* era in which they are no longer legally prohibited from discriminating on the basis of content, broadband providers (and other powerful conduits for expression) have increasingly engaged in acts of censoring, blocking, or degrading speech and content on the Internet.

Content Regulation by Broadband Providers

Incidents of censorship and other discrimination by broadband providers are difficult to establish or document with precision. First, because average users are generally unaware that their broadband provider is blocking content, and because they may not know what content is being blocked, it is difficult to identify instances of content restriction. Second, providers, when questioned, may simply deny that they are blocking disfavored content and refuse to provide the information necessary for Internet users to confirm or deny such restrictions—or to allow subscribers to make informed decisions about whether to switch to a less censorial provider (assuming that another such provider is available).[16] Notwithstanding these difficulties, several instances of alleged discrimination by broadband providers and other conduits of Internet expression have been identified. In particular, broadband providers have censored expression on matters of *political and societal importance* that undoubtedly would be protected by the First Amendment if restricted by a public actor. They have also censored expression that is *critical of them, or that potentially threatens their commercial interests,* expression which is also highly valuable within our constitutional framework.

Censorship of Political and Other Socially Valuable Expression

Comcast—one of the nation's leading broadband Internet providers—has restricted the transmission of politically charged, time-sensitive communications to its subscribers. In one incident, AfterDowningStreet, a web based organization that advocates an end to the war in Iraq, sought to communicate with thousands of its supporters regarding its then-imminent plans to lobby Congress to consider impeachment proceedings against President Bush on the third anniversary of the incident involving the "Downing Street memos."[17] Only after several weeks had elapsed did the organization become aware that intended recipients of its email communications who had Comcast email accounts had not received these communications. As a result of Comcast's failure to deliver these emails, AfterDowningStreet's attempts to set up time-sensitive conference calls were frustrated, as were its plans to lobby Congress.

Comcast's censorship of these emails was especially troubling given Comcast's dominance in the Washington, D.C., area.

It ultimately became apparent to AfterDowningStreet that Comcast had filtered the email that Comcast email subscribers received and censored all communications that contained the term *www.AfterDowningStreet.org.* To make matters worse, neither the intended recipients nor the sender of the email communications was informed that Comcast was censoring these communications. Only after several weeks, when members of the organization and other interested parties failed to show up for meetings and other events, did AfterDowningStreet begin to suspect that its communications were being thwarted by Comcast.

When confronted with the problem, Comcast first refused to discuss it at all, citing its policy of not discussing such matters with members of the press.[18] Ultimately, after repeated inquiries from AfterDowningStreet, Comcast pinned responsibility for this censorship on BrightMail, the company responsible for maintaining software filters for Comcast email accounts. BrightMail (a division of Symantec) in turn claimed that it had chosen to block email from AfterDowningStreet or with *AfterDowningStreet.org* in the text because it had allegedly received complaints about email communications sent by AfterDowningStreet (while refusing to make available any such complaint). To make matters worse, BrightMail serves not just Comcast but other major ISPs (including Cox Cable and AOL) and apparently imposed this same restriction on email accounts serviced by these other ISPs as well. As a result of this censorship, AfterDowningStreet was thwarted in its objectives and lost members and substantial support.[19]

This instance of censorship, like many others, is particularly troubling because of the lack of transparency to the affected senders and recipients. If you are unaware that Comcast is censoring your speech, you lack the information that might prompt you to switch to another broadband provider—if indeed one is available to you. As Seth Kreimer—who has criticized such "censorship by proxy"—explains, such "private censorship takes place at low levels of visibility. It is neither coordinated nor reviewed. Often, neither speakers nor listeners will know that the message has not been conveyed, and there is no way to determine how dialogue has been deformed."[20] Comcast's censorship of AfterDowningStreet's messages is also troubling because of the possibility that individuals hostile to AfterDowningStreet's message might have effectively shut out its speech by relaying "complaints" to Comcast or BrightMail about such messages.[21] If Comcast (or its proxies) intentionally censored such political speech because of its unpopularity or because it was subject to user complaints, this would constitute a substantial distortion of the marketplace for expression upon which our liberal democracy depends.

A month after the incident involving AfterDowningStreet, another antiwar organization experienced difficulties communicating via email with Comcast subscribers. The organization MeetwithCindy, headed by Cindy Sheehan, an antiwar advocate whose son was killed in the war in Iraq, had its email communications censored by Comcast, Cox, and other email providers.[22] Emails that contained the term *meetwithcindy.org* were blocked by Comcast, Cox, and others. Once again, as with the AfterDowningStreet incident, neither the sender nor the intended recipients of the communications were informed that the emails were being censored, as such blocking was implemented in a manner that was not transparent either to the sender or to the intended recipients.

Nor is such censorship limited to restricting left-leaning or anti-Bush expression. Two other major Internet service providers—SBC Global and Earth-Link—blocked delivery of emails from conservative news sites.[23] Notwithstanding the fact that EarthLink and SBC Global's subscribers had expressly chosen to receive email and news updates from conservative news site News-WithViews, these ISPs blocked emails from this source, and SBC Global also apparently blocked emails from at least four other conservative newsletters.[24]

Other ISPs and Internet gatekeepers have thwarted the ability of individuals to engage in expression on matters related to the war in Iraq, as well as the (unrelated) events of 9/11. Shortly after the war began, Internet service provider Vortech censored the news site YellowTimes.org because it had posted pictures of U.S. prisoners captured by the Iraqis.[25] Similarly, in the wake of the commencement of hostilities, Google censored all images of U.S. soldiers torturing Iraqi prisoners of war.[26] Shortly after the September 11 terrorist attacks, AOL and Yahoo! censored message boards that hosted anti-American and anti-Islam postings.[27]

In another example of blatant censorship of political speech, AT&T—one of the country's largest broadband providers—censored its live Lollapalooza cablecast of a Pearl Jam concert performance. During the performance, lead singer Eddie Vedder added lyrics mildly critical of President Bush, including "George Bush, leave this world alone" and "George Bush, find yourself another home" (in place of "Teacher, leave those kids alone," in its performance of "Daughter," which morphed into a cover of Pink Floyd's "Another Brick in the Wall"). In webcasting the Pearl Jam performance, AT&T censored

Vedder's anti-Bush lyrics,[28] apparently believing that they would be offensive to some viewers. When such censorship was ultimately discovered, AT&T claimed that the censorship was the result of a "mistake."[29]

Internet gatekeepers have also censored speech on religious and societal matters. Network Solutions, Inc. (NSI), one of the most popular U.S. domain name registrars and gatekeepers for acquiring a website in the first place,[30] suspended the domain name registration and shut down the website of Dutch lawmaker Geert Wilders because NSI believed that the website available under the domain name (www.fitnathemovie.com) was *going to be used* to make available a short film critical of Islam. At the time NSI suspended the domain name, however, the only content available on the website was a picture of the Koran, along with the text "Allahu Akhbar" (God is Great), and the words "Geert Wilders presents Fitna—Coming Soon."[31] Apparently, news of the website's existence and the film's content led NSI to suspend the account preemptively.[32] NSI stated that it suspended the domain name in response to complaints it had received and because the content that it believed was going to be made available under the domain name might violate its terms of service,[33] which prohibit, among other things, the "posting or storage of . . . objectionable material of any kind or nature."[34]

On the related issue of content discrimination by a wireless carrier, Verizon—one of the nation's two largest wireless carriers—rejected the request from NARAL Pro-Choice America to allow Verizon cell phone customers voluntarily to receive the organization's text messages. Asserting its authority to block messages from any group that seeks to "distribute content that, in [Verizon's] discretion, may be seen as controversial or unsavory to any of our users," Verizon initially refused to facilitate the transmission of such messages to *willing* recipients of NARAL Pro-Choice America's messages. Text messaging has become an extremely popular tool used by advocacy groups and political organizations to reach out to their supporters, and Verizon's actions accordingly had a powerful detrimental effect on the ability of this advocacy group to communicate with willing recipients of its messages.[35] Only after Verizon's decision was subject to public exposure and criticism in the mainstream media—including in a front-page article in the *New York Times*—did the company reverse course. Even while doing so, Verizon steadfastly maintained that it enjoys the discretion to determine which text messages to facilitate and which to prohibit.[36]

Censorship of Expression That Criticizes or Competes with
Providers' Commercial Interests

Conduits of Internet expression have also engaged in acts of censoring expression that they believe threatens their commercial or business interests—including expression that is critical of them.

In one such instance, AOL—once the nation's (and the world's) largest Internet service provider—blocked emails sent by those who opposed certain AOL email policies.[37] AOL blocked emails containing links to an online petition by the organization DearAOL.com, a web-based coalition of six hundred organizations (including the AFL-CIO) that was critical of AOL's proposed email policies. DearAOL.com opposed AOL's proposal to create a two-tiered mail system composed of (1) a pay-per-send system that would allow senders to route around AOL's spam filters and (2) a lower-tier free system that would not. Messages sent to AOL users that included a link to "DearAOL.com" were not delivered by AOL, while messages without such links were successfully delivered.[38]

In a similar incident involving (nearby) Canadian broadband provider Telus, Canada's second-largest telecommunications company censored expression that was critical of its business interests. Telus, which was then involved in a heated labor dispute with the Telecommunications Workers Union, blocked access to the website of Voices for Change, an organization supporting the union. In blocking the Voices for Change website, Telus also blocked access to over 750 other sites that shared an IP address with Voices for Change, including a U.S.-based breast cancer site, recycling sites, and alternative Medicare sites.[39]

In a much-discussed incident, Madison River Communications, a midwestern DSL provider, blocked hundreds of its subscribers from accessing Vonage, a Voice over Internet Protocol (VoIP) provider. Madison River did so by engaging in port blocking—a type of blocking that enables Internet providers to block content based on the Internet port over which the content is transmitted. Because VoIP is transmitted over a distinct Internet "port,"[40] broadband providers can easily implement port-blocking technology to block VoIP transmissions from providers with which they may be in direct competition. These blockages prevented Vonage customers—who relied on their broadband providers to facilitate their telephone communications—from making any calls at all, even to 911.[41] Vonage has also claimed that at least two other broadband providers have blocked its subscribers' calls.[42]

At least two major broadband network operators—Verizon and AT&T—include clauses in their terms of service authorizing them to terminate the accounts of subscribers who criticize them or their business partners.[43]

Broadband providers have also thwarted the transmission of content and applications that they believe will harm their commercial interests. Comcast, for example, engaged in acts of secretly degrading, delaying, and outright blocking its subscribers' ability to upload files to share with other users via peer-to-peer file-sharing technology. Comcast's interference with file sharing by users applied across the board, to authorized and unauthorized, legal and illegal file sharing. Comcast prohibited, among other things, subscribers' ability to download the King James Bible using a popular file-sharing program.[44] It also prohibited independent songwriters, movie producers, and software developers from using file-sharing technology to share their work with others. When a Comcast user engaged in sending packets to others using file-sharing technology, Comcast shut down the connection between that user and other non-Comcast users, by using deep packet inspection technology to interfere with communications at the transport layer. As Vuze, Inc.—a primary source of legal video downloads whose services were affected by Comcast's actions—explains: "Comcast does this by hacking into its own network and using a clandestine "Man in the Middle" tactic whereby each party is sent a communication "RST" (reset) message which falsely tells the other party to shut down the connection."[45] As a result of such interference, each affected user's computer received a message invisible to the user that looked like it came from another computer instructing it to stop communicating. The message, however, actually originated with Comcast. As MSNBC characterized Comcast's interference, "if it were a telephone conversation, it would be like the operator breaking into the conversation, telling each talker in the voice of the other: 'Sorry, I have to hang up. Good-bye.'"[46]

In a similar incident, broadband provider BellSouth prohibited its subscribers from accessing MySpace.com, the phenomenally popular social networking site, and YouTube, the most popular site for posting and accessing user-generated videos,[47] apparently because of concerns about bandwidth consumption.

In what was apparently a ham-handed attempt to combat spam, DSL provider Verizon blocked nearly all email from certain regions in Europe and Asia—without telling its subscribers of its plan to do so. Verizon only agreed to remove legitimate ISPs from its software filter's blacklist long after would-be recipients discovered that these emails were being censored.[48]

In another recent incident, Comcast blocked the access of subscribers in the Boston area to Google and associated Gmail services. When subscribers complained about the blockage, Comcast's customer support personnel blamed Google and suggested that Comcast subscribers switch from Gmail to Comcast email.[49]

Several broadband providers have also publicly expressed their intentions to sell preferential Internet access speed to the highest bidder, or to reserve the same for their own (or affiliated) content, and to (respectively) degrade Internet access for those unwilling to pay for this privilege. AT&T's Project Lightspeed and Verizon's FiOS, for example, reserve substantial portions of last-mile bandwidth for the broadcast downloading of their own preferred video services.[50]

In a similar vein, Bill Smith, chief technology officer of BellSouth, claimed that his company enjoys the discretion to charge a company like Yahoo! for the opportunity to have its search engine site load faster than that of Google, and to degrade the quality of a rival VoIP provider unless such a rival pays BellSouth's asking price.[51]

· · ·

Under current First Amendment jurisprudence and telecommunications policy, the preceding restrictions of content or applications by broadband providers and other powerful gatekeepers of Internet expression are legally permissible—given the Supreme Court–sanctioned removal by the FCC of common carriage nondiscrimination obligations from broadband providers and the general demise of the affirmative conception of the free speech guarantee within First Amendment jurisprudence. Decisions about what speech to censor or degrade, and what speech to transmit or favor, are now left solely to the discretion of the companies providing broadband Internet access—in most cases, for most residential Internet users, the cable-DSL duopoly—and to the other powerful private conduits of speech on the Internet. And because of ill-advised trends in First Amendment jurisprudence over the past few decades toward the negative conception of the free speech guarantee, censorship of expression by broadband providers and other powerful "private" Internet speech conduits is no longer held to be in violation of the First Amendment.

Censorship by Dominant Search Engines

Beyond broadband providers, other powerful private conduits of Internet expression are also engaging in acts of censorship. Google, in its capacity both as the dominant Internet search engine and as the operator of its popular news aggregation site, has engaged in various acts of censorship. Like providers of broadband Internet access, Internet search engines enjoy substantial control over critical pathways and forums for communication on the Internet. Although a diverse range of expression exists on the Internet, such expression is accessed by individuals primarily by the use of Internet search engines. Like broadband providers, Internet search engines thus also enjoy the sort of "bottleneck" or "gatekeeper" control or "control over critical pathways of communication"[52] that cable operators enjoy over the market for cable television, and which the Supreme Court expressed concern about in 1994 in *Turner Broadcasting System* v. *F.C.C.* In that case, the Court upheld against First Amendment challenge government intervention into the market for cable television to protect the free speech interests of the public. Although search engines (like the cable operators in *Turner*) do not enjoy absolute control over the content to which their users have access on the Internet (users can type in the domain name associated with a website, if they know it), they nonetheless exert significant control over the information their users are able to access.

As the largest and most popular Internet search engine in the United States, Google serves as the first place most people turn to find information on the Internet, and it now enjoys the dominant position in the search engine market.[53] Its main search engine is the portal to which U.S. Internet users turn more than six billion times each month for information,[54] and Google serves as the gatekeeper for such information. However, Google's policies regarding the content that it indexes limit users' access to certain types of information.

Censorship by Google News

In addition to providing links to web pages as results for search terms, Google makes information available through its popular service Google News. Google News is a computer-generated news site that aggregates headlines from over 4,500 English-language news sources worldwide, with such information purportedly gathered and displayed via objective, computerized search algorithms. In particular, and unlike a newspaper publisher, Google News maintains, "[O]ur headlines are selected entirely by computer algorithms, based on factors like how often and where a story appears online. Google News has no human editors selecting [or prioritizing] stories. . . . "[55] Google claims that because such news articles are "selected and ranked by computers, . . . stories are sorted without regard to political viewpoint or ideology."[56] Millions of U.S. Internet users rely upon Google's representations that it presents news headlines in an unbiased manner. Indeed, the service of providing news and other information on matters of public importance is critical to the development of an informed electorate. Yet despite its apparent commitment to neutrality in aggregating and presenting the news, Google News has allegedly censored the content of several news sites.

In one such incident, Google News discontinued listing stories from Inner City Press, a United Nations–focused media organization, after an Inner City Press staffer questioned Google on its failure to sign on to the human rights and anti-censorship principles of the Global Compact. When questioned by Inner City Press regarding this censorship, Google simply responded, "We periodically review news sources, particularly following user complaints, to ensure Google News offers a high quality experience for our users. When we reviewed your site we've found that we can no longer include it in Google News."[57]

In another incident involving political speech, PrisonPlanet.com claimed that Google censored various news stories about prominent actor Charlie Sheen's criticisms of the government's response to 9/11. Not until Google was criticized in a radio broadcast for such censorship did Google index websites reporting on Sheen's comments.[58]

Google News has used geolocation technology to block content from being accessed not only within speech-restrictive countries such as China but also within the United States. The World Prout Assembly website claims, for example, that a news article discussing efforts in Congress to use U.S. military force to end genocide in Darfur was accessible via a Google News link in other countries but was blocked by Google News for users seeking access to it in the United States.[59] The *New Media Journal* has also been blocked by Google News, in connection with articles that were critical of Islam.[60]

Given the importance that information on public affairs serves in producing an informed electorate capable of the task of democratic self-government, and given Google News's express promise to provide such information in an objective, unbiased, uncensored manner in which (unlike a newspaper publisher) it is not performing an editorial function, these acts of censorship are particularly troubling.

Censorship in Google's General Search Engine
and Sponsored Links

Google has also engaged in acts of manipulating its search results and rankings and censoring its associated "sponsored links"—the brief text messages that are keyed to search terms entered by Google users. In an example of the first, SearchKing, a search engine optimization website, alleged that Google reduced its "PageRank" from eight to zero—thereby effectively banishing it from the universe of sites accessible via a Google search—because Google perceived SearchKing as a competitor.[61] Google's search engine has also banished from existence websites that are critical of its practices.[62]

In addition, Google has censored the sponsored links it makes available on its site. Because of Google's predominance in the search engine market, the ability to secure a sponsored link responsive to Internet users' interests and keyed to search terms is a critically important vehicle for expressing one's message on the Internet. Indeed, for many advocacy groups and less well-known causes whose sites do not otherwise enjoy substantial web traffic, sponsored links serve as an important means of drawing attention to their content and their cause. Google has wielded its power in connection with the billions of searches users perform each month to restrict such expression—including political speech that would fall within the core of the First Amendment's protection. Referring to its policy of refusing to accept sponsored links that contain "sensitive issues" or that "advocate against any individual, group, or organization,"[63] Google has refused to host a range of political, religious, and critical social commentary in the form of the sponsored links themselves, as well as the websites linked to by these sponsored links.[64] Google has required prospective content providers to alter the content within their sponsored link text—as well as within their websites themselves—as a condition for hosting such links. Furthermore, Google's speech regulations and restrictions apply not only to Google's site but also to Google's partners, including America Online, Ask Jeeves, Netscape, CompuServe, AT&T, *The New York Times,* and EarthLink.[65]

One of the "sensitive issues" on which Google substantially restricts communications is the discussion of abortion. Although Google apparently accepts sponsored links on abortion-related topics from certain religious and pro-choice viewpoints, it refuses to accept sponsored links that discuss abortion from a religious viewpoint or that make any reference to religion.[66] Thus an individual searching for the term *abortion* within Google's search engine will be presented on Google's home page with sponsored links on abortion from one viewpoint or perspective but not from others.[67] The Christian Institute, a British lobbying and education organization, recently sought to purchase a link from Google that would have read, "UK abortion law—news and views on abortion from the Christian Institute. www.christian.org.uk." Adhering to its policy of not accepting sponsored links for websites that contain "abortion and religion-related content" together, Google refused to allow the organization to acquire the link. The Christian Institute has brought suit against Google, claiming that Google's refusal to accept its sponsored link violates Britain's anti-discrimination laws.[68]

Google also singles out for special treatment links that are sponsored by the Church of Scientology and requires that particular language appear in links sponsored by this church. No other religion is subject to the requirement that particular language be contained within its sponsored links.[69]

Google has substantially restricted political expression in its sponsored links. In implementing its policy of refusing to host sponsored links that "advocate against any individual, group, or organization," Google has wielded this power to restrict speech in favor of certain political positions. W. Frederick Zimmerman, who maintains a political website called the Zimmerblog, sought to advertise his book *Basic Documents About the Detainees at Guantanamo and Abu Ghraib*, which contained the full text of several key court opinions, including *Hamdi v. Bush, Rumsfeld v. Padilla*, and *Rasul v. Bush*, as well as various applicable Geneva Convention documents. Once Google became aware of the material Zimmerman was linking to via this sponsored link, it suspended Zimmerman's account, informing him that "Google policy does not permit the advertisement of websites that contain 'sensitive issues.'"[70] Similarly, Google refused to allow Republican Senator Susan Collins's campaign to acquire a sponsored link that was critical of left-leaning advocacy group MoveOn.org. Collins wished to acquire sponsored links with text such as "Help Susan Collins stand up to the MoveOn.org money machine." Google apparently declined to allow such sponsored links on the grounds that they contained the trademark-protected term *MoveOn.org*. Yet Google has allowed others to refer to trademark-protected terms in a critical manner (and such critical references would clearly be protected by the First Amendment).[71]

In another such incident, John Perr, author of the Perrspectives website, which contains "left-of-center" political commentary, sought to advertise his website via a Google-sponsored link with an advertisement titled "The Liberal

Resource—Analysis, Commentary, and Satire—Complete Liberal Resource Center." The linked-to website contained an article written by Perr that was critical of George W. Bush and that characterized the president as "secretive, paranoid, and vengeance-filled." Once Google became aware of this language within Perr's article, it informed Perr that his link was being removed because it linked to a website that contained text that was critical of Bush and therefore inappropriately "advocates against an individual, group, or organization."[72]

Similar incidents of Google restricting political expression in the form of sponsored links abound. Political activist Christopher Langdon sought and was refused the right to purchase from Google sponsored links for two political websites: (1) www.ncjusticefraud.com, in which Langdon claimed that the attorney general of North Carolina lied to the United States Supreme Court; and (2) www.chinaisevil.com, a website maintained by Langdon that is critical of the Chinese government. Google's refusal to allow Langdon to secure a sponsored link to the latter site is noteworthy in light of Google's collaboration with the Chinese government to create a censored version of Google's search engine for use within China.[73]

When *The Nation* sought to secure a sponsored link headlined "Bush Lies," Google refused, referring again to its policy against links that advocate against any individual, group, or organization.[74] When the owner of a T-shirt shop in Los Angeles sought to secure a sponsored link from Google, he was told that Google would not accept his link unless he removed from his site all T-shirts with slogans critical of George W. Bush.[75] When Unknown News sought to link to a site providing anti-Iraq-war bumper stickers with a sponsored link headlined "Who Would Jesus Bomb?," Google censored the link, claiming (with unintended irony) that it was in violation of its policy against "sites that promote hate, violence, racial intolerance, or that advocate against any individual, group, or organization." When Unknown News responded to Google's decision by explaining that it merely "advocates against the killing of thousands of Iraqis," Google (apparently implementing its own version of the Fairness Doctrine)[76] explained that it would only reinstate the link if the website was edited "to show both sides of the argument" over attacking Iraq.[77]

Google's policy of refusing to host sponsored links that advocate against any individual, group, or organization has impaired the ability of nonprofit advocacy organizations to communicate their message to Internet users. Because many advocacy groups advocate against other entities, it is difficult for such entities to express their message in a manner that complies with Google's policy. For example, the nonprofit environmental group Oceana sought to secure a sponsored link criticizing Royal Caribbean Cruise Line's environmental policies under the headline "Help us protect the world's oceans." Two days after hosting Oceana's sponsored link, apparently in response to pressure from Royal Caribbean, Google pulled the Oceana advertisement, per its policy prohibiting links criticizing groups or companies.[78]

• • •

In short, Google—as the dominant Internet search engine and news aggregator—enjoys and exercises substantial control over the content of news headlines presented via Google News and over search result links and sponsored links that appear on Google News's and Google's main search page—the first place to which U.S. citizens turn over six billion times a month for information on the Internet.[79]

Censorship by ISPs Under the Digital Millennium Copyright Act

In addition to broadband providers, dominant search engines, and news aggregators censoring Internet content at their own volition, many ISPs are induced by content owners to censor content in accordance with a recent amendment to the Copyright Act. The overwhelming majority of ISPs accede to such requests, given the strong incentives for them to do so provided under that amendment. Prior to the passage of the Digital Millennium Copyright Act (DMCA), service providers had no particular incentive to accede to censorship requests made by content owners. Thus when the Church of Scientology in 1995 objected to the critical use of the church's texts by a disaffected Scientology minister, the church's request that the minister's ISP remove such allegedly infringing texts fell on deaf ears. In the absence of any particular incentive to comply with this request, Netcom chose to protect the free speech and fair use rights of the former minister who posted texts critical of the church and refused to censor such expression.[80]

Service providers' decision-making calculus was radically altered in 1998 by Congress's passage of the DMCA.[81] Section 512 of the DMCA establishes a quid pro quo that facilitates censorship and that benefits and protects ISPs at the expense of the free speech and fair use rights of Internet users. The Act grants service providers the means to limit their liability for direct and indirect copyright infringement if they agree to remove content posted by their subscribers that content owners claim is infringing.[82] Under the notice and take-down provisions of Section 512, a copyright owner may provide a notice to a service provider that it believes the service provider is hosting or otherwise facilitating infringing content.[83] Upon receipt of such notice, the service provider must expeditiously cease its hosting (or other means of facilitating) such allegedly infringing content in order for the service provider to secure the benefits of the statute's limitations of liability. Although the statute also provides a mechanism for the Internet user who made such content available to defend his or her use (via a "counter-notification"[84]), this mechanism is problematic and has had limited effect on the censorship of content enabled under Section 512.[85]

Prior to the passage of the DMCA in 1998, in order to secure the removal of allegedly infringing content made available on the Internet, a copyright owner would have needed to prevail in a copyright infringement lawsuit (or prevail on the ISP to remove such content). Armed with the DMCA, copyright owners today merely need to send a notice to the ISP requesting take down, and the ISP that facilitates such content—having the incentive to secure the limitations of liability promised it under 512—will likely readily comply, by "expeditiously" removing or disabling access to the content.[86] In effect, this provision enables a copyright owner to secure the equivalent of a temporary restraining order—a court order mandating that the allegedly infringing content be removed but without benefit of judicial process.

In another powerful example of "censorship by proxy,"[87] thousands of copyright owners have successfully induced ISPs to censor critical or unflattering uses of their copyrighted content—even in cases in which such uses would clearly be considered non-infringing, fair uses under the Copyright Act. After the passage of the DMCA, for example, when the Church of Scientology sought to wield its power under Section 512 to censor allegedly infringing content, it was readily able to do so. In 2003, the Church submitted a 512 notice and take-down request to Google, requesting that Google remove the anti-Scientology website Xenu.net from its index—so that this site critical of the Church would essentially be rendered invisible to the vast majority of Internet users who rely on Google to present the world of Internet content to them. Under the DMCA regime, Google complied with the church's request and removed its link to the site—so that users searching for information on Scientology via Google's search engine would no longer be presented with this critical website on the search results page.[88]

Under the DMCA notice and take-down regime, copyright owners—and businesses more generally—have wielded their rights under Section 512 to censor speech that is critical of them. In another example of such censorship, after the controversial 2000 presidential election, Diebold—the manufacturer of much-criticized voting machines—successfully wielded Section 512 to induce many ISPs to censor discussions of flaws in its voting machines that were critical of and embarrassing to Diebold—even where such discussions were clearly protected as fair use.[89] Indeed, the use of Section 512 to suppress and silence the Internet speech of one's critics is apparently becoming a commonplace tactic for businesses. A 2005 *Forbes* magazine article encourages businesses that are criticized online to

> Attack the host. Find some copyrighted text that a blogger has lifted from your web site and threaten to sue his Internet service provider under the Digital Millennium Copyright Act. That may prompt the ISP to shut him down.[90]

A recent detailed analysis of the thousands of uses of Section 512 to secure take downs of content by ISPs reveals a "high incidence of questionable uses of the process . . . to create leverage in a competitive marketplace, to protect rights not given by copyright . . . , and to stifle criticism, commentary and fair use, [resulting in a] continuous and perhaps unquantifiable effect on public discourse."[91]

• • •

How exactly do broadband service providers and other Internet speech conduits censor Internet expression on the basis of its content or other characteristics? In the next section I explain the role that broadband providers serve in facilitating the transmission of expression, how private entities came to own and control the conduits for expression over the Internet, and the ways in which they are able to censor or otherwise discriminate against information and expression on the basis of content.

The Fundamentals of Internet Data Transmission

All information over the Internet is transmitted via "packet switching," a method by which computers break apart data into variable-size "packets" and forward these packets through connecting computers to recipient computers that, in turn, reassemble them.[92] Each such packet contains its own source, destination, and reassembly information.[93] Using packet-switching technology, large pieces of information (such as a song, movie, or document) are broken into various packets, and those packets are dispersed and communicated via different pathways, until they reach their ultimate destination and are reassembled.[94] Using the Transmission Control Protocol/Internet Protocol (TCP/IP), developed by the U.S. Department of Defense's Advanced Research Projects Agency (DARPA), various computer networks are able to interconnect and exchange data using packet-switching technology. To implement the TCP/IP interconnection protocol, individual networks must be interconnected by interface devices called switchers or routers.[95] Packets of data are then transmitted from one interface device to another via transmission links.[96]

The interconnection of computer networks via the TCP/IP protocol grew markedly during the 1970s and 1980s under the aegis of the National Science Foundation (NSF), driven largely by the desire of scientists and other researchers to communicate via electronic mail.[97] The NSF and DARPA collaborated on various projects to connect U.S. universities to the Internet. In 1988, the NSF collaborated for the first time with a consortium of private-sector organizations to complete a long-distance wide-area network (known as the NSFNET backbone). With substantially increased usage of this network, in 1992 traffic on NSFNET was near capacity, and the consortium of private-sector entities established a private organization called Advanced Networks and Services to build a new "backbone" with substantially greater capacity. This marked the first time that a private entity, instead of a U.S. government agency, substantially owned the computers and transmission lines of the Internet backbone.[98] Shortly thereafter, in 1993 the NSF concluded that the Internet was growing too fast for the NSF to continue managing it, and decided to delegate the management of the Internet backbone to private, commercial operators. Around this time, the prohibition on the exchange of commercial activity on the Internet was lifted,[99] and the conditions were in place for the development of the Internet as we know it, with the ownership and control of the Internet's infrastructure transferred from U.S. government entities to private hands. By 1995, this growing network of private, commercial Internet backbones had replaced the NSFNET backbone, marking in effect the privatization of the Internet's infrastructure.[100]

The Internet presently comprises thousands of individual networks that are overwhelmingly privately owned.[101] Packets of data travel over the Internet from their originating computer across various networks and routers until they reach a "last mile" Internet service provider and are thereby directed to an end-user computer. These "last mile" ISPs serve to connect end users to the various networks composing the Internet backbone.

In the early days of the Internet's commercial development, most users were connected to the Internet via a narrowband or dial-up telephone connection and a modem, through which information was transmitted over the traditional telephone system's copper wire lines. Over the past decade, users have increasingly begun to connect to the Internet using significantly faster broadband technologies, via coaxial cable wirelines, digital subscriber lines (DSL), wireless technology, fiber-optic wirelines, and broadband-over-power-line technologies, among others.

Discrimination Against Internet Content

As Internet content becomes more bandwidth-intensive and as last-mile broadband providers seek to advance their own commercial interests, these providers increasingly have the incentive and the ability to discriminate against different types of content and applications that they are charged with transmitting. To do so, ISPs must be able to discern relevant information about such content and applications. Recall that such content is broken down into component packets before it is transmitted. Each packet's header contains the Internet Protocol (IP) address of its source and destination, as well as several pieces of information pointing to the type of program or application needed to open or access the content.[102] "Deep packet inspection" technologies are now being developed and employed to examine the content contained in packets and to search for and take certain actions based on designated key words. These technologies can be implemented by ISPs to discover information about certain types of content in packets, and, on the basis of that information, to block, filter, or otherwise discriminate against that content.[103]

Broadband providers have the ability, the incentive, and—if the status quo is maintained—the legal authority to discriminate against disfavored Internet content in a variety of ways. While historically ISPs have transmitted content over their pipes in one of two content-neutral, nondiscriminatory methods—either a "first-in-first-out" or a "best efforts" basis[104]—ISPs are now developing means to discriminate against data on the basis of the data's source, destination, users' identity, data type, port, or content. Such means of discrimination include outright blocking or dropping disfavored data or delaying the transmission of such data by sending it over a more heavily used connection.[105] For certain types of latency-sensitive[106] applications such as VoIP or bandwidth-intensive video content, an ISP's decision to degrade or delay transmission is tantamount to blocking such data. Conversely, an ISP might choose to favor certain data on the basis of certain of its characteristics. For example, an ISP might grant prioritization of transmission to its own content or to affiliated or favored content—in the process (relatively) degrading the transmission of unaffiliated or disfavored content. Such prioritization and degradation can be implemented by providing separate physical or logical channels for different types of data (sending preferred data over a lightly used connection, reserving capacity or bandwidth for preferred data, or sending disfavored data over a heavily trafficked connection).[107]

It is quite difficult for content providers or end users to know for certain whether broadband providers are discriminating against their content. While it is rather straightforward for an intended recipient to determine if content is being outright blocked (once the recipient is clearly notified by some other means that such content has been sent and he or she is expecting to receive it), it is more difficult for the sender to make such a determination. And, it is very difficult for the sender or the recipient to determine whether information is degraded in its transmission by an ISP. As Lawrence Lessig explains, Internet users may interpret ISPs' degradation of content simply as "congestion" on the network, and may not be able to perceive—or respond to—ISPs' acts of intentional degradation.[108]

ISPs that serve as email providers or website hosts can also block content in emails or websites by using filtering software, and can use "packet sniffers"[109] to block access to other types of connection protocols. Filtering software can block content using a variety of methods. First, and most simply, such software can block particular disfavored words or phrases, such as sexually related terms. Such software could be configured simply to block all websites or emails that contain any designated disfavored words. These days, software filters have advanced beyond simply blocking content on the basis of the presence of particular words and now employ sophisticated (albeit quite imperfect[110]) algorithms to determine which content to block, although they still suffer from substantial underblocking and overblocking problems.[111] The algorithms or processes that filtering software programs employ to determine which content to block are created by those who design such software and constitute a substantial portion of the program's value. As such, they are typically protected as trade secrets. Thus an ISP implementing filtering software developed by a third party typically has no way of knowing which content will actually be blocked by the software or the criteria used by the software to filter out content. More important, Internet users who depend upon the ISP for communicating with others have no way of determining which content or applications will be blocked by such upstream filtering. You never know what you are missing.

In summary, with the use of deep packet inspection technology, packet sniffers, and software filters, broadband providers and other conduits for Internet speech have the technological means to censor and otherwise discriminate against the expression that they are charged with facilitating. Broadband providers, which enjoy monopoly or duopoly status in residential markets,[112] have the incentive to restrict speech that disfavors their market (or other) interests and to facilitate speech that favors their interests. And, given the recent actions by the FCC and the Supreme Court to remove constraints on the discretion of Internet speech conduits, such conduits enjoy the legal authority to censor or otherwise discriminate against whatever expression they choose.

* * *

In sharp contrast to the utopian vision of the Internet as an open, public forum that enables individuals to exercise their free speech rights in an unprecedented manner, the Internet is actually in danger of becoming a forum in which speech is subject to control by a few dominant actors. Historically, the FCC would have imposed the common carriage doctrine's nondiscrimination requirements on such conduits, or courts might have treated such dominant players as state actors controlling access to public forums. With the recent contraction of these doctrines, broadband providers such as Comcast are able to select and promote content of their choosing and to censor disfavored content. Similarly, Internet search engines such as Google—which serve as the gatekeepers to billions of web pages for the vast majority of Internet users— enjoy unfettered power to censor the speech that is made available to users via their portal. And, after the passage of the Digital Millennium Copyright Act, ISPs have an even greater incentive to censor speech. Because these are private restrictions on speech, the negative conception of the First Amendment renders the state impotent to address or remedy such censorship. In contrast, under an affirmative conception of the First Amendment, the state would enjoy the power to insert itself into the market for Internet speech to regulate private conduits where necessary to ensure that channels remain open for the nondiscriminatory communication of information and ideas.

2 The First Amendment's Free Speech Guarantee

ANY DISCUSSION OF THE MEANING OF THE FIRST AMENDMENT'S free speech guarantee might well begin with the text itself: "Congress shall make no law . . . abridging the freedom of speech, or of the press. . . . " This seemingly straightforward mandate has been subject to volumes of theories of interpretations since its adoption—theories of why freedom of expression is so highly valued in our society, of what types of expression fall within the scope of the Amendment's protection, and of what types of entities are prohibited from abridging the freedom of expression. While these interpretational questions are all interrelated, I focus my attention on the latter inquiry— exactly which types of entities are prohibited from abridging individuals' freedom of expression? Should powerful "private" conduits of expression be held to fall within the scope of this prohibition, in addition to "Congress"? If so, is the state permitted to regulate to ensure the free flow of information in the hands of these private entities? Under what circumstances? Should we trust the state to regulate in order to advance these goals? In this chapter I focus on this interpretational strand of First Amendment theory and on what I refer to as the affirmative and negative conceptions of the First Amendment.

Simply stated, under the negative conception of the First Amendment, freedom of expression is a "negative liberty,"[1] and the state's primary (or only) role is a negative one—to get out of the way and to allow (well-functioning, competitive) marketplaces for speech to flourish free of state intervention. Under the affirmative conception, in contrast, the state is justified in doing more than nothing; rather, it is justified in intervening in marketplaces for speech to achieve important societal goals—to bring about conditions necessary for democratic self-government—by prohibiting discrimination by powerful conduits of expres-

sion or by facilitating expression from a multiplicity of viewpoints and deliberation and debate on matters of public and societal importance.

The negative and affirmative conceptions of the First Amendment each
enjoyed predominance at various stages of free speech jurisprudence over the
past one hundred years. The prevalence of one over the other has depended on
many factors, including the stage of development of the mediums for expression at issue and the philosophical and economic theories dominant among
policymakers and justices. Whereas the affirmative conception flourished in
the early days of the broadcasting regime and the Supreme Court's early adoption of the state action and public forum doctrines in the mid-twentieth century, the negative conception currently enjoys predominance.

Milton, Mill, and Holmes: "Free Trade in Ideas" and the Roots of the Negative Conception

The negative conception of the First Amendment has its roots in Justice Oliver
Wendell Holmes's "free trade in ideas" or "marketplace of ideas" theory of the
First Amendment. Under the negative conception, the free speech guarantee is best fulfilled by placing primacy on the individual speech decisions of
market actors, unfettered by state interference—and *state* interference only.
Holmes, in turn, was strongly influenced by his intellectual predecessors,
John Milton and John Stuart Mill. Milton, while primarily renowned as one
of the greatest English poets, was also an outspoken opponent of state censorship. In response to a statute passed by the English parliament that prohibited
publication of any book without government approval, Milton argued forcefully in favor of freedom of expression against governmental censorship. In
this representative passage from his *Areopagitica,* Milton set forth the foundation for the marketplace of ideas conception of freedom of expression, on
which Mill and Holmes later relied:

> And though all the winds of doctrine were let loose to play upon the earth, so
> Truth be in the field, we do injuriously by licensing and prohibiting to misdoubt
> her strength. Let her and Falsehood grapple; who ever knew truth put to the
> worse, in a free and open encounter?[2]

Two centuries later, John Stuart Mill carried forth Milton's metaphor in his
opposition to government censorship and expressly adopted a "free trade in
ideas" conception of the free speech guarantee:

But the peculiar evil of silencing the expression of an opinion is, that is robbing the human race; posterity as well as the existing generation; those who dissent from the opinion, still more than those who hold it. If the opinion is right, they are deprived of the opportunity of exchanging error for truth; if wrong, they lose, what is almost as great a benefit, the clearer perception and livelier impression of truth, produced by its collision with error.[3]

According to this early articulation of the free trade in ideas or marketplace conception, entrusting members of society with the power to express and form their opinions and decisions free of state censorship is the most effective means of achieving the societal goal of ultimate truth.

As noted, the free trade in ideas conception espoused by both Milton and Mill strongly influenced Justice Oliver Wendell Holmes, who authored a number of influential decisions in the early twentieth century that heralded the emergence of modern First Amendment jurisprudence. Under Holmes's conception of free speech, only when individuals are able to express themselves without state intervention can a number of competing views freely collide and compete in the marketplace of ideas, with the most meritorious ideas winning out in this competition. The role for the state in this model is simply to refrain from interfering with the marketplace (beyond remedying any market failures or imperfections that arise). The kernels of this conception of the First Amendment were articulated by Holmes in a series of opinions written in the early days of modern First Amendment jurisprudence. In his first noteworthy First Amendment opinion, Justice Holmes dissented from a decision upholding the prosecution of five individuals for encouraging resistance to the United States's position in World War I. In *Abrams* v. *United States*,[4] Holmes emphasized the importance of a robust marketplace of ideas constituted by individuals' free speech decisions, free of state censorship:

[T]he ultimate good desired is better reached by *free trade in ideas*—the best test of truth is the power of the thought to get itself accepted in the competition of the market. . . . That at any rate is the theory of our Constitution. It is an experiment, as all life is an experiment. . . . While that experiment is part of our system, I think that we should be eternally vigilant against attempts to check the expression of opinions that we loathe and believe to be fraught with death. . . .[5]

In these early influential First Amendment opinions, Justices Holmes adopted the marketplace of ideas or free trade in ideas theory in opposition to government censorship, which happened to be the major form of censorship with which speakers were then confronted. Since that time, the free trade in ideas metaphor has generally been advanced to support a conception of the free speech guarantee in which the government—and only the government—is prohibited from restricting the free trade in ideas.[6] According to this conception, speech and the ideas embodied in speech are conceptualized in a manner analogous to other market goods, upon which market forces should be allowed to operate freely. Under this conception, the state does best by trusting the market to bring about the proper allocation of all such goods as a result of the competition in the marketplace. This model functions "in much the same way as the Darwinian theory of evolution: the assumption is that after combat, the best ideas will emerge triumphant."[7]

Modern adherents to the negative conception of the First Amendment share this approach. According to such theorists, the same laissez-faire approach that economic theory applies with respect to economic goods in the market applies to speech. The recent trend toward deregulation in communications law, discussed further on, embodies an endorsement of this negative conception. Under this conception, "the First Amendment requires . . . a free speech market or a system of unrestricted economic markets in speech [in which] government must respect the forces of supply and demand."[8] Unfettered competition in the marketplace for speech is the appropriate mechanism for bringing about First Amendment goals—with "unfettered" essentially meaning unfettered by the state. Under the negative conception, the First Amendment imposes limits solely on state action that restricts the free trade of ideas. Restrictions on speech imposed by private entities—so long as they do not rise to the level of antitrust violations—are not considered interferences with the free speech guarantee. Rather, consistent with the importance placed on private ownership of property under this conception, restrictions on speech imposed by private entities are conceptualized as market forces themselves that must be allowed to operate freely. In essence, "it is as though the First Amendment placed a zone of non-interference around each individual, and the state—and the state alone—was prohibited from crossing that boundary."[9] Under the negative conception, speech restrictions imposed by private entities—such as broadcasters or broadband providers—are not inconsistent with the right to freedom of expression, but rather are conceptualized as the legitimate prerogative of the winners of the competition in the market. Just as we should not be concerned if market forces lead to the dominance by two major brands of toothpaste (and the demise of consumers' third and fourth favorite brands), we should not be concerned if market forces lead to the dominance of two major broadcasters or broadband providers, where the winners get the spoils—including the power to censor disfavored expression. Accordingly, in the negative conception of the First Amendment, the primary (or only) justification for government intervention in the marketplace for speech, like in economic markets, is provided under antitrust law. The state is only justified in breaking up interferences with the operation of the free market for speech and protecting against monopolistic effects within such markets.[10]

This negative conception of the First Amendment has been subject to trenchant criticisms. Jerome Barron, an early and influential critic of the free trade conception, contends that in the modern communications era, in which the power to speak is controlled by a handful of dominant corporate media players, the marketplace is impoverished and poses dangers to free expression. Accordingly, protection against government censorship is insufficient. Rather, to render the marketplace for speech meaningful, the government must do more than nothing; it must intervene to grant individuals access to the media, to secure meaningful opportunities for individuals to compete and be heard within this marketplace:

> There is inequality in the power to communicate ideas just as there is inequality in economic bargaining power. . . . The "marketplace of ideas" has rested on the assumption that protecting the right of expression [from government censorship] is equivalent to providing for it. But changes in the communications industry have destroyed the equilibrium in that marketplace. A realistic view of the First Amendment requires recognition that a right of free expression is somewhat thin if it can be exercised only at the sufferance of the managers of mass communications.[11]

Barron claims that because of inadequacies in the marketplace for ideas in the era of mass communications dominated by a few market players, government intervention to ensure meaningful access to the marketplace is necessary. If powerful media entities—broadcasters, major metropolitan newspapers, or, today, broadband providers—can restrict access to the marketplace, then even on its adherents' own terms the marketplace conception of the free speech guarantee is not viable. Although the ease of entry and access to the Internet medium might at first blush render Barron's critiques of the marketplace metaphor inapt in this forum, in fact the control that powerful gate-keepers exercise over Internet speech renders Barron's critique as timely as when it was first advanced.[12]

The critique that Barron advances of the negative conception essentially accepts and works from within the premise that a marketplace of speech to which individuals have meaningful access[13] and in which the free flow of expression is unrestricted will result in the attainment of truth at a societal level.[14] Other critiques of the negative conception of the First Amendment strike at the heart of the marketplace model by challenging its initial premise.

Public Deliberation, Democratic Self-Government, and the Affirmative Conception of the First Amendment

The negative conception of the First Amendment, which garnered widespread support among policymakers and Supreme Court justices in recent decades, has been subject to vigorous criticism by those who conceptualize the First Amendment as advancing a different set of values—public, nonmarket values that are central to democratic self-government. Affirmative conception theorists contend that speech that is valuable within our democratic system may not be adequately protected within a marketplace model, in which we essentially treat speech like other commodities and entrust speech decisions solely to the market. Under the affirmative conception of the free speech guarantee, as Cass Sunstein explains:

> It is important to ask . . . whether unregulated markets actually promote a well-functioning system of free expression. . . . Such a system is closely connected to the central constitutional goal of creating a deliberative democracy. In such a system, politics is not supposed merely to protect pre-existing private rights . . . [or] to aggregate existing private preferences. . . . Instead it is designed to have an important deliberative feature, in which new information and perspectives influence social judgments about possible courses of action [and through which] both collective and individual decisions can be shaped and improved. . . . The system of free expression is the foundation of this process. One of its basic goals is to ensure broad communication about matters of public concern among the citizenry at large and between citizens and representatives.[15]

In his writings espousing an affirmative conception of the free speech guarantee, Sunstein builds upon the theory of the First Amendment advanced by Alexander Meiklejohn, who placed substantial emphasis on the importance of free speech within our system of self-government. According to Meiklejohn's theory, freedom of expression is protected precisely because—and to the extent that—it contributes to the process of self-government:

> [The] principle of the freedom of speech springs from the necessities of the program of self-government. It is not a law of Nature or of Reason in the abstract. It is a deduction from the basic American agreement that public issues shall be decided by universal suffrage.[16]

According to Meiklejohn's theory, for self-government to function effectively, members of the polity must be exposed to a wide variety of conflicting viewpoints on matters of public importance, so that they can evaluate and develop for themselves informed opinions on such matters. Accordingly, "conflicting views must be expressed, not because they are valid, but because they are relevant."[17]

While Meiklejohn would have limited the First Amendment's protection to speech involving the consideration of matters of public interest,[18] his intellectual successors who advance various affirmative conceptions of the First Amendment, including Cass Sunstein and Owen Fiss, would extend First Amendment protection to more speech on the grounds that freedom of expression on a broader range of matters of public and societal importance is essential to our system of self-government. Sunstein advances a model for a system of free expression that embodies a commitment to "broad and deep attention to public issues" and to "public exposure to an appropriate diversity of views."[19] He criticizes the marketplace model for its failure to embody the values that constitute the core of our system of democratic self-government. First, he claims, dissident or other countermajoritarian speech—which ipso facto is at a disadvantage in a marketplace model—may not be sufficiently protected within such a model. Second, individuals in their speech decisions may not choose to consume or produce an objectively desirable amount of speech necessary for meaningful democratic self-government bearing on public affairs. For example, in the market for expression on television, individuals may choose to watch game shows or sitcoms instead of presidential debates or in-depth analyses of the war with Iraq. If subjected purely to individual consumption choices and market forces, expression bearing on matters of public importance may not secure sufficient audiences and may lose out in market competition. As Sunstein considers these issues:

Imagine . . . a new country . . . proposed the following explicit rule: The right to speak will be allocated to those people to whom other people are willing to pay enough to entitle them to be heard. Suppose in other words that the allocation of speech rights was decided through an ordinary pricing system, like the allocation of soap, or cars, or candy. It would follow that people would be prevented from speaking, or from having significant access to listeners, if other people were not willing to pay enough to entitle them do so. . . . . The hypothesized system of allocation, based on private willingness to pay, would . . . significantly endanger political deliberation.[20]

In other words, affirmative conception theorists claim that we should not trust a system of free speech characterized by free markets to facilitate the discussion of and deliberation on matters of public and societal importance that is necessary for a well-functioning system of democratic self-government, nor to ensure that a diversity of viewpoints (including unpopular, dissident, counter-majoritarian viewpoints) are able to be expressed. On the affirmative conception of the free speech guarantee, the state is justified in intervening in the market to bring about an objectively desirable amount of speech on matters of public and societal importance.

Whereas Sunstein advances essentially a paternalistic justification for the affirmative conception of the free speech guarantee, other theorists view speech on matters of public importance as a proper object of self-paternalism. Lee Bollinger contends that members of the polity may justifiably turn to public institutions to alter and override their individual speech consumption decisions. He explains that there is more than one way for individuals to exercise choice: they may exercise choice by flipping the channel to the sitcom instead of the presidential debate, but they may also exercise a higher-level, more deliberative choice by voting for legislators who support state intervention in the market to facilitate deliberation and debate on matters of public importance. Such self-paternalism is nonetheless a choice, and a more considered one at that. As Bollinger contends:

It may fairly be asked by people who strongly favor the free market approach exclusively, if there is no market failure . . . , then why should we permit government regulation . . . when it seems entirely possible for people to implement their desires through the market system: If people want balanced discussion of public issues, then let them demand it. And if they don't demand it, then perhaps we should assume they don't want it. . . . [T]he question is whether the majority may, if it chooses, sensibly turn to public institutions and regulations as a means of altering to some degree the choices they see themselves making in the open market. . . . [21]

Self-paternalism in such instances supports citizens' higher-order determinations that it is in their best interests as citizens in a democracy for the state to intervene in speech markets. Implementing an institutional structure that respects both citizens' immediate choices and their higher-order, more considered choices is nothing new:

> [T]he issue cannot be whether or not it is wise for society to set up different, or special, social institutions for the purpose of fostering certain values that are thought likely to be undervalued by any other method of social decision-making, for that is the common view of the First Amendment and the Supreme Court.[22]

The affirmative conception of the First Amendment recognizes that individuals have a right to participate in democratic self-government by expressing their views, and in turn by being exposed to a diversity of viewpoints, on matters of societal and public importance. These rights create correlative, affirmative obligations on the part of would-be powerful censors—whether public or private—to facilitate a diverse range of speech on matters of societal and public importance. The state is justified in regulating powerful private conduits and private owners of forums for speech where necessary to facilitate such speech. Whereas the negative conception erects a barrier to state intervention in the marketplace for speech to preserve the laissez-faire ordering of the market, the affirmative conception guards against both public and powerful private censorship of expression within the "marketplace" for expression. In essence, under the affirmative conception, in order to advance the core free speech goals that are essential to a well-functioning democracy, the state may need to do more than nothing—more than itself not censoring speech.

Freedom of Expression for Whom— Speakers or Conduits of Speech?

The affirmative conception of the First Amendment prioritizes the expressive interests of individuals over the expressive interests of conduits for expression, such as broadcasters or broadband providers in today's speech market. Certain affirmative conception theorists arrive at this result by separating the analysis of freedom of expression into two components that are accorded different levels of protection—broad protection for freedom of speech for individuals, and limited protection for freedom of the press for conduits of expression.[23] Under this approach, freedom of speech for individuals is granted near-absolute protection against restrictions by both public and powerful private censors, while freedom of the press is granted more limited protection and rendered subservient to the goals of advancing debate and deliberation on matters of public importance. In evaluating instances in which a speech conduit—a broadcaster or broadband provider—restricts an individual's freedom of expression, this approach does not equally weight the First Amendment "rights" of the conduit against those of the speaker; rather, it considers whether the restrictions by the speech conduit serve or disserve deliberative democracy. If the speech restrictions thwart the goals of deliberative democracy, then the conduit's free press rights would be limited in favor of speakers' free speech rights. Under this understanding of the affirmative conception of the First Amendment, conduits' exercise of their "rights" to dominate or monopolize the relevant forum for expression impoverishes discussion and debate on matters of public and societal importance, and the conduits' free press rights should be limited in favor of individuals' free speech rights.

Under the affirmative conception, the right to free speech creates duties on the part of public and powerful private speech conduits to facilitate speech. The state and other potentially powerful censors of speech have the obligation not to discriminate against speech and, further, to take affirmative steps to facilitate a diverse range of speech on matters of public and societal importance. In contrast to the negative conception, under which individuals' speech may be censored by forces that predominate in the marketplace, the affirmative conception views such speech restrictions as illegitimate. The state has the right and the duty to intervene in order to check censorship by powerful private conduits and forums for expression to advance the preeminent free speech goals of facilitating public deliberation and debate.

To understand the differences between these two conceptions of the First Amendment, consider an example in which the market for broadcast television or broadband service is dominated by two or three powerful private actors, each of which favors the president's policy with respect to the war in

Iraq. Suppose further that a senator who opposes the war seeks time to air her views or to send mass emails or text messages regarding her position on the war. Proponents of the negative conception would maintain that the configuration of (pro-war) broadcasters and broadband providers is the legitimate outcome of the competition in the marketplace (barring antitrust violations). These conduits' right to make whatever speech decisions they choose is a prerogative that they have rightfully secured by prevailing in this competition. If the state were to intervene in such decisions—by enacting a statute requiring equal time or other forms of protection for the expression of the senator's antiwar views or prohibiting broadband providers from restricting such expression—this would constitute unconstitutional state interference in the marketplace for expression. Only the state's regulation of speech to prevent censorship, not the conduits' censorship itself, would be considered a First Amendment violation under the negative conception.

Under the affirmative conception, in contrast, the restriction by powerful private conduits of the senator's speech would constitute a violation of the free speech guarantee that would warrant state intervention. It is the limitation by powerful speech regulators of public discussion and debate, and the denial of the right to be heard on matters of public importance, that constitutes the First Amendment violation, not the state intervention to protect the senator's right to be heard. The affirmative conception evaluates state intervention in the marketplace for speech according to its impact on the free speech values of public deliberation and debate, rather than by its interference with the decisions of powerful private speech conduits. As Owen Fiss explains, "Autonomy may be protected, but only when it enriches public debate, and it might well have to be sacrificed when, for example, the speech of some drowns out the voices of others. . . . "[24] Accordingly, the affirmative conception concerns itself with public as well as powerful private restrictions of speech. When individuals' assertions of a First Amendment right to speak conflict with speech conduits' assertions of a First Amendment right to restrict speech, individuals' free speech rights may trump the conduits' rights if the exercise of the former would enrich the public debate whereas the exercise of the latter would impoverish the public debate. The affirmative conception rejects the formalistic distinction between public and private regulation of speech and evaluates both types of regulation in terms of their effect on the public deliberation and debate necessary for effective democratic self-government.

The State Action Question

One of the strongest criticisms of the affirmative conception grows out of the text of the First Amendment itself, which, by its terms, only prohibits Congress (and other governmental entities) from regulating speech. If affirmative conception theorists are to successfully maintain that the First Amendment is to regulate powerful private actors, they must respond to the criticism that only governmental entities may be regulated under the express terms of the First Amendment. While I set forth the doctrinal underpinnings of the state action doctrine in greater detail in Chapter 5, I explore the general theoretical contours of this doctrine here.

The state action doctrine enjoys a long and complicated history in our constitutional jurisprudence. Essentially, the doctrine is best understood as the vehicle through which courts enforce the public-private distinction necessary to ensure a zone of personal autonomy for individuals within a liberal democracy. This zone of autonomy allows private entities to act as they choose, free from the limits and dictates of the Constitution.[25] Viewed in this light, the state action doctrine maintains the boundary between the public and the private that is integral to liberal political theory.[26] Under the doctrine as interpreted in the First Amendment context, on the public side, the state—and those entities that are functionally equivalent to the state—are prohibited from restricting expression. This prohibition on censorship by the state and by those with attributes of state power is necessary to protect expressive freedom for individuals. Individuals' expressive freedom, in turn, is necessary for democratic self-government to flourish. On the private side, individuals must enjoy freedom of expression for themselves (as well as the freedom to regulate the expression of others on their property).[27] This expressive autonomy enjoyed by private actors is essential to advance the goal of facilitating a wide and diverse array of viewpoints on matters of societal and public importance that is integral to a well-functioning democracy. In essence, the public-private distinction forged by the state action doctrine leaves "private persons and institutions . . . presumptively free to act in accordance with manifold and differing values,"[28] a freedom that is integral to our system of democratic self-governance.

The difficult question, of course, is where and how to draw the line between the public and private. Under what circumstances should a nominally private entity such as a broadband provider be treated like a private individual, who must be accorded freedom of expression (and freedom to regulate others' expression on his or her property)? And under what circumstances should such an entity be treated as the functional equivalent of the state, such that its power to regulate the expression of others may be held in check by constitutional norms?

Those who espouse a negative conception of the First Amendment generally adopt a restrictive interpretation of the state action doctrine and draw the public-private line so as to regulate only the speech regulations of the government itself, leaving all private speech regulators—regardless of their power to control or distort public deliberation and debate—immune from scrutiny. Julian Eule and Jonathan Varat, for example, contend that only government entities should be subject to First Amendment scrutiny; all other entities should enjoy the discretion to regulate whatever speech they choose, regardless of the consequences of such regulation.[29] These theorists would leave it to the market to decide whether to impose checks on the censorial actions of owners of powerful private forums and conduits for expression, and extol the expressive freedom enjoyed by such entities as essential to individual autonomy and liberty.

Affirmative theorists, in contrast, eschew the formalism inherent in the negative conception's interpretation and maintain that the state action doctrine is best understood as the vehicle through which courts should balance (and in fact actually do balance) the interests of those who are seeking to regulate versus the interests of those whose expression is to be regulated. These theorists claim that, in resolving state action questions, courts should (and actually do) balance the competing claims on either side, instead of engaging in a formalistic analysis of the governmental or nongovernmental status of the actor involved.[30] As the Supreme Court itself articulated this balancing test in its seminal First Amendment state action decision, in *Marsh* v. *Alabama:* "[w]hen we balance the constitutional rights of owners of property against those of the people to enjoy [First Amendment freedoms], we remain mindful of the fact that the latter occupy a preferred position."[31]

Consistent with this substantive analysis of the public-private distinction, in construing the state action doctrine in the First Amendment context, I maintain that courts should abandon a formalistic approach and should undertake a balancing of the relevant competing interests. As I set forth in greater detail in Chapter 5, this interpretation of the state action doctrine requires courts to evaluate the privacy, property, and free speech interests of the entity engaged in the challenged regulation of speech against the free speech and access interests of those seeking to exercise their expressive freedoms, much as the Supreme Court did in *Marsh v. Alabama.*

To illuminate this point, consider another example of two different schemes for defining and regulating private property and free speech rights. In both states A and B, citizens frequently gather in large, privately owned shopping centers like the Mall of America. Many citizens pass through the common areas and thoroughfares within these large centers. Suppose that individuals protesting the administration's conduct in connection with the war in Iraq wish to pass out leaflets and gather signatures in connection with the antiwar movement.[32] In state A, suppose that the applicable laws grant such large suburban shopping centers the right to exclude any speech of their choosing, and the owners of the shopping centers—who do not wish to antagonize the administration—ban the protestors and threaten them with trespass prosecution if they continue to protest.[33] State B's laws, in contrast, limit these large municipal shopping centers' right to exclude speech reasonably exercised on matters of public importance.[34] State A and state B also have divergent policies for the regulation of broadcast stations and broadband providers. State B's laws require stations to devote a certain portion of airtime to issues of public importance and to strive toward balanced coverage of such issues, and prohibit broadband providers from discriminating against content.[35] State A, in contrast, grants broad license to stations to air the speech of their choosing, and grants broadband providers the right to censor or otherwise discriminate against the speech of their choosing. A coalition of individuals opposing the war in Iraq seeks to purchase airtime on stations in states A and B to air a message setting forth reasons for opposing the war. Because of state B's regulatory regime, the coalition is granted airtime on stations in state B. Stations in state A, however, refuse to allow the antiwar coalition to air its message.[36] Similarly, an antiwar group seeks to disseminate its message via email[37] or cablecast of a protest march.[38] In state B, broadband providers are prohibited from discriminating against such content. In state A, they are not.

Under the substantive interpretation of the state action doctrine that I advanced earlier, in determining whether the speech restrictions by state A's shopping centers, broadcasters, and broadband providers constitute state action in violation of the First Amendment, courts should look beyond the private label enjoyed by such speech regulators and should undertake a meaningful substantive inquiry into and balancing of the rights and interests at stake. In so doing, they should evaluate (1) the free speech and property interests supporting the mall, broadcaster, or broadband providers' speech restriction as against (2) the free speech interests of the would-be speaker as well as the free speech interests of members of the public in accessing such expression. Under this affirmative conception of the state action doctrine, the states' regimes are evaluated by balancing the rights of the forum owners against the rights of the would-be speakers, and by considering the effects of private regulation of speech on the free flow of information on matters of public and societal importance. On this metric, state A's regulatory regime is less desirable because it restricts the free flow of information and contributes to the impoverishment of public debate, whereas state B's regime—albeit one that regulates the speech decisions of private entities—is preferable because of its salutary effect on the free flow of information and on public deliberation and debate.

Affirmative conception theorists such as Onora O'Neill emphasize that both state A and state B regulate speech, whether directly or indirectly. Therefore, it is inaccurate to claim that state B's regime regulates speech while state A's regime does not. State A's acts of establishing a regulatory regime that grants and enforces private entities' power to restrict speech itself constitutes a regulation of speech (albeit an indirect one). In essence, the negative conception theorists' Holy Grail of zero regulation of speech is a conceptual myth:

> No society can institutionalize zero-regulation of public discourse. The choice can only be between differing patterns of regulation. . . . Supposed attempts to do this by laissez-faire communications policies merely assign the regulation of communication to non-state powers. [Doing so secures] a particular configuration of freedom of expression, which . . . does not guarantee the expression of diverse views.[39]

Put another way, state B's property and free speech laws do not constitute "government intervention" into speech where none existed before.[40] The state-conferred and enforced property rights that enable large shopping centers, broadcasters, and broadband providers to exclude expression that they disfavor are not natural or God-given, but rather are themselves creations of law. As Cass Sunstein puts it, "laissez faire is no less a conceptual myth for speech than it is for property."[41] The choice therefore is between two different regulatory regimes for public discourse, not between regulation and zero-regulation.

Accordingly, the choice between different speech regulatory regimes should be assessed substantively by balancing the competing rights at stake and by considering the regimes' comparative effects on the free flow of information and expression, not by attending to formalistic distinctions between "state" and "nonstate" regulation of expression.

Criticisms of the Affirmative Conception of the First Amendment

The affirmative conception of the First Amendment, and the regulation of nominally private actors that it contemplates, is subject to criticism on a variety of fronts. First, as discussed, in abandoning a sharp distinction between government and nongovernment actors, and maintaining that the latter may be subject to regulation under the First Amendment, this theory impinges on the zone of autonomy that liberal democracies accord to private actors. Second, in eschewing a bright line between public and private actors, and calling on courts constantly to weigh and balance the interests of the competing claimants, this theory introduces great uncertainty and substantial costs into First Amendment law.

In response to these criticisms, defenders of the affirmative conception maintain that the actors whose speech restrictions are to be regulated are not truly private and thus do not merit having their personal autonomy respected. If it is an issue of the Mall of America's personal autonomy and free speech interests versus the free speech interests of those seeking to peacefully protest the war on such property, the latter interests are clearly more deserving of protection in our constitutional scheme. Second, defenders of the affirmative conception would respond that courts *already* (implicitly or explicitly) balance in evaluating the merits of state action cases, and it would be intellectually more honest and conceptually more clear for them to do so explicitly, as did the Supreme Court in *Marsh*.

Another powerful criticism of the affirmative conception is that it contemplates government regulation of speech—the very evil that the First Amendment was intended to avoid. If, under the affirmative conception, the government has the power to determine which speech "contributes to public deliberation and debate," and which does not, this power allows the government too great of a role in the marketplace for expression. Similarly, if the state is allowed ultimately to determine when each side of a particular position has been adequately represented—as under the fairness doctrine regime[42]—such a regime embodies the danger that the state will place its hand on the scales to alter the debate to favor its own viewpoints.

While it may plausibly be maintained that government intervention in broadcasters' speech decisions—for example, to achieve such amorphous goals as representation of diverse and competing viewpoints—reposes excessive power in the government to shape debate, government regulation of private speech conduits merely to prohibit censorship of and discrimination against those seeking to express themselves via the conduits' pipes does not embody this danger. The nondiscrimination obligations imposed on powerful private conduits of expression under the common carriage doctrine and the state action doctrine merely impose on such conduits the duty not to discriminate on the basis of content—whatever content is sought to be expressed by those seeking to utilize such conduits. Under the application of such doctrines, decisions regarding which content is to be expressed are left up to members of the public—not to the conduit for such expression, and not to the state.

In the next chapter, I analyze several free speech doctrines that implement an affirmative conception of the First Amendment to varying degrees. The Supreme Court has articulated powerful justifications for adopting an affirmative conception and should continue to recognize the importance of these justifications in its First Amendment jurisprudence in the twenty-first century.

3 Embracing the Affirmative First Amendment

IN THIS CHAPTER, I ANALYZE THE STRANDS OF THE AFFIRMATIVE conception of the First Amendment in the Supreme Court's foundational First Amendment jurisprudence and the FCC's speech regulations. Courts and policymakers should reconsider the important free speech values embodied in the affirmative conception and embrace these values in regulating powerful private conduits of Internet expression. I illuminate the Supreme Court's and the FCC's early adoption of the affirmative conception of the First Amendment by examining the evolution of five doctrines—*the public forum doctrine, the state action doctrine, the fairness doctrine, must carry regulations,* and the *common carriage doctrine.* These doctrines were predominately adopted and strengthened in the mid-twentieth century but substantially weakened by the end of the twentieth century, leading to the current contours of Internet speech regulation in which private entities control speech on the Internet unconstrained by state regulation.

The public forum doctrine imposes affirmative obligations on the state not to discriminate against speakers or speech on certain public property in order to facilitate public discussion and debate. The state action doctrine extends these and other obligations to powerful private actors who serve the same relevant functions as the state. The fairness doctrine charges broadcasters with the obligation to provide balanced and fair coverage of issues of public importance to enhance public deliberation and debate, while must carry regulations require cable operators to carry broadcast coverage of local and public affairs programming to ensure public access to a multiplicity of information sources. The common carriage doctrine charges private conduits for communication such as telecommunications providers with the obligation to facilitate all legal communications in a nondiscriminatory manner. These doctrines either directly impose affirmative obligations on the state to facilitate free speech or countenance state intervention into the decisions of private conduits for speech where necessary to ensure the free flow of information and expression. As such, these doctrines serve the ultimate goal of facilitating the conditions essential to the enterprise of democratic self-government. Under each of these doctrines, the state is permitted, and in some circumstances required, to do more than nothing—more than simply refrain from censoring speech itself. Rather, these doctrines constitute a coherent system of laws and policies regulating powerful conduits and forums, allowing the state to take meaningful affirmative steps to facilitate the free flow of information and expression and to check censorship by powerful public or private regulators. In examining these doctrines, I survey the landscape of the obligations historically imposed on conduits for expression, with an eye toward prescribing the obligations that should be imposed upon conduits for Internet expression.

The Public Forum Doctrine

The public forum doctrine mandates that the state facilitate and not discriminate against speech by requiring that certain public property be available for "uninhibited, robust, and wide-open"[1] discussion and debate on matters of public and societal importance. This doctrine, which grows out of the 1939 case of Hague v. CIO,[2] imposes obligations on the state to facilitate free speech within places that traditionally are devoted or well-suited to the expression and exchange of ideas, such as public parks, sidewalks, and streets, as well as within places that the state has chosen to open up for expressive purposes. Because, in real space, there is a mixture of publicly owned and privately owned property, the public forum doctrine in real space serves the critical role of ensuring that there will always be some places where people can meaningfully exercise their First Amendment right to free speech. Because of the public forum doctrine, even if all private property owners were permitted to discriminate against the speech of their choosing, there would remain some publicly owned places conducive to expressive purposes that the state must preserve as open spaces for public discussion and debate.

Since the Supreme Court's adoption of the public forum doctrine in the mid-twentieth century, the state and state actors[3] have been constitutionally required to facilitate speech and to refrain from suppressing it within such forums on the basis of its content or viewpoint. The availability of such forums in which individuals are ensured the meaningful right and opportunity to express themselves and where members of the general public are—willingly or unwillingly—exposed to such expression has been central to freedom of expression and to democratic self-government "from time immemorial."[4] Significantly, the public forum doctrine removes the protection of free speech rights from the market and ensures that individuals enjoy the meaningful opportunity to express themselves, even if they cannot afford to purchase such a right within the relevant marketplace for expression. As the Supreme Court emphasized in *Hague*,[5] the state may not restrict speech within publicly owned places that are quintessentially well-suited for public discussion and debate within democracies.

The balance between publicly owned and privately owned spaces, however, does not carry over to cyberspace, which, as discussed previously,[6] is composed almost entirely of privately owned spaces and privately owned conduits for expression, such as Comcast, Verizon, and Google. And, as I explain in Chapter 4, even the very few publicly owned forums for Internet expression have not been considered to be "public forums" for First Amendment purposes by the courts. Because of the radically different public-private balance on the Internet and courts' unwillingness to impose public forum obligations even on publicly owned Internet forums for expression, the important values embodied in the public forum doctrine have been substantially eroded in recent years.

To understand those important values and their potential loss in cyberspace, I examine the genesis of the public forum doctrine and its development in the mid-twentieth century. The seminal public forum case, *Hague* v. *CIO*,[7] grew out of a dispute between members of the Committee for Industrial Organization (now part of the AFL-CIO) and Jersey City, New Jersey, which was hostile to the message that the CIO sought to communicate. Members of the CIO sought to conduct meetings in public venues in Jersey City to explain to city workers the purposes and benefits of the National Labor Relations Act, and to distribute pamphlets on the subject. CIO members repeatedly sought from the city and were repeatedly denied permission to lease the city hall to conduct public meetings or distribute their pamphlets in city streets and other similar public places. When CIO members, undeterred by the city's recalcitrance, continued attempting to express their message, the mayor ordered them arrested and literally ferried out of the city on boats bound for New York.

In response to the CIO's claim that the city violated its First Amendment rights, the city argued, relying on the 1897 case of *Davis* v. *Commonwealth of Massachusetts*,[8] that its right to exclude people from city property was as absolute as that of a private property owner to exclude people from his or her home, and that it therefore enjoyed the power to exclude from city property whichever citizens it chose for whatever reasons it chose. In *Davis*, a preacher challenged a Boston ordinance that prohibited anyone from making "a public address" on public grounds without a permit. Davis had been convicted for speaking in Boston Common without a permit, and Oliver Wendell Holmes, then a justice on the Massachusetts Supreme Judicial Court, held that the legislature, "as representative of the public," could exercise control over the uses that members of the public could make of public places. Holmes explained that for the legislature to "forbid public speaking in a highway or public park is no more an infringement of the rights of a member of the public than for the owner of a private house to forbid it in his house."[9] The United States Supreme Court affirmed, holding that Davis had no right to use the Common "except in such mode and subject to such regulations as the legislature . . . may have deemed proper to prescribe."[10]

In *Hague,* the CIO contended that the city should be charged with different duties than those of a private owner of property—that is, the duty to facilitate the expression of members of the public, even those whose message it disliked. This time, the Supreme Court agreed. The Court explained that the existence and flourishing of our form of democratic self-government require that citizens enjoy meaningful opportunities to express themselves and meaningful venues available to them in which to express their views on matters of public importance:

> The very idea of a government, republican in form, implies a right on the part of its citizens to meet peaceably for consultation in respect to public affairs and to petition for a redress of grievances. . . . Citizenship of the United States would be little better than a name if it did not carry with it the right to discuss national legislation and the benefits, advantages, and opportunities to accrue to citizens therefrom.[11]

Accordingly, the *Hague* Court rejected Jersey City's claim that its right to exclude was as absolute as that of a private property owner. Rejecting the holding of *Davis,* the Court adopted what is now known as the public forum doctrine and charged the city with the obligation to facilitate speech without discrimination on certain types of public property:

> Wherever the title of streets and parks may rest, they have immemorially been held in trust for the use of the public, and time out of mind, have been used for purposes of assembly, communicating thoughts between citizens, and discussing public questions. Such use of the streets and public places has, from ancient times, been a part of the privileges, immunities, rights, and liberties of citizens. The privilege of a citizen of the United States to use the streets and parks for communication of views on national questions . . . must not, in the guise of regulation, be abridged or denied.[12]

Within these "traditional public forums," individuals are guaranteed not just the right in theory but the meaningful opportunity to express themselves.[13]

Eight months after the *Hague* decision, the Supreme Court solidified its newly articulated public forum doctrine in the case of *Schneider* v. *State*.[14] In *Schneider*, individuals who handed out leaflets on a public street announcing a protest were convicted of violating an ordinance prohibiting the distribution of leaflets on public streets. The municipality defended the ordinance on the grounds that it was designed to prevent littering. Rejecting the municipality's argument, the Court first explained that the government has an obligation to facilitate speech within places that are well-suited to such expression, even in cases in which other places (less well-suited to expression) are available. Justice Roberts wrote:

> The streets are *natural and proper places* for the dissemination of information and opinion; and one is not to have the exercise of his liberty of expression in appropriate places abridged on the plea that it may be exercised in some other place.[15]

The Court found the municipality's justification of convenience for restricting expression on a public street insufficient, given the importance that freedom of expression serves in our system of democratic self-government:

> Municipal authorities, as trustees for the public, have the duty to keep their communities' streets open and available for the movement of people and property. . . . So long as legislation to this end does not abridge the constitutional liberty of one rightfully upon the street to impart information through speech or the distribution of literature, it may lawfully regulate the conduct of those using the

street. . . . *[F]reedom of speech and freedom of press [are] fundamental personal rights and liberties.* [M]ere legislative preferences . . . respecting matters of public convenience [are] insufficient to justify such ordinance as diminishes the exercise of *rights so vital to the maintenance of democratic institutions.*[16]

The Court emphasized that the government must facilitate expression within "natural and proper places" for expression, even if doing so will impose costs and inconvenience.

In both *Hague* and *Schneider,* the Supreme Court rejected a negative conception and adopted an affirmative conception of the state's role in implementing the First Amendment. As Richard Posner explains, "[u]ntil fairly recently it was assumed that the purpose of the First Amendment was the negative one of preventing undue interference with private markets in ideas rather than the positive one of promoting the effective functioning of such markets. The 'public forum' doctrine, however, requires the government in some cases to make public facilities available for persons wanting to express themselves."[17] In its foundational public forum jurisprudence, the Court underscored the importance that the unrestricted, uncensored free flow of information serves in our system of democratic self-government. If the government enjoyed the discretion to censor expression of its choosing, this power would impair the free flow of information and ideas. After *Hague* and *Schneider,* the state could no longer exclude undesirable or unpopular expression from public places. The state's discretion, unlike that of a private homeowner, was limited by the public forum doctrine to ensure that citizens could assemble, communicate their thoughts, and express their views regarding public affairs on public property such as streets, sidewalks, parks, and other "natural and proper places for the dissemination of information and opinion."[18]

Not all public property enjoys public forum status, however. Property such as government-owned office buildings, state prisons, and places that are not held open by the government or traditionally used for expressive purposes are not regulated as public forums in which the state is obligated to facilitate citizens' free speech rights.[19] But within government-owned property that has traditionally been available for expressive purposes, such as public parks, streets, sidewalks, or public property that the state has made available for expressive purposes, such as auditoriums and concert halls, all speakers are permitted to express themselves from whatever viewpoints and on whatever subjects they choose.[20] It is within these public forums that citizens enjoy the fullest and most meaningful protection of their right to free expression. The government is required to permit all manner of speech within the scope of the First Amendment's protection[21]—regardless of the content of such speech—within public forums, and any restrictions on speech within such forums are subject to the strictest judicial scrutiny.[22]

The ability to express oneself within a public forum is among the most important components of the First Amendment's protection for free speech. As Stephen Gey explains:

> The public forum doctrine . . . derives from the most basic mythological image of free speech: an agitated but eloquent speaker standing on a soap box at Speakers' Corner, railing against injustices committed by the government, whose agents are powerless to keep the audience from hearing the speaker's damning words. [P]rotecting such speakers is essential to preserving a Western democratic culture, because democracy can only flourish if citizens are free to speak Truth to Power. . . . Although the dynamics of real public forums may never have been as pure and honorable, the essential reality grasped by the public forum doctrine remains as valid today as it was when thousands of Socialists packed into Union Square in the early days of [the twentieth] century to hang on every word of great progressive orators such as Eugene Debs. [E]very culture must have venues in which citizens can confront each other's ideas and ways of thinking about the world.[23]

Given that real space consists of a mixture of private and public property and contains some public forums for expression, in real space all speakers are guaranteed a forum within which to express their views and potentially to reach a broad general audience. The mandate that the government preserve forums for nondiscriminatory exercise of the right of free speech provides a crucial safeguard for free expression in real space. Speakers can enter public parks, streets, and sidewalks and express themselves with the assurance that their speech cannot be censored by the forum owner on the basis of viewpoint or subject matter.

This powerful embodiment of the affirmative conception of the First Amendment has been substantially weakened in recent times, both in real space and in cyberspace. First, the Supreme Court has been reticent to extend the public forum doctrine to nontraditional, government-owned forums for expression in real space (such as airport terminals[24]). Second, in real space, many forums for expression in cities and towns that were formerly state-owned (such as municipal town squares) are increasingly being taken over by private entities (such as shopping malls and gated community "town squares"), and the courts have declined to extend public forum obligations to such entities under the state action doctrine.[25] Further, in cyberspace, the balance between public and private spaces has shifted almost entirely to the private,[26] with the consequence that there are virtually no public spaces on the Internet that are even *candidates* to be considered as public forums. Finally, in a recent decision, the Supreme Court declined to impose public forum obligations on the state in its capacity of providing a forum for Internet expression.[27] In Chapter 4 I examine the Court's contraction of the public forum doctrine and the associated curtailment of affirmative obligations imposed on the state to facilitate expression in the context of both real space and cyberspace. I contend that courts should conceptualize the (small percentage of) public conduits of Internet expression as public forums with attendant obligations to facilitate speech without discrimination.

The State Action Doctrine

Whereas the public forum doctrine imposes obligations on the state to facilitate speech and to refrain from discriminating against it within state-owned forums that are natural and proper places for expression, the state action doctrine imposes similar obligations on powerful private actors. Under the state action doctrine, the fact that would-be forums and venues for expression are nominally "private" does not necessarily excuse them from the obligation to facilitate and refrain from discriminating against expression. When private actors perform functions that have traditionally or exclusively been performed by the state, they are charged under the state action doctrine with obligations—including those imposed under the public forum doctrine—to facilitate expression. First recognized in the First Amendment context in the mid-twentieth century in *Marsh* v. *Alabama*,[28] the state action doctrine rejects the proposition that powerful private entities can discriminate against whatever speech they choose free of First Amendment constraints because of their nominally private status.

With the increased shift in real space from publicly owned forums for expression (actual town squares) to privately owned forums (shopping malls and gated community "town squares"), the state action doctrine—if properly interpreted and applied—guarantees that members of the public will be assured of the opportunity to engage in expression on matters of public and societal importance in places well-suited to expressive activity, regardless of the public-private balance of property ownership. And, with the near-complete shift in cyberspace from public to private ownership of forums and conduits for expression, the state action doctrine is becoming increasingly necessary to impose obligations on forum and conduit owners on the Internet to facilitate expression. With the resurgence of the negative conception of the First Amendment, however, the state action doctrine has been substantially limited in recent years, both in real space and in cyberspace. I will briefly review the state action doctrine in general, and then analyze the contours of, and the important values embodied in, the doctrine as applied to powerful "private" property owners as implemented in the early years of modern First Amendment jurisprudence.

Under the state action doctrine, courts generally will impose constitutional obligations upon actors other than the government in certain limited circumstances: (1) where the actor is a government corporation; (2) where the actor performs "public functions" or functions that have been traditionally or exclusively performed by the government (such as the management of cities or towns or other property well-suited to public gathering); or (3) where the state has authorized, facilitated, encouraged, or otherwise become entangled or entwined with private unconstitutional conduct.[29] In these circumstances, courts refuse to allow the state to evade its constitutional obligations to protect the freedom of expression (or other constitutional rights) by resorting to the corporate form, by delegating such public functions to private entities, or by encouraging such private entities to violate constitutional rights. As the Court explained in *Lebron* v. *National Railroad Passenger Corp.*,[30] "[I]t surely cannot be that the government is able to evade the most solemn obligations imposed in the Constitution" by repositing the authority for public functions in a "private" corporation or otherwise delegating such functions to a "private" entity. The state action doctrine is thus designed to "flush out a state's attempt to evade its responsibilities by delegating them to private entities."[31]

The seminal state action decision in the First Amendment context is the 1946 case of *Marsh* v. *Alabama*,[32] in which the Supreme Court began to re-examine formalistic distinctions between public and private regulations of speech and scrutinized the restrictions on expression imposed by an entity wielding extensive power over individuals' expression. In *Marsh,* the Supreme Court treated a private entity that performed certain government functions and that exercised the power to regulate the free flow of information within its property as the equivalent of the state for First Amendment purposes. *Marsh* involved restrictions on expression imposed by a privately owned "company town," a phenomenon of the Deep South in the early twentieth century, in which economically ailing regions encouraged capital investments by allowing corporations actually to build and operate towns.[33] Though privately owned and maintained, such towns "had all the characteristics of any other American town," including "streets, sidewalks, sewers, public lighting, police and fire protection, business and residential areas, churches, postal facilities, and schools."[34] The town of Chickasaw, Alabama, was one such company town, with "nothing to distinguish [it] from any other town and shopping center, except the fact that the title to the property belong[ed] to a private corporation."[35] The streets and sidewalks of the town—which under the recently inaugurated public forum doctrine[36] would be considered public forums— were privately owned and regulated by Gulf Shipbuilding Corp.

Grace Marsh, a Jehovah's Witness, came onto a sidewalk in Chickasaw and sought to distribute literature to express her religious views.[37] A Chickasaw official warned her that she could not engage in such expression on the town's sidewalks or streets—nor anywhere else in the town— without a permit, and that no permit would ever be issued to her. Marsh was asked to leave the sidewalk and the town, but refused to do so. She was subsequently arrested and charged with violating state trespass law.

Marsh claimed that the private town's restriction of her free speech and free exercise rights, aided by the enforcement of the state trespass law, abridged her First Amendment rights. The Supreme Court agreed. In inaugurating its state action First Amendment jurisprudence, the Court rejected a formalistic understanding of the public-private distinction and held that the town's nominally private status did not insulate its restrictions of speech from First Amendment scrutiny. In extending the First Amendment's protections to individuals as against powerful private regulators of speech, the Court emphasized that the streets, sidewalks, and other places within the town—which would have constituted public forums if owned by the state—were "accessible to and freely used by the public in general" and served the same functions as such places serve when publicly owned.[38] The Court held that, notwithstanding the fact that such places were privately owned, they were "built and operated primarily to benefit the public" and "their operation is essentially a public function."[39] Accordingly, the speech regulations by the town owner within such places were subject to First Amendment scrutiny. Condemning unfettered regulation of speech by powerful private forums for expression, the Court explained,

> Ownership does not always mean absolute dominion. The more an owner, for his advantage, opens up his property for use by the public in general, the more do his rights become circumscribed by the statutory and constitutional rights of those who use it. . . . Whether a corporation or a municipality owns or possesses the town, the public in either case has an identical interest in the functioning of the community in such a manner that the channels of communication remain free. . . . Many people in the United States live in company-owned towns. These people, just as residents of municipalities, are free citizens of their State and country. *Just as all other citizens they must make decisions which affect the welfare of community and nation. To act as good citizens they must be informed. In order to enable them to be properly informed their information must be uncensored.* There is no more reason for depriving these people of the liberties guaranteed by the First and Fourteenth Amendments than there is for curtailing these freedoms with respect to any other citizen. . . . *When we balance the constitutional rights of owners of property against those of the people to enjoy freedom of the press and religion, as we must here, we remain mindful of the fact that the latter occupy a preferred position.* The circumstance that the property rights to the premises where the deprivation of liberty, here involved, took place were held by others than the public is not sufficient to justify the State's permitting a corporation to govern a community of citizens so as to restrict their fundamental liberties.[40]

The *Marsh* Court therefore adopted an affirmative conception of the First Amendment and acted to ensure that even within privately owned forums for expression, the "channels of communication remain free" and available so as to enable individuals to become informed and to "act as good citizens" within our system of democratic self-government. In scrutinizing the private speech restrictions at issue, the Court looked to the functions and uses served by the forum. Because such property was open to the public and because members of the public had an interest in keeping the channels of communication open and uncensored to enable them to make well-informed decisions, restrictions on speech within such forums were subject to meaningful First Amendment scrutiny.

The Court also recognized that the state was indirectly involved and implicated in empowering the private entity to restrict expression. The state had expressly empowered Gulf Shipbuilding to exercise broad control over individuals' expression, and was prepared to enforce its trespass laws to support such broad private control. In so doing, the state became substantially involved and intertwined with the exercise of power over individuals' lives that Gulf Shipbuilding enjoyed. As the Supreme Court characterized the situation, this was an instance in which "the State [was] permitting a corporation to govern a community of citizens so as to restrict their fundamental liberties."[41] The Court recognized that a system in which the state conferred upon a powerful private entity the power to restrict the expression of those within its property was tantamount to one in which the state itself was restricting such expression.

Marsh places primacy on the government's affirmative obligations under the First Amendment to facilitate the free flow of expression and to protect the preconditions of democratic self-government, even where doing so means regulating the speech restrictions of powerful private entities. The Court held that individuals, in order to participate meaningfully in democratic self-government, must have access to uncensored information and open channels of communication. For the purposes of advancing this goal, it does not matter whether the restrictions on speech are imposed by powerful public or private forum owners. Rather, the dispositive inquiry is whether the speech regulations by the powerful regulator at issue interfere with the open channels of communication essential for individuals to participate meaningfully in democratic self-government.

The primacy that the *Marsh* Court placed on preserving open channels of communications to secure the preconditions for democratic self-government was carried forward in the 1968 case of *Amalgamated Food Employees Union* v. *Logan Valley Plaza*.[42] *Logan Valley* involved circumstances in which a private entity was far less powerful in the control it exercised over individuals' lives than was Gulf Shipbuilding, and far less comprehensive in the types of government-like functions it served. *Logan Valley* concerned a small-scale shopping center with two stores in place, one of which sought to censor expression that was critical of it. This case involved the picketing of Weis Supermarket, a non-union supermarket located within the shopping center. The shopping center had no publicly owned sidewalks or streets adjacent to the targeted supermarket—no nearby traditional public forums for expression—so the picketers' staged their picket on the private property next to the supermarket, where the customers picked up their groceries, and the adjacent portion of the parking lot.[43] Members of the Amalgamated Food Employees Union picketed Weis by carrying signs (truthfully) stating that the supermarket was non-union and that its employees were not receiving union wages or benefits.

The owners of the supermarket and the shopping center instituted a legal proceeding to prohibit this expression. The lower court granted an injunction prohibiting such expression, finding that expressive activity constituted a trespass that was not privileged by the First Amendment.[44] Once again, as in *Marsh,* both the state-defined trespass law (which granted the property owner the right to exclude others from its property) and the state court's enforcement of this law were at issue.

The Supreme Court reversed the state court's decision upholding the protestors' convictions for trespass. It first compared the features and characteristics of the places where the expressive activity occurred in *Logan Valley* to the place where the expressive activity involved in *Marsh* occurred, and found them to be functionally similar for purposes of the First Amendment inquiry, explaining, "[w]e see no reason why access to a business district in a company town for the purpose of exercising First Amendment rights should be constitutionally required, while access for the same purpose to property functioning as a business-district should be limited. . . . "[45] Because the Logan Valley shopping center enjoyed the same relevant features as the streets and sidewalks in *Marsh*—and as public forums such as sidewalks and streets in actual cities and towns—the Court found that the private speech regulations were subject to First Amendment scrutiny:

> If the shopping center premises were not privately owned but instead constituted the business area of a municipality, which they to a large extent resemble, petitioners could not be barred from exercising their First Amendment rights there on the sole ground that title to the property was in the municipality. . . . [S]treets, sidewalks, parks, and other similar public places are so historically associated with the exercise of First Amendment rights that access to them for the purpose of exercising such rights cannot constitutionally be denied broadly and absolutely. . . . [46]

Even though these streets and sidewalks were privately owned, they nonetheless remained the types of places where individuals needed to be able to exercise their free speech rights, free of public or private interference.

As in the *Marsh* decision, the Court in *Logan Valley* looked to the functional characteristics of the property at issue, instead of to the formalistic distinction between public and private ownership of such property, in determining whether and how to protect free speech values. The Court looked to the characteristics of the property on which the speech regulation occurred, the functional similarities between such private forums and public forums, the openness of the property to the public, and the suitability of such property for expressive purposes, instead of simply to whether the property was held "privately" or "publicly." Recognizing the importance of preserving places such as sidewalks and streets—whether publicly or privately owned—as forums for open communication on matters of public and societal importance, the Court held the private owners to the same standards as public owners of forums of expression. The Court went on to explain that the evolution in the ownership of such forums for expression from public to private ownership called for an evolving and functional interpretation of the First Amendment's state action doctrine:

> The large-scale movement of this country's population from the cities to the suburbs has been accompanied by the advent of the suburban shopping center. . . . [Absent the application of the First Amendment's state action doctrine,] [b]usiness enterprises located in downtown areas would be subject to on-the-spot public criticism for their practices, but businesses situated in the suburbs could largely immunize themselves from similar criticism by creating a cordon sanitaire of parking lots around their stores. Neither precedent nor policy compels a result so at variance with the goal of free expression and communication that is at the heart of the First Amendment.[47]

Decisions such as *Marsh* and *Logan Valley* that treat powerful private speech regulators as state actors do not require that *all* speech restrictions by such actors are unconstitutional. Just as governmental entities are permitted to impose time, place, or manner regulations on expression, so too are those deemed "state actors" under First Amendment jurisprudence permitted to impose reasonable, content- and viewpoint-neutral regulations on expression.[48] Nominally private property owners that have opened their property to the public and that serve government-like functions are prohibited from distorting the public debate by discriminating against speech on the basis of its viewpoint or content, but are still free to engage in reasonable content-neutral regulation of speech.

The First Amendment state action doctrine was applied and extended through the 1960s, but was curtailed in several Supreme Court decisions in the 1970s.[49] Following this trend of declining to treat private speech forums and conduits as state actors for First Amendment purposes, courts have declined to subject private Internet actors' speech restrictions to any scrutiny whatsoever under the First Amendment. As I explain in Chapter 5, courts' refusal to treat private conduits of Internet speech as state actors insulates the censorship and discrimination by such conduits from meaningful First Amendment scrutiny, and fails to ensure the open channels of communication necessary to our system of democratic self-government.

The Fairness Doctrine

The fairness doctrine, adopted and implemented by the FCC in the early days of broadcast radio and television, imposed obligations on privately owned radio and television broadcasters to facilitate a broad range of speech on matters of public importance via the airwaves. In the early years of broadcast, the FCC took the position that "one of the most vital questions of mass communication in a democracy is the development of an informed public opinion through the public dissemination of news and ideas concerning the vital public issues of the day."[50] To achieve these goals, the FCC in 1949 adopted a series of regulations that came to be known as the "fairness doctrine," which required broadcast licensees to serve as fiduciaries for the public interest and which granted a (conditional) right of access to (certain) members of the public on certain matters of public importance. The fairness doctrine was aimed at ensuring that radio and television broadcasters' coverage of controversial issues of public importance was balanced and fair. Conceptualized under the fairness doctrine as public trustees, broadcasters were required to afford a reasonable opportunity for discussion of competing points of view and controversial issues of public importance, and were prohibited from using their licenses purely to serve their private interest by advancing biased viewpoints on such issues. The fairness doctrine further required that broadcasters actively seek out issues of importance to their local community and to air programming that focused on these issues. The Commission implemented these broad mandates in 1967 by promulgating rules defining matters such as political editorializing. In further implementing the public trustee conception of broadcasters, the FCC in 1971 established rules requiring broadcasters, as part of their application for license renewal, to report on their efforts to identify and air programming on issues of concern to their community.

In its central case upholding the fairness doctrine, the Supreme Court espoused an affirmative conception of the First Amendment in approving of this substantial state intervention in these broadcast forums for expression. In *Red Lion Broadcasting* v. *F.C.C.,*[51] the Court ruled on a challenge to the constitutionality of the fairness doctrine. Challenged were those aspects of the fairness doctrine that required broadcast stations to provide notification and a right of access—an opportunity to respond—when "during the presentation of views on a controversial issue of public importance, an attack is made upon the honesty, character, integrity, or like personal qualities of an identified person or group."[52] The *Red Lion* case arose in 1964, when Pennsylvania radio station WGCB aired a broadcast in which the Reverend Billy James Hargis condemned the author of a book that was critical of presidential candidate Barry Goldwater and suggested that the author had Communist affiliations. When the author, Fred Cook, heard of the broadcast, he concluded that he had been "personally attacked" within the meaning of the fairness doctrine regulations and demanded that the station provide him with the opportunity to reply. When the radio station refused to comply, Cook raised this matter with the FCC, which determined that the broadcast in question indeed constituted a personal attack within the purview of the fairness doctrine and that Cook enjoyed a right to reply.

The broadcasters challenged the fairness doctrine regulations as interpreted by the FCC, contending that the regulations abridged their First Amendment right to free speech and free press. In rejecting this challenge, and in prioritizing the free speech interests of members of the public over the free speech interest of the broadcasters, the Supreme Court explained that "differences in the characteristics of new media justify differences in the First Amendment standards applied to them."[53] Because a limited number of broadcast frequencies exist, the Court held, the state is justified in treating the chosen licensees as proxies or fiduciaries for members of the public at large. Accordingly, the individual broadcast licensee "has no constitutional right . . .

to monopolize a radio frequency to the exclusion of his fellow citizens."[54] The state can therefore require a licensee to "share his frequency with others and to conduct himself as a proxy or fiduciary with obligations to present those views and voices which are representative of his community and which would otherwise, by necessity, be barred from the airwaves."[55]

In balancing the First Amendment right of the broadcasters to select what speech to air against the rights of the viewers and listeners to be informed on a broad range of public issues, the Court held that the rights of members of the public—the viewers and listeners—were paramount. In so doing, the Court adopted an affirmative conception of the First Amendment that placed primary importance on the role of free expression in facilitating democratic self-government and expressed hostility toward restrictions of free speech by public or private speech conduits:

> It is the purpose of the First Amendment to preserve an uninhibited market-place of ideas in which truth will ultimately prevail, rather than to countenance monopolization of that market, whether it be by the Government itself or a private licensee. Speech concerning public affairs is more than self-expression; it is the essence of self-government. It is the right of the public to receive suitable access to social, political, esthetic, moral, and other ideas and experiences which is crucial here.[56]

With respect to this particular "marketplace of ideas," the Court expressed serious doubt about whether an unregulated market would facilitate speech conducive to discussion and debate on matters of public importance. It emphasized the First Amendment goal of "producing an informed public capable of conducting its own affairs"[57] and was skeptical about whether this goal could be achieved in a market dominated by the "private interests" of broadcasters:[58]

> Nor can we say that it is inconsistent with the First Amendment goal of producing an informed public capable of conducting its own affairs to require a broadcaster to permit answers to personal attacks occurring in the course of discussing controversial issues, or to require that political opponents of those endorsed by the station be given a chance to communicate with the public. Otherwise, station owners and a few networks would have unfettered power . . . to communicate only their own views on public issues, people and candidates, and to permit on the air only those with whom they agreed. Freedom of the press . . . does not sanction repression of that freedom by private interests. . . . The right

of free speech of a broadcaster ... does not embrace a right to snuff out the free speech of others. . . . Congress need not stand idly by and permit those with licenses to ignore the problems which beset the people or to exclude from the airwaves anything but their own views of fundamental questions.[59]

The *Red Lion* Court gave little credence to the claims of the broadcasters that they themselves enjoyed the First Amendment right to use "their" frequencies to broadcast the content of their choosing and to deny access to whomever they chose. The Court had no difficulty subordinating the First Amendment rights of the broadcasters to the First Amendment rights of prospective speakers and members of the public. It similarly rejected the broadcasters' arguments that enforcement of the fairness doctrine would serve as a disincentive for them to cover controversial public issues. In responding to this latter argument, the Court evidenced little tolerance for such "threatened timorousness" on the part of the broadcasters, and suggested that the FCC could respond to broadcasters' reticence in this regard by exercising its power to condition the grant or renewal of broadcast licenses on the licensee's "willingness to present representative community views on controversial issues."[60]

Although the *Red Lion* case arose in a context in which there arguably existed technological barriers to broad public participation in the market for speech, the Supreme Court did not limit the state's role to merely serving as a "traffic cop" in allocating the broadcast spectrum. Rather, the Court broadly approved of the state's role of facilitating deliberation and debate on matters of public importance in the face of censorship by powerful private conduits for expression. It emphasized "the public interest in . . . the presentation of vigorous debate of controversial issues of importance and concern to the public."[61] More generally, the Court adopted the fundamental premise of the affirmative conception of the First Amendment that "speech concerning public affairs is . . . the essence of self-government."[62] As First Amendment theorist Stephen Holmes explains, in the Court's analysis

> [G]overnment action was not justified solely by the desirability of escaping from the "state of nature" of unregulated speech use. Regulation was meant to establish not mere order but, rather, a certain kind of order, maybe even a just order. At stake in public oversight of broadcasting was not merely efficient coordination but also some sort of moral norm: . . . an obligation to serve the public interest.[63]

The *Red Lion* decision signaled the Supreme Court's approval of state intervention into forums for expression in order to generally facilitate discussion and debate on controversial issues of public importance. The Supreme Court has also countenanced more specific rights of access to the airwaves to advance goals fundamental to democratic self-government. In the 1981 case of *C.B.S. v. F.C.C.,*[64] the Court considered a challenge to a federal statute authorizing the FCC to require broadcasters to sell airtime to legally qualified political candidates. Section 312(a)(7) of the Communications Act of 1934, as added by Title I of the Federal Election Campaign Act of 1971, authorized the FCC to revoke a broadcaster's license in the case of its "willful or repeated failure to allow reasonable access to or to permit purchase of reasonable amounts of time for the use of a broadcasting station by a legally qualified candidate for Federal elective office on behalf of his [or her] candidacy."[65] In reliance on this statutory right of access, the Carter-Mondale Presidential Committee requested that CBS, ABC, and NBC provide time for it to air a thirty-minute program in the prime-time evening slot in early December 1979, to enable Carter to formally announce his reelection campaign and to outline the record of his first term. Each of the stations refused, and the presidential committee filed a complaint with the FCC charging that the networks violated their obligation to provide "reasonable access" under the statute. The FCC agreed, as did the Supreme Court.

Rejecting the broadcasters' arguments that the statute unconstitutionally restricted their editorial discretion, the Supreme Court held that the statute created an affirmative, promptly enforceable right of reasonable access for candidates. Once again, in balancing the free speech interests of the broadcasters against the free speech interests of the political candidates and the electorate, the Court recognized that although broadcasters were entitled to exercise "the widest possible journalistic freedom" consistent with their public duties, "[i]t is the right of viewers and listeners, not the right of broadcasters, which is paramount."[66] The Court emphasized that this limited, statutory right of access to the media for political candidates "makes a significant contribution to freedom of expression by enhancing the ability of candidates to present, and the public to receive, information necessary for the effective operation of the democratic process."[67] Accordingly, the Court upheld against First Amendment challenge Congress's intervention in the broadcast medium for expression to ensure that this "important resource . . . will be used in the public interest."[68]

The rights of access to the broadcast medium that Congress, the FCC, and the Supreme Court approved in *Red Lion* and *C.B.S.* v. *F.C.C.* represent the high-water mark of the acceptance of the affirmative conception of the First Amendment. In the past two decades, the FCC and the courts have rejected many aspects of the affirmative conception (and have abandoned the fairness doctrine in particular).[69] This sea change was partly brought about by the fact that broadcast spectrum is no longer scarce, and partly by a philosophical shift toward the negative conception of the First Amendment, in which courts and policymakers increasingly entrust the protection of free speech rights to the market.

Must Carry Obligations

Although not as protective of individuals' free speech interests as those imposed under the fairness doctrine, must carry obligations imposed by the FCC on cable systems operators and approved of by the Supreme Court also represent a significant—and recent—recognition of the affirmative conception of the First Amendment. The 1994 case of *Turner Broadcasting System* v. *F.C.C.*[70] involved a challenge brought by several cable systems operators to the must carry provisions of the Cable Television Consumer Protection and Competition Act of 1992 (the Cable Act).[71] The Cable Act required cable systems operators to carry the signals of local commercial and noncommercial educational public broadcast television stations, without charge, on a continuous, uninterrupted basis and in the same numerical channel position as when these programs were broadcast over the air.[72]

In passing the Cable Act, Congress evidenced concern about the concentration of economic power in the cable industry and about how this concentration of power endangered the ability of local broadcast stations to compete for viewing audiences. Congress found that local broadcast television was "an important source of local news, public affairs programming, and other local broadcast services critical to an informed electorate" and that noncommercial local broadcast television "provides educational and informational programming to the Nation's citizens."[73] Congress found that state intervention into the market for speech in cable television was necessary to ensure that the electorate continue to receive information necessary to produce citizens well informed on matters of public concern.

In response to the cable systems operators' assertions that the must carry provisions unconstitutionally infringed their free speech rights to make editorial decisions as to which content to carry, the FCC defended the statute on a market dysfunction rationale. The FCC claimed that imperfections and dysfunctions in the market for cable television justified affirmative government intervention, just as imperfections in the market for broadcast televising justified intervention in the form of the fairness doctrine. While ultimately upholding key provisions of the statute, the Court rejected the comparison between the type of market dysfunction in the broadcast market and that in the cable television market, and took the occasion to refine and clarify its basis for upholding government intervention in the broadcast market in *Red Lion.* The Court explained that economic causes for market dysfunction were not a sufficient basis for justifying affirmative government intervention into the market, whereas technologically imposed causes of market dysfunction as were present in the broadcast market—the scarcity inherent in the broadcast spectrum—were a sufficient basis for affirmative government intervention. If as a result of economic conditions a particular medium of expression evolves to be dominated by one entity that enjoys control over speech within that medium, such de facto control by itself is an insufficient ground on which to justify affirmative government intervention into that market. If, however, the technical conditions of a particular medium of expression limit opportunities for competition in the market, then government intervention in such a market is justified. The Court explained that "the special physical characteristics of the broadcast transmission, not the economic characteristics of the broadcast market, are what underlie our broadcast jurisprudence [upholding state intervention into the broadcast market]."[74] The Court concluded that the economic conditions of the cable television market, which by their nature limited the number of participants in this medium of expression, were by themselves insufficient to justify government intervention into this market.

While declining to hold that the economic sources of market dysfunction at issue in *Turner* justified the same reduced scrutiny that the Court applied to the regulations in *Red Lion,* the Court did find that certain features of the cable television market justified state intervention into this market (and less-than-strict scrutiny of such state intervention). It also held, once again, that in balancing the First Amendment rights of the cable operators against

those of members of the public, the latter prevailed. In particular, the Court
rejected the analogy that the cable operators sought to draw between their
First Amendment rights and those of newspaper publishers. In opposing the
statute, cable operators referred to the Court's holding in *Miami Herald* v.
Tornillo[75] that a requirement that newspapers publish content not of their
choosing unconstitutionally intruded upon the editorial prerogative of the
newspapers. Cable operators claimed that they enjoyed free speech rights regarding the content they chose to carry that were analogous to those enjoyed
by newspaper publishers, and that the same strict scrutiny the Court applied
to the regulations in *Tornillo* were applicable in this case. The Court disagreed. It held that although both newspapers and cable operators may enjoy
economic monopoly status in a given geographical locale, the cable operator
enjoys much greater control over access to its medium, and accordingly enjoys
much greater power to affect the free speech rights of members of the public:

> A daily newspaper, no matter how secure its local monopoly, does not possess
> the power to obstruct readers' access to other competing publications—whether
> they be weekly local newspapers or daily newspapers published in other cities.
> Thus, when a newspaper asserts exclusive control over its own news copy, it
> does not thereby prevent other newspapers from being distributed to willing
> recipients in the same locale.
>
> The same is not true of cable. When an individual subscribes to cable, the
> physical connection between the television set and the cable network gives the
> cable operator bottleneck, or gatekeeper, control over most (if not all) of the
> television programming that is channeled into the subscriber's home. Hence,
> simply by virtue of its ownership of the essential pathway for cable speech, a ca-
> ble operator can prevent its subscribers from obtaining access to programming
> it chooses to exclude. A cable operator, unlike speakers [or publishers] in other
> media [such as newspaper publishers], can thus silence the voice of competing
> speakers with a mere flick of the switch.
>
> *The potential for abuse of this private power over a central avenue of commu-*
> *nication cannot be overlooked. Each medium of expression . . . must be assessed*
> *for First Amendment purposes by standards suited to it, for each may present*
> *its own problems. The First Amendment's command that government not im-*
> *pede the freedom of speech does not disable the government from taking steps*
> *to ensure that private interests not restrict, through physical control of a critical*
> *pathway of communication, the free flow of information and ideas.*[76]

Cable operators (and other broadband providers) today continue to enjoy bottleneck or gatekeeper control over another central avenue of communication—the Internet—and such control justifies state intervention into the Internet medium for expression as well.

Because of the control that cable operators exercised over this "critical pathway of communication" and the consequences of such control for the "free flow of information and ideas," the Court concluded that intermediate, not strict, scrutiny was the proper level of scrutiny to apply to the regulations in this case. Such intermediate scrutiny (merely) required the Court to find, in order to uphold the regulations, that the speech regulations at issue served an important government interest and that the restriction of First Amendment freedoms of the cable systems operators was no greater than necessary to achieve that interest.[77]

The Court readily identified three important government interests that were advanced by the Act: (1) preserving local broadcast television, (2) *promoting the widespread dissemination of information from a multiplicity of sources,* and (3) promoting fair competition in the market for television programming.[78] In particular, with reference to the second interest, the Court recognized a government purpose "of the highest order" in ensuring public access to "a multiplicity of information sources."[79] On this point, the *Turner* Court explained that "it has long been a basic tenet of national communications policy that the widest possible dissemination of information from diverse and antagonistic sources is essential to the welfare of the public."[80]

The first two interests countenanced by the Court evidence its recognition of an affirmative conception of the state's role in advancing First Amendment values. The Court also approved of state intervention in the market characterized by private actors' speech decisions. It explained that the First Amendment "does not disable the government from taking steps to ensure that private interests not restrict, through physical control of a critical pathway of communication, the free flow of information and ideas."[81] Specifically, the Court rejected the negative conception of the First Amendment articulated by Justice O'Connor in her dissent, in which she stated,

> It is for private speakers and listeners, not for the government, to decide what fraction of their news and entertainment ought to be of a local character and what fraction ought to be a national (or international) one. And the same is true of the interest in diversity of viewpoints. . . . [82]

Rejecting this articulation of the negative conception of the First Amendment, the majority approved of the state's intervention into this market for speech to protect the free flow of information and ideas and to secure broad public exposure to a multiplicity of information sources—values it held were central to the First Amendment.

The *Turner* Court was unable to conclude on the record before it that the Act's provisions were narrowly tailored to advance these interests, and remanded for further consideration. Reviewing the case after remand, the Court, per Justice Kennedy, credited evidence that the potential harms Congress had sought to remedy were real, that the must carry regulations served the government's important interests directly and effectively, and that the regulations did not burden substantially more of the cable operators' speech than necessary to further these interests. It credited the lower court's findings that cable operators had already dropped, refused to carry, or adversely repositioned local broadcasters, and that this situation would grow worse absent regulation.[83] The Court recognized that broadcast television "has been an essential part of the national discourse on subjects across the whole spectrum of speech, thought, and expression,"[84] and that the regulation at issue was appropriately tailored to preserve this important source of expression.

In his concurring opinion, Justice Breyer addressed in detail the contention that the must carry regulations impermissibly restricted the free speech rights of the cable operators. He acknowledged that compulsory carriage "extracts a serious First Amendment price—amounting to the suppression of speech . . . by . . . interfer[ing] with the protected interests of the cable operators to choose their own programming."[85] Yet, he explained, there were other, weightier First Amendment interests on the other side of the balance, the side of the public—specifically, the statute's purpose of advancing the national communications policy of protecting "the widest possible dissemination of information from diverse and antagonistic sources." Justice Breyer explained that

> [This national communications] policy, in turn, seeks to *facilitate the public discussion and informed deliberation, which, as Justice Brandeis pointed out many years ago, democratic government presupposes and the First Amendment seeks to achieve.* . . . Indeed, *Turner* [below] rested in part upon the proposition that assuring that the public has access to a multiplicity of information sources is a governmental purpose of the highest order, for it promotes values central to the First Amendment.[86]

Justice Breyer concluded that although there were important First Amendment interests "on both sides of the equation," the statute struck a reasonable balance between potentially speech-restricting consequences for cable operators and speech-enhancing consequences for members of the public.[87]

In summary, in upholding the must carry regulations, the Court approved of state intervention into a market for speech where there were no technological barriers to competition, but where the conduits exercised bottleneck or gatekeeper control over the content accessible by members of the public. In so doing, the Court championed the goal of bringing about the "widest possible dissemination of information from diverse and antagonistic sources" in order to facilitate public discussion and informed deliberation, which "democratic government presupposes and the First Amendment seeks to achieve."[88]

The Common Carriage Doctrine

The common carriage doctrine—like the state action doctrine, the fairness doctrine, and must carry obligations—imposes obligations on private speech conduits to facilitate the expression of others. Like the public forum doctrine, the common carriage doctrine "ensures open, non-discriminatory access to the means of communication."[89] The common carriage doctrine imposes affirmative obligations on privately owned communications conduits to facilitate such communications without discrimination. Notwithstanding the fact that such entities are privately owned, the common carriage doctrine prohibits them from exercising the discretion to determine which communications to facilitate and which to censor (thereby rejecting the claim that such conduits enjoy First Amendment rights of their own to exercise editorial discretion). Since the beginning of the modern communications era in the 1930s, the FCC has imposed obligations on providers of interstate communications services (such as telephone and telegraph companies) to facilitate the transmission of all legal content. The United States Postal Service has also been regulated as a common carrier that is required to facilitate the transmission of all legal content and is prohibited from discriminating against such content.[90]

Under the doctrine of common carriage, the state has historically imposed affirmative obligations on private entities engaged in transportation, communications, and other important public service functions to facilitate the free flow of information and commerce without discrimination or censorship.

Through this doctrine, the state has bridged the gap between public and private entities and imposed affirmative duties on entities that provide important communication and transportation functions for the benefit of the public. While the common carriage doctrine historically applied to those carrying goods on behalf of others, it has evolved throughout the centuries to extend to those facilitating communications and transmitting information on behalf of others. As such, the common carriage doctrine is one of the most important representations of the affirmative conception of the free speech guarantee. Under this doctrine, individuals' ability to communicate is affirmatively protected by the state instead of relegated to the dictates of private speech conduits. Rather than granting private communications conduits the discretion to regulate speech however they see fit, the doctrine countenances affirmative government intervention into this market for expression by requiring that such conduits carry all legal content without discrimination. As Ithiel de Sola Pool explains, the common carriage doctrine embodies the affirmative conception of the free speech guarantee by requiring that communications be facilitated free of censorship:

> [T]he law of common carriage protects ordinary citizens in their right to communicate. [This doctrine] rests on the . . . assumption that, in the absence of regulation, the carrier will have enough monopoly power to deny citizens the right to communicate. The rules against discrimination are designed to ensure access to the means of communication. . . . [T]his element of civil liberty is central to the law of [common carriage].[91]

The common carriage status of transportation and communications providers benefits members of the public by granting them access to communications conduits under a nondiscrimination principle. As Jerome Barron characterizes this benefit, individuals who rely on common carriers to facilitate their communications "benefit from the democratic egalitarianism that characterizes the non-discriminatory access principle associated with common carrier law."[92] As such, the common carriage model is "the paradigm of mandatory access to a communications medium."[93]

The common carriage doctrine has played a critical role in regulating communications providers over the past several decades. Recently, however, courts and policymakers have begun to curtail common carriage obligations imposed on telecommunications providers—in particular, on broadband providers. In the absence of common carriage regulations or other laws or policies imposing similar obligations, broadband providers will continue to enjoy the power to restrict Internet communications however they see fit. To understand the importance of the obligations imposed under the doctrine of common carriage and what is at stake in the FCC's and the Court's recent abandonment of that doctrine for broadband providers, I will analyze the doctrine's foundational principles.

The common carriage doctrine in the United States has its roots in the early English law of common carriage,[94] under which private entities that served the public in the performance of important public functions similar to those assumed by the government were charged with certain affirmative obligations. By imposing affirmative obligations on certain private entities to facilitate the transport—and ultimately the communications—of others, the common carriage doctrine rejected the principle that private entities may regulate transportation and communication however they choose, with their conduct held in check by the market only.

In the mid-1880s, Congress began to regulate American telegraph companies in a manner akin to common carriers. Even though telegraph companies (like broadband service providers today) did not enjoy monopoly power within their market, Congress conditioned certain valuable privileges for telegraph companies on their agreement to be subject to common carriage obligations.[95] And in 1893, the Supreme Court ruled that, like common carriers, telegraph companies were required to provide service without discrimination.[96] Two decades later, in the Mann-Elkins Act of 1910, Congress extended common carrier obligations to a host of early telecommunications providers—telegraph, telephone, and cable providers.[97]

Congress overhauled the regulation of telecommunications providers in the Communications Act of 1934,[98] which charged the newly created Federal Communications Commission with regulatory authority over telecommunications providers (telegraph and telephone companies), regardless of whether they enjoyed monopoly power, and imposed additional common carriage regulations on such providers.[99] Under the 1934 Act, as the Supreme Court later explained, common carriers are charged with the obligation to serve as transparent conduits for all (legal) content originated by others; accordingly, any regulation that is sought to be imposed that prohibits common carriers from transmitting legally protected content is subject to strict scrutiny.[100] The role of a common carrier such as the telephone company is neither to generate content nor to make editorial or qualitative decisions regarding which content to carry and which to censor. Common carriers are prohibited from "mak[ing] individualized decisions, in particular cases, whether and on what terms to deal,"[101] and do not enjoy independent First Amendment rights to exercise editorial discretion. Unlike newspaper publishers, for example, common carriers are not entitled to engage in editorial discretion to determine which content to transmit and which to censor.[102] Common carriers are distinct from publishers or other editors who enjoy their own First Amendment rights to exercise editorial discretion in their selection and exclusion of content.[103]

Throughout the mid-twentieth century, common carriage nondiscrimination obligations were applied to traditional conduits of communication such as telephone companies. In the early 1970s, the FCC began to consider whether and to what extent to impose common carriage obligations on computer-assisted processes and services. As discussed in greater detail in Chapter 6, in a series of "Computer Inquiries," the FCC essentially created two categories of computer-assisted communications services—basic services and enhanced services. "Basic" (later, "telecommunications") services,[104] such as telephone and facsimile services, were those that offered straightforward transmission services, and those offering such services were regulated as common carriers and made subject to the requirement that they not discriminate on the basis of content. "Enhanced" (later, "information") services were those in which computer-processing applications were implemented to act on a subscriber's information, and providers of such services were made exempt from common carriage nondiscrimination requirements.

In the formative years of the development and commercial use of the Internet, entities providing access to the Internet, such as telephone companies providing dial-up Internet access, were subject to common carriage requirements that prohibited them from discriminating against any and all (legal) content. However, as users migrated from narrowband, dial-up Internet access to broadband Internet access, the FCC embarked on a path of gradually removing common carriage obligations from broadband Internet service providers, and the Supreme Court countenanced the removal of these obligations in its *Brand X* decision in 2005. The result is that today, no provider of broadband Internet access is subject to common carriage obligations. In a drastic reversal of both this nation's long history of regulating telecommunications providers as common carriers and the regulation of Internet access providers as common carriers in the Internet's formative years, today no providers of broadband Internet access are subject to such regulation.

• • •

Through its adoption of these five doctrines, the Supreme Court historically recognized the importance of the affirmative conception of the First Amendment, in which the state is empowered to do more than simply refrain from itself censoring speech. But recent trends in the Court's First Amendment jurisprudence are jeopardizing this conception of the free speech guarantee, as I explore in the following chapters.

4   A Place to Speak Your Mind[1]

PUBLIC FORUMS ARE THE PLACES IN REAL SPACE—SUCH AS THE National Mall or Lafayette Square—where you are guaranteed the right under the First Amendment to express yourself and speak your mind. The Supreme Court adopted and strengthened the public forum doctrine in the mid-twentieth century, but has substantially weakened it in recent years. And this (now anemic) doctrine applies only within *public* places. So what happens to this guaranteed right to express yourself when virtually no places are publicly owned? Practically all forums and conduits for speech on the Internet are in private hands, and all speech occurring within those places is subject to private regulation, unchecked by the First Amendment and the public forum doctrine. Virtually no places exist on the Internet to serve as "public forums." As a result, the free speech values historically embodied within the public forum doctrine, and the state's affirmative role of providing speakers with meaningful forums from which to express themselves, have been essentially nonexistent on the Internet.

Along with the loss of public forums in cyberspace comes the loss of meaningful protection for free speech under the First Amendment. In particular, the government's abdication of control over Internet speech regulation results in the loss of protection for speech that is insufficiently protected within an unregulated market for speech—that is, unpopular and poorly subsidized speech. In real space, such speech is protected by the existence of public forums, access to which is open to all and within which restrictions on speech are subject to exacting scrutiny. The existence of government-owned property as a forum for speech available to all comers provides an important guarantee for such speech. Yet today, as increasingly more speech takes place not in real space but in cyberspace, the affirmative constitutional protections for free speech that exist in real space are in danger of being sacrificed. In the words of Justice Kennedy:

> Minds are not changed in streets and parks as they once were. To an increasing degree, the more significant interchanges of ideas and shaping of public consciousness occur in mass and electronic media. The extent of public entitlement to participate in those means of communication may be changed as technologies change. . . . [2]

To make matters worse, the Supreme Court recently declined to accord public forum status (and therefore declined to extend meaningful First Amendment protection) to even the comparatively minor portion of public "property" on the Internet. In *American Library Association* v. *United States*,[3] the Court held that public libraries' provision of Internet access via publicly owned computers did not constitute a public forum and that restrictions on speech in that context were therefore not subject to meaningful First Amendment scrutiny.

Despite the common perception among members of the public and Internet law scholars that the Internet is a forum for free expression of unprecedented scope and importance, in fact there are essentially no places on the Internet where free speech is actually constitutionally protected against censorship by those with the actual power to censor such expression. In this chapter I explore the Court's ill-advised contraction of the public forum doctrine, both in real space and in cyberspace.

The development of the public forum doctrine has become quite complex in recent years. Since the inception of this doctrine, the Court has rendered the doctrine intricate and rather convoluted. This case law breaks out forums into the following categories: (1) traditional public forums, (2) designated public forums, and (3) nonpublic forums. "Traditional" public forums consist of streets, sidewalks, parks, and other places that "have immemorially been held in trust for the use of the public, and, time out of mind, have been used for purposes of assembly, communicating thoughts between citizens, and discerning public questions."[4] "Designated public forums" consist of public property that has not "immemorially" been used for expressive purposes but which the government has explicitly opened and designated as a place for public expressive activity.[5] The government may choose, for example, to open up property within a public school,[6] university meeting facilities,[7] or munici-pal theaters[8] as forums for expression in general or for expression on certain designated subjects. Within a limited-purpose designated public forum, once the government has defined the subject-matter limitations of the forum, regu-lation of such property is subject to the same stringent limitations as those governing a traditional public forum.[9] Thus within traditional public forums such as streets, sidewalks, and parks, and with designated public forums such as public meeting places devoted to expression on particular subjects, indi-viduals enjoy their most robust rights of free expression. Government restric-tions on speech within both types of public forums are subject to the most stringent scrutiny under the First Amendment, such that no speech restric-tions will be upheld unless they serve compelling government interests and are the least restrictive means of restricting such speech. The Supreme Court has also made clear that, in order to constitute a designated public forum, the place in which speech occurs need not be an actual physical place. Rather, public forums may also include virtual forums, such as funding and solici-tation schemes,[10] the airwaves,[11] and cable television.[12] The third category of publicly owned forums are nonpublic forums, places such as military bases, jail grounds, and federal workplaces, that the government owns but which it has not opened up for expressive activity on the part of the public.

In general, the classification of a forum into one type of forum or another all but determines the free speech rights of the parties seeking to express themselves on such property. If a forum is deemed to fall within the tradi-tional or designated public forum category, courts will apply strict scrutiny to content-based or viewpoint-based regulations of speech within such forums and will almost certainly strike down such regulations. Regulations of speech within nonpublic forums, on the other hand, are subject to reduced scrutiny and will most likely withstand constitutional challenge.

The Contraction of the Public Forum Doctrine in Real Space

Although the public forum doctrine was meaningfully applied in the years following its initial adoption, in recent years it has been substantially cur-tailed by the Supreme Court.[13] In particular, instead of adopting a functional interpretation of the concept of "traditional public forums" that would enable it to extend to new media the protections that "from time immemorial" have extended to "rights so vital to the maintenance of democratic institutions," the Court has refused to extend "traditional public forums" beyond actual, real space streets, sidewalks, and parks, rendering this category very narrow in real space (and a dead letter in cyberspace). Second, the Court has been slow to infer that the state has created a "designated public forum" by acts of "intentionally opening a nontraditional forum for public discourse,"[14] and has interpreted this category extremely narrowly (both in real space and cyberspace).

The case of *International Society for Krishna Consciousness* v. *Lee* is illustrative. In that case, members of the International Society for Krishna Consciousness (ISKCON) sought to engage in their religious practice of *sankirtan,* which involved "going into public places, disseminating religious literature, and soliciting funds to support the religion."[15] The public places they chose in which to distribute literature and solicit funds were three major New York area airports: Kennedy, La Guardia, and Newark, all of which were owned and managed by the Port Authority of New York and New Jersey. These airports and associated terminals serve as thoroughfares for approximately one hundred million passengers annually, along with other members of the public. The Port Authority adopted a regulation prohibiting both the repetitive distribution of literature and the solicitation of funds within the airport terminals, and ISKCON sought a declaratory judgment that the regulation violated its members' First Amendment rights.

As with most cases involving regulation of speech on public property, the disposition of *ISKCON* v. *Lee* turned on whether airport terminals constituted a public forum. A majority of the Supreme Court, in a complex series of opinions, essentially answered in the negative. ISKCON advanced a functional interpretation of the public forum doctrine that emphasized the historic, speech-facilitating nature of transportation nodes (for example, rail and bus stations, wharves, and Ellis Island), and contended that such sites historically served as important forums for expression. Justice Rehnquist rejected this functional interpretation of the doctrine in favor of a narrower reading, and concluded for the Court that "given the lateness with which the modern air terminal has made its appearance, it hardly qualifies for the description of having immemorially . . . time out of mind been held in trust and used for purposes of expressive activity."[16] Accordingly, Rehnquist concluded, airport terminals did not constitute a "traditional public forum." Furthermore, according to Rehnquist, airport terminals did not constitute "designated public forums" because the government owners were (not surprisingly) contesting their use for expressive purposes, and they could not be said to have been "intentionally opened by their operators to such [expressive] activity."[17] Of course, in nearly every public forum case before the courts, the government will be contesting the exercise of free speech rights on government property and will contend that it did not take the requisite steps to create a "designated public forum." Having concluded that the airport terminals were nonpublic forums, Rehnquist merely evaluated the Port Authority's ban on distribution of literature and solicitation of funds under a "reasonableness" standard, under which the bans were readily upheld.

Justice Kennedy (writing for himself and Justices Blackmun, Stevens, and Souter) criticized Rehnquist's miserly interpretation of the public forum doctrine, on the grounds that it left "almost no scope for the development of new public forums absent the rare approval of the government."[18] He explained that the purposes of the public forum doctrine cannot be given effect unless the Court undertakes an objective, functional inquiry, based on the "actual, physical characteristics and uses of the property."[19] Under such an inquiry, the Court should recognize that open public spaces and thoroughfares that are suitable for discourse such as airport terminals should be conceptualized as public forums, whatever their historical pedigree. Absent such a functional interpretation, the public forum doctrine "retains no relevance in times of fast-changing technology."[20] In lieu of the strict "traditionality" inquiry adopted by Chief Justice Rehnquist, Justice Kennedy advanced a functional, evolving interpretation of the public forum doctrine, under which the Court should take into account the fact that airport terminals are among the few public spaces where people have extended contact with other members of the public, and which, like streets, have areas that are "open to the public without restriction."[21]

Justice Kennedy went on to criticize Rehnquist's interpretation of "designated public forums," under which the government is granted the discretion to "restrict speech by fiat."[22] Under Rehnquist's analysis, if the government does not expressly designate property as a public forum (and thereby assume the burden not to regulate speech on that property), the public enjoys no meaningful free speech rights on such property. This reading of the "designated public forum" doctrine allows the government to easily evade its affirmative obligations under the First Amendment. Rehnquist's failure to "recognize the possibility that new types of government property may be appropriate forums for speech will lead to a serious curtailment of our expressive activity,"[23] as Justice Kennedy explained:

> [U]nder the Court's view, the authority of the government to control speech on its property is paramount, for in almost all cases the critical step in the Court's analysis is a classification of the property that turns on the government's own definition or decision, unconstrained by an independent duty to respect the speech its citizens can voice there. . . .
>
> *The Court's approach is contrary to the underlying purposes of the public forum doctrine. The liberties protected by our doctrine . . . are essential to a functioning democracy. . . . Public places are of necessity the locus for discussion of public issues, as well as protest against arbitrary government action. At the heart of our jurisprudence lies the principle that in a free nation citizens must have the right to gather and speak with other persons in public places. The recognition that certain government-owned property is a public forum provides open notice to citizens that their freedoms may be exercised there without fear of a censorial government, adding tangible reinforcement to the idea that we are a free people. . . .*
>
> [T]he policies underlying the [public forum] doctrine cannot be given effect unless we recognize that open, public spaces and thoroughfares that are suitable for discourse may be public forums, whatever their historical pedigree and without concern for a precise classification of the property.[24]

Justice Kennedy went on to lament the Court's unwillingness to construe the public forum doctrine to encompass public forums in new media in the 1996 case of *Denver Area Educational Telecommunications Consortium* v. *F.C.C.*[25] In that case, the Court scrutinized various FCC orders implementing provisions of the Cable Television Consumer Protection and Competition Act governing "indecent" and obscene programming. One of the challenged FCC orders permitted cable operators to prohibit patently offensive or indecent programming on public access channels—channels that were available at low or no cost to members of the public. Justice Kennedy contended that these public access channels met the definition of a "designated public forum"— "property that the State has opened for expressive activity by part or all of the public"[26]—and therefore that cable operators' speech restrictions within such forums (as expressly authorized by the FCC) were subject to stringent scrutiny. First, he explained, even the nominally private ownership of these forums did not insulate them from the reach of the public forum doctrine: "[p]ublic access channels . . . are public fora even though they operate over property to which the cable operator holds title."[27] Second, he explained that in providing public access channels under their franchise agreements,

> [C]able operators therefore are not exercising their own First Amendment rights. [Rather,] [t]hey serve as conduits for the speech of others. . . . Treating [public] access channels as public fora does not just place a label on them. . . . It defines the First Amendment rights of speakers seeking to use the channels. When property has been dedicated to public expressive activities, by tradition or government designation, access is protected by the First Amendment.[28]

Justice Kennedy went on to explain that the purpose underlying the public forum doctrine—to ensure open, nondiscriminatory access to the means of communication—was evident in the legislation under which the FCC was regulating and that the public forum doctrine must be meaningfully extended to new media:

> Giving Government free rein to exclude speech it dislikes by delimiting public fora (or common carriage provisions) would have pernicious effects in the modern age. Minds are not changed in streets and parks as they once were. To an increasing degree, the more significant interchanges of ideas and shaping of public consciousness occur in mass and electronic media. The extent of public entitlement to participate in those means of communication may be changed as technologies change; and in expanding those entitlements the Government has no greater right to discriminate on suspect grounds than it does when it effects a ban on speech against the backdrop of the entitlements to which we have been more accustomed.[29]

Justice Kennedy concluded that in order for the First Amendment to remain meaningful within new technologies, the public forum doctrine—like the common carriage doctrine—must be extended to these new technologies, to prevent government (and government-like actors operating public forums) from exercising the power to discriminate against disfavored expression.

In summary, in a series of recent cases the Supreme Court has curtailed the obligations imposed on the government to facilitate expression in public "places." First, the Court has refused to adopt a functional interpretation of the "traditional public forum" category, thus rendering this category ineffectual for new media such as the Internet. Second, the Court has substantially deferred to government actors in its determinations of which public places will be conceptualized as "designated public forums," in the process returning perilously close to the doctrine embodied in *Davis* in which the state enjoyed the same rights as private property owners to determine which expression to prohibit and which to allow on its property.[30] The Court's recent public forum jurisprudence fails to recognize the importance of preserving spaces where members of the public can engage in the free exchange of ideas, without fear of government censorship, that is essential to democratic self-government.

The Contraction of the Public Forum Doctrine in Cyberspace

However bleak is the picture of public forums in real space, it is bleaker still for cyberspace. The vast majority of speech forums in cyberspace are privately owned and regulated, with the consequence that virtually no public places exist that are even candidates for the public forum designation. One might suppose that the small number of actually public Internet spaces would be regulated as public forums. Yet in recent challenges to speech regulations imposed by government actors within public Internet spaces, courts—including the Supreme Court—have concluded that such spaces are not public forums and that governmental regulations of speech within these forums are immune from meaningful First Amendment scrutiny. Most notably, in the *American Library Association* v. *United States*[31] case decided in 2003, the Supreme Court held that Internet access provided by public libraries did not constitute a public forum, and therefore that speech restrictions imposed within such forums were immune from meaningful First Amendment scrutiny.

In *American Library Association* v. *United States,* plaintiffs challenged the constitutionality of the Children's Internet Protection Act (CIPA), which required all public libraries that provide Internet access to their patrons to impose software filters upon such access—or else forgo substantial federal funding. CIPA makes the use of software filters by public libraries and schools a condition on their receipt of two kinds of federal subsidies: grants under the Library Services and Technology Act (LSTA) and "E-rate" discounts for Internet access and support under the Telecommunications Act.[32] To receive LSTA funds or E-rate discounts, public libraries and schools are required to certify that they are using technology protection measures like software filters that prevent patrons from accessing visual depictions that are obscene; child pornography; or, in the case of minors, "harmful to minors."[33] With respect to adults' use of Internet-accessible computers, CIPA provides that a library official is permitted to "disable the technology protection measure concerned, during use by an adult, to enable access for bona fide research or other lawful purpose."[34] However, CIPA's amendments to the E-rate program do not permit libraries or schools to disable filters to enable bona fide research or other lawful use for minors.

The algorithms and process employed by filtering software to restrict access to certain content are created by those who design such software and constitute a substantial portion of the programs' value to consumers. As such, they are typically protected as trade secrets. Thus a library implementing a filtering software program typically has no way of knowing which websites will actually be rendered inaccessible by the program. Although the library may choose to configure the software to filter out certain pre-defined categories of websites (such as "Adult/Sexually Explicit"), the library has no way of knowing the criteria used by the software developers to select which websites fall into this category, nor which websites will actually be found to fall within this category.

The constitutionality of CIPA was initially considered by a special three-judge panel, which first found that the use of the filtering software programs mandated by CIPA erroneously block a huge amount of speech that is protected by the First Amendment,[35] estimating the number of web pages erroneously blocked to be "at least tens of thousands."[36] Filtering software programs, the court found, "block many thousands of Web pages that are clearly not harmful to minors, and many thousands more pages that, while possibly harmful to minors, are neither obscene nor child pornography."[37] Indeed, the government's expert himself acknowledged that popular filtering software packages over-block at rates between nearly 6 percent and 15 percent (in other words, between 6 and 15 percent of blocked web pages contained no content that met even the software's own definitions of sexually themed content, let alone the constitutional definitions of obscenity or child pornography).[38] Furthermore, the court concluded that software filtering programs inevitably over-block harmless Internet content, which adults and minors have a First Amendment right to access, and under-block obscene and child pornographic content, which neither adults nor minors have a First Amendment right to access. This is in part because the categories used by such software for filtering purposes are broader than the constitutional categories of unprotected speech defined by CIPA and in part because of the imperfections in filtering software technology.[39]

The court went on to find that the provisions of CIPA permitting libraries to unblock wrongfully blocked sites upon request were insufficient to render the statute constitutional.[40] In addition to the constitutional infirmities inherent in refusing to permit libraries to unblock wrongfully blocked sites for minors,[41] the court found that many adult patrons would be "reluctant or unwilling to ask librarians to unblock Web pages or sites that contain only materials that might be deemed personal or embarrassing, even if they are not sexually explicit or pornographic."[42] Because libraries were not required under CIPA's scheme to permit Internet users to make anonymous unblocking requests, the vast majority of patrons confronted with wrongfully blocked sites apparently declined to request the unblocking of such sites.[43] Furthermore, even where unblocking requests were submitted and acted upon, the unblocking process took too long—between twenty-four hours and one week. The court concluded that

> [T]he content-based burden that the library's use of software filters places on patrons' access to speech suffers from the same constitutional deficiencies as a complete ban on patrons' access to speech that was erroneously blocked by filters, since patrons will often be deterred from asking the library to unblock a site and patron requests cannot be immediately reviewed.[44]

The court also undertook a forum analysis of the requirements imposed on libraries by CIPA, explaining that the threshold determination was whether libraries' provision of Internet access constituted a traditional public forum, a designated public forum of some type, or a nonpublic forum.[45] Because under the Supreme Court's public forum jurisprudence the category of traditional public forums appears to be limited to streets, sidewalks, public parks, and other such public places that have "immemorially been held in trust for the use of the public for expressive purposes,"[46] the court concluded that libraries' provision of Internet access could not fall within this category.

The court then considered whether libraries' provision of Internet access constituted a "designated public forum"—a forum the libraries opened up and designated for expressive and communicative purposes—in which case the speech restrictions would be subject to stringent First Amendment scrutiny. The court easily distinguished libraries' provision of Internet access from non-public forums—government-owned property not opened up for expressive purposes, such as military bases, jail grounds, and the federal workplace[47]—and found that the purpose of a public library's provision of Internet access is "for use by the public . . . for expressive activity, namely, the dissemination and receipt by the public of a wide range of information."[48] It concluded that the government's provision of Internet access in a public library constituted a designated public forum.[49]

The court then considered the level of First Amendment scrutiny that was applicable to the speech regulations CIPA imposed within this designated public forum. It explained that if the government had only intended to facilitate a narrow range of speech within the designated public forum at issue, then the government's restriction of speech within such a forum to that narrow range would be accorded substantial deference. That is, once the government has opened its property for use for a particular range of expressive purposes, its restrictions limiting expressive uses to this range of expression are to be accorded substantial deference. As the Supreme Court explained by way of example on the related subject of government-subsidized speech, "[w]hen Congress established the National Endowment for Democracy to encourage other countries to adopt democratic principles, it was not constitutionally required to encourage competing lines of political philosophy such as communism and fascism."[50] Rather, only speech that was within the scope for which the forum was designated was permitted within that forum, and speech that fell outside of this designated range could constitutionally be excluded by the government. Conversely, the broader the range of speech the government facilitates within a designated public forum, the less deference courts will accord to the government's content- or viewpoint-based restrictions on speech within that forum. Thus "when the government creates a designated public forum to facilitate speech representing a diverse range of viewpoints, the government's decision selectively to single out particular viewpoints for exclusion is subject to strict scrutiny."[51] The court concluded that libraries' provision of Internet access fell within the latter category of designated public forums—that is, those in which a broad range of expression was permitted and within which the government's speech regulations are subject to strict First Amendment scrutiny.

Referring to the Supreme Court's decision in *Rosenberger* v. *Rectors and Visitors of the University of Virginia,*[52] the court explained,

> [T]he more widely the state opens a forum for members of the public to speak on a variety of subjects and viewpoints, the more vulnerable is the state's decision selectively to exclude certain speech on the basis of its disfavored content, as such exclusions distort the marketplace of ideas that the state has created in establishing the forum. . . . [W]here the state designates a forum for expressive activity and opens the forum for speech by the public at large on a wide range of topics, strict scrutiny applies to restrictions that single out for exclusion from the forum particular speech whose content is disfavored.[53]

Applying the *Rosenberger* Court's analysis, the court explained that libraries' provision of Internet access to their patrons—in contrast to their provision of print materials—enables their patrons to receive speech on a "virtually unlimited number of topics, from a virtually unlimited number of speakers, without attempting to restrict patrons' access to speech that the library, in the exercise of its professional judgment, determines to be particularly valuable."[54] Libraries' provision of Internet access enables patrons to receive speech on a broad and diverse range of topics, and the restrictions on sexually themed expression imposed by mandatory software filters within this forum are subject to strict First Amendment scrutiny. Accordingly, the court rejected the government's argument that libraries' content-based decisions implemented via filtering software are merely subject to reduced scrutiny. It concluded,

> Within this "vast democratic forum" which facilitates speech that is "as diverse as human thought," software filters single out for exclusion particular speech on the basis of its disfavored content. These content-based restrictions on patrons' access to speech are subject to strict scrutiny.[55]

Applying strict scrutiny to libraries' filtering of certain sexually themed speech, the court found that the use of filtering software mandated by CIPA "erroneously blocks a huge amount of speech that is protected by the First Amendment."[56]

The Supreme Court reversed, holding that CIPA's restrictions on speech were not unconstitutional,[57] on the basis of its determination that these speech restrictions were not imposed within a public forum. Chief Justice Rehnquist, who authored a plurality opinion in which Justices O'Connor, Scalia, and Thomas joined, held that the provision of Internet access in public libraries did not constitute a public forum and that strict scrutiny was therefore not warranted.[58] Rehnquist first explained that Internet access in public libraries did not constitute a "traditional public forum" within the constitutional meaning of that term because "this resource—which did not exist until quite recently—has not immemorially been held in trust for the use of the public [or], time out of mind, . . . been used for purposes of assembly, communication of thoughts between citizens, and discussing public questions."[59]

He went on to explain that Internet access in public libraries did not constitute a "designated public forum," a forum in which "the government [has made] an affirmative choice to open up its property for use as a public forum."[60] Rehnquist found, with little elaboration and despite the American Library Association's arguments to the contrary,[61] that "a public library does not acquire Internet terminals in order to create a public forum for web publishers to express themselves, [but rather] . . . to facilitate research, learning, and recreational pursuits by furnishing materials of requisite and appropriate quality."[62] He observed that "even if appellees had proffered more persuasive evidence that public libraries intended to create a forum for speech by connecting to the Internet, we would hesitate to import the public forum doctrine . . . wholesale into the context of the Internet."[63]

Having concluded that libraries' provision of Internet access did not constitute a public forum, Rehnquist analyzed CIPA's constitutionality under a framework of reduced scrutiny, and merely inquired into whether libraries' use of filtering software was "reasonable,"[64] which he readily found that it was. Despite the fact that the libraries themselves contended that they had provided Internet access to their patrons in order to facilitate communication and exchange on a "virtually unlimited number of topics," Rehnquist declined to extend public forum status to the publicly owned Internet forum at issue and declined to extend meaningful scrutiny to the government's content-based exclusions from that forum effected by the implementation of mandatory software filters.

The Court's refusal to recognize the public forum status of libraries' provision of Internet access establishes a dangerous, speech-restrictive precedent for the Internet. In this rare instance of public ownership and control over an Internet speech forum, in which the public entity acknowledges that it created the forum to facilitate the exchange of ideas among members of the public on a virtually unlimited number of topics, the Court nonetheless held that no public forum was created and that speech restrictions within the forum were immune from meaningful First Amendment scrutiny. If no public forum for expression is found in these circumstances, it is unlikely that a public forum will ever be recognized in the context of the Internet.

Indeed, following the Supreme Court's decision in the *American Library Association* case, courts appear unwilling to hold that public provision of Internet access constitutes a public forum. In *Nickolas* v. *Fletcher*,[65] for example, blogger Mark Nickolas challenged the state of Kentucky's decision to prohibit state employees from accessing blogs on state-owned computers. The Kentucky state government had initially allowed its employees to access the Internet for business and limited personal use, while implementing commercial filtering software to prohibit access to pornographic sites and chat rooms. On June 20, 2006, Nickolas was quoted in *The New York Times* expressing views that were critical of Governor Fletcher's administration. Immediately after that date, the state prohibited state employees from accessing blog sites (by selecting "blogs/newsgroups" from the list of categories to be blocked by its commercial filtering software), while continuing to allow employees to access mainstream news websites. Nickolas challenged this restriction that prohibited state employees from accessing his and other blogs, claiming that this action effected an unconstitutional restriction of speech within a designated public forum.

The court rejected Nickolas's argument that the state's provision of Internet access constituted a traditional public forum or a designated public forum. Because state employees were only allowed to use the Internet for business and limited personal use, the court concluded that this use was not for "open communication or the free exchange of ideas between members of the public," and therefore the forum at issue was not a "traditional public forum."[66] Second, the court ruled that because the state restricted Internet access to categories such as pornography and chat rooms, it was not providing "open access to any website" but rather was providing "limited access at its discretion," and therefore was not creating a "designated public forum."[67] In this contorted application of the public forum doctrine, the court held that because the state was restricting access to *some* Internet expression based on content, the state was ipso facto constitutionally permitted to restrict access to *any* Internet expression it chose.

The court thus held that the government's challenged speech restrictions occurred within a nonpublic forum and, following *American Library Association* v. *United States,* that the state's restrictions on speech within this nonpublic forum need only be "reasonable" and viewpoint-neutral. Despite Nickolas's assertion that the state's ban on blogs was implemented the same day he was quoted in the *New York Times* criticizing the governor, the court held that the state's actions restricting access to blog sites was reasonable and viewpoint-neutral,[68] and not in violation of the First Amendment.

The legacy of the Supreme Court's ill-advised public forum analysis in *American Library Association* v. *United States* appears to be that even public entities such as public libraries and state governments that control Internet speech forums will not be held to meaningful First Amendment scrutiny. Restrictions of speech within Internet forums—whether by public or private actors—simply are no longer constitutionally prohibited. As a result, the important functions served by the First Amendment—and by the public forum doctrine in particular—are in danger of being seriously eroded in cyberspace.

Restoring the Values of the Public Forum within Cyberspace

The Supreme Court's current public forum jurisprudence, both in real space and in cyberspace, has all but abandoned its original mandate from *Hague* v. *CIO* that citizenship in our form of government requires that public places be held open and made available for individuals to assemble, communicate, and discuss matters of public and societal importance. The public forum doctrine as it exists today is insufficient to protect individuals' right to engage in the exchange of information and ideas that is essential to our form of self-government. Courts' refusal to extend public forum status to (and meaningful First Amendment protection within) Internet forums managed and controlled by the state all but decimates meaningful protection for expression on the Internet. As Justice Kennedy warned, "minds are not changed in streets and parks as they once were." Today, they are often changed on the Internet. Courts should rethink their public forum analysis to impose meaningful limitations on state actors' discretion to restrict speech within the Internet forums they control, and should apply a functional instead of a historically literal analysis of what constitutes a "traditional public forum." As the lower court in *American Library Association* explained,

> The provision of Internet access . . . shares many of the characteristics of traditional public fora that uniquely promote First Amendment values. . . . Regulation of speech in streets, sidewalks, and parks is subject to the highest scrutiny not simply by virtue of history and tradition, but also because the speech-

facilitating character of sidewalks and parks makes them distinctly deserving of First Amendment protection. Parks and sidewalks are paradigmatic loci of First Amendment values in large part because they permit speakers to communicate with a wide audience at low cost. . . . Similarly, . . . a speaker can, via the Internet, address the public, for little more than the cost of Internet access. . . .

The Internet promotes First Amendment values in the same way that the historical use of traditional public fora for speaking, handbilling, and protesting [does]. . . . A faithful translation of First Amendment values from the context of traditional public fora such as sidewalks and parks to the distinctly non-traditional public forum [of the Internet] . . . requires that content-based restrictions on Internet access . . . be subject to the same exacting standards of First Amendment scrutiny as content-based restrictions on speech in traditional public for such as sidewalks, town squares, and parks.[69]

Courts should recognize that the Internet is the functional equivalent of the public town square—a place that permits speakers to communicate with a wide audience at low cost—and should meaningfully translate the values underlying the public forum doctrine from real space to cyberspace. Government provision of Internet access for general information purposes, such as that offered by public libraries or by municipalities offering municipal broadband, should be held to constitute a public forum in which restrictions on expression are subject to meaningful First Amendment scrutiny.

Unless and until the federal courts rethink the public forum doctrine so as to provide meaningful protection for freedom of expression, states should, through their courts or legislatures, define public forums to encompass Internet forums that are generally open to the public for free speech purposes. In this regard, the example of California is illustrative. Concerned with what it found to be a "disturbing increase in lawsuits brought primarily to chill the valid exercise of the constitutional right of freedom of speech,"[70] in 1992 the California legislature enacted a statute aimed at deterring "strategic lawsuits against public participation," or SLAPP suits.[71] This statute grants individuals the right to speak and petition freely within "public forums"—whether publicly or privately owned—free from harassing and meritless lawsuits aimed at chilling such speech. California's anti-SLAPP statute grants individuals the right to "dismiss at an early stage nonmeritorious litigation meant to chill the valid exercise of constitutional rights of freedom of speech and petition in connection with a public issue."[72] The statute defines an "act in furtherance of a person's right of petition or free speech" to include "any written or oral statement or writing made in a place open to the public or a public forum in connection with an issue of public interest."[73]

In interpreting its anti-SLAPP statute, the California courts in a number of instances have held that Internet forums constitute public forums. In *National Technical Systems* v. *Schoneman*,[74] for example, the California Court of Appeal held that an Internet bulletin board constituted a public forum. In that case, National Technical Systems Inc. (NTS) brought a defamation suit against Brett Schoneman, its former vice president, for statements that Schoneman had posted about NTS on the Yahoo! Finance message board. Schoneman brought a motion to strike the lawsuit under California's anti-SLAPP statute, claiming that his statements arose out of First Amendment activity, were made in "a public forum in connection with an issue of public interest," and were therefore protected. The California Court of Appeal granted Schoneman's motion to strike, holding that the statute's definition of "public forum" as a place open to the public and in which information on matters of public interest were freely exchanged encompassed Internet bulletin boards or chat rooms that are open to the public.

The Court reached similar holdings in *ComputerXpress* v. *Jackson*[75] and in *Bidbay* v. *Spry*,[76] concluding that Internet chat rooms and message boards (even where privately owned) constitute public forums when they are "open to the public or to a large segment of the interested community."[77] California's anti-SLAPP statute accordingly grants individuals the right to express themselves without fear of reprisal or censorship by public or private speech regulators. Although California's anti-SLAPP statute was originally designed to deter lawsuits that merely threatened to chill free expression, its invocation to deter actions that actually censor free expression—such as the removal of disfavored content by an Internet speech regulator—is an even more significant form of protection for individuals' free speech rights. With the technological tools available to Internet actors to censor speech with the click of a mouse, such censorship tools present an even greater harm to speakers than lawsuits designed to chill their speech. Following California's lead, in the face of the Supreme Court's unwillingness to protect the values inherent in the public forum doctrine, states should define public forums (whether under their state constitutions or state legislation) to encompass Internet forums for expression that are in fact open to the public.

· · ·

Contrary to the widely held perception of the Internet as one great public forum in which individuals can express themselves without fear of censorship, with the Supreme Court's recent contraction of the public forum doctrine, even government restrictions on speech within expressive Internet forums have been rendered immune from meaningful First Amendment scrutiny. With the demise of public ownership, and of public forums, in cyberspace, important constitutional safeguards for speech that were formerly embodied in the public forum doctrine are in danger of being seriously eroded in cyberspace. Courts should reverse this trend by adopting a functional interpretation of the public forum doctrine to render these crucial safeguards for free speech meaningful in the Internet age.

5   When Private Becomes Public

WHEN A PRIVATE ENTITY ACTS LIKE A GOVERNMENT AND enjoys government-like power to censor speech, under what circumstances should it be treated like the government and have its speech restrictions subject to First Amendment scrutiny? In the mid-twentieth century, the Supreme Court set forth the circumstances in which it was appropriate to subject private actors who censor speech to constitutional scrutiny. Under the state action doctrine, the Court explained that sometimes private entities act so much like the government that they should be regarded as such for constitutional purposes. However, consistent with the negative conception of the First Amendment, beginning in the 1970s the Court declined to treat powerful private speech regulators as state actors for First Amendment purposes. Subsequent courts have declined to subject private *Internet* speech restrictions—such as those imposed by Comcast or Google—to meaningful scrutiny under the First Amendment. In this chapter, I explore the Court's recent, ill-advised refusal to consider powerful private actors as state actors for First Amendment purposes, both in real space and then in cyberspace.

The mid-twentieth century cases of *Marsh* and *Logan Valley,* discussed in Chapter 3, represent the high-water mark of the Supreme Court's treatment of private speech regulators as state actors for First Amendment purposes. Shortly after the *Logan Valley* decision, in *Lloyd* v. *Tanner,*[1] the Supreme Court scaled back its protection of free speech against regulation by powerful private actors.

Lloyd involved individuals' efforts to peacefully distribute leaflets in a large shopping mall to protest the Vietnam War, less than six months after the

Logan Valley decision was handed down (which protected expression in similar circumstances). This time, the protestors sought to exercise their rights within Lloyd Center, a shopping mall complex that was much larger and more comprehensive than Logan Valley, encompassing fifty acres and containing sixty establishments, including offices of doctors, dentists, lawyers, bankers, travel agents, and persons offering a variety of other services.[2] The private company that acquired Lloyd Center purchased the land from the city of Portland, which vacated eight acres of public streets to make room for the shopping mall complex. (Notably, if the city had maintained ownership of this property, individuals seeking to exercise their free speech rights on the Portland streets would have enjoyed the right to do so under the public forum doctrine.) Given the extent of goods and services available at this centrally located shopping center, "for many Portland citizens, Lloyd Center [would] so completely satisfy their wants that they would have no reason to go elsewhere for goods or services."[3] Indeed, because of the Center's ability to reach such large audiences, presidential candidates from both major parties selected the Lloyd Center as the forum from which to reach the broadest audience of Portland residents (and received permission to do so).

Recognizing the Center's potential for reaching a broad audience of Portland citizens, several protestors sought to distribute antiwar materials on the mall's walkways. The owners of the complex instructed their security guards to warn the protestors that they would be arrested unless they ceased their activities. The protestors brought suit, seeking declaratory relief and claiming that the First Amendment privileged their expressive activities. Although the case arose within months of the *Logan Valley* decision, this time the Court privileged the shopping center's property rights over the free speech rights of members of the public. The Court distinguished *Logan Valley* on the grounds that the picketers in that case were expressing themselves on a subject matter that was directly related to the shopping center's operations—the non-union status of the Weis supermarket—in circumstances in which "no other reasonable opportunities for the picketers to convey their message to their intended audience were available."[4] In contrast, the Court explained, the protestors in *Lloyd* were not protesting on a matter related to the shopping center's operations, and therefore had reasonable alternatives to convey their message to their intended audiences (such as by distributing their literature on the public streets and sidewalks adjacent to Lloyd Center).

Despite the Court's attempt to distinguish *Logan Valley* from *Lloyd*'s facts, it is difficult to explain the divergent outcomes in *Logan Valley* and *Lloyd* as anything other than a deliberate doctrinal shift by the Court, with the effect of insulating speech regulation by powerful private forums of expression from First Amendment scrutiny.[5] Indeed, the circumstances of *Lloyd* present a stronger case for recognition of free speech rights. Lloyd Center took over a larger swath of public land, comprehended a greater offering of goods and services, and involved the most highly valued of speech—"pure expression of political beliefs," in the words of the district court.[6] This doctrinal shift toward the negative conception of the First Amendment is particularly troubling because it coincides with the trend toward increased takeover of public forums by private entities. As Justice Marshall warned in his dissent,

> It would not be surprising in the future to see cities rely more and more on private business to perform functions once performed by government agencies. The advantage of reduced expenses and an increased tax base cannot be overstated. As governments rely on private enterprise, public property decreases in favor of privately owned property. It becomes harder and harder for citizens to find means to communicate with other citizens.[7]

Indeed, since the *Lloyd* decision was handed down in the early 1970s, private entities have assumed greater ownership and control of forums for communication and expression, in real space and cyberspace, and exercise such control unchecked by the First Amendment, as a result of the contraction of the state action doctrine begun in *Lloyd*.

In a further blow to the state action doctrine, in the 1973 case of *C.B.S. v. D.N.C.*[8] the Court made clear that it would continue to narrowly construe the doctrine in the First Amendment context. Although this case is generally viewed as involving the unsuccessful invocation of the fairness doctrine, it is also noteworthy in that it further limits the state action doctrine in the First Amendment context. In this case, the Democratic National Committee (DNC) and other antiwar organizations sought radio and television airtime to express their views in opposition to the Vietnam War. The organizations claimed that the fairness doctrine—and the First Amendment more generally—prohibited the radio and television stations involved from refusing to sell them airtime to express their views on the war. The case involved a consolidation of appeals from FCC decisions brought by the DNC and the Business Executives Move for Vietnam Peace (BEM). BEM had filed a complaint with the FCC alleging that radio station WTOP had refused to sell it airtime to broadcast a series of brief announcements expressing its views on the Vietnam War. It was the policy of WTOP (and many other broadcasters) to refuse to sell advertising time for announcements to those who wished to express views on controversial issues of public importance such as the Vietnam War. The DNC had also filed a request with the FCC seeking a declaratory ruling under the First Amendment and the Communications Act that a broadcaster may not refuse to sell airtime to responsible entities wishing to comment on controversial public issues.[9] The FCC denied both requests, and BEM and the DNC appealed to the D.C. Circuit. That court held that a policy banning paid announcements on controversial public issues (while allowing other paid advertisements) violated the First Amendment.

In a complex series of opinions, the Supreme Court sided with the broadcasters, concluding that neither the fairness doctrine nor the First Amendment required the broadcasters to grant airtime to these organizations to express their views on controversial issues of public importance such as the Vietnam War. In so doing, the Court concluded that the challenged action of the broadcasters did not constitute state action in violation of the First Amendment despite the substantial intertwined relationship between the state and the broadcasters.

The state action aspect of the decision was sharply criticized by Justice Brennan, who argued that the broadcasters were so intertwined with the government as to render them state actors for First Amendment purposes. In an analysis with important implications for our consideration of broadband providers and other powerful Internet speech conduits, Justice Brennan explained that the reach of the First Amendment should not depend upon any "formalistic 'public-private' dichotomy, but rather upon more functional considerations concerning the extent of government involvement in, and public character of, a particular 'private' enterprise."[10] In contending that the broadcasters' refusal to facilitate these antiwar announcements constituted state action, Brennan observed that the characteristics of the broadcast industry revealed an "extraordinary relationship between the broadcasters and the federal government"—including the public nature of the airwaves; the government-conferred, quasi-monopolistic status of broadcast licensees; and the FCC's approval of the challenged broadcaster policy. On the basis of the confluence of these various indicia of government action, Justice Brennan concluded that the government had "so far insinuated itself into a position of participation in [the challenged] policy that the absolute refusal of broadcast licensees to sell air time to groups or individuals wishing to speak out on controversial issues of public importance must be subjected to the restraints of the First Amendment."[11] He contended that the First Amendment should be interpreted to provide members of the public with the meaningful opportunity to express themselves—even via privately owned conduits for expression:

> It is only through free debate and free exchange of ideas that government remains responsive to the will of the people and peaceful change is effected. . . . The public have a strong First Amendment interest in the reception of a full spectrum of views—presented in a vigorous and uninhibited manner—on controversial issues of public importance. . . . [T]he most effective way to insure this uninhibited, robust, and wide-open debate is by fostering a free trade in ideas by making our forums of communication readily available to all persons wishing to express their views. . . . Indeed, the availability of at least some opportunity for editorial advertising is imperative if we are ever to attain the free and general discussion of public matters [that] seems absolutely essential to prepare the people for an intelligent exercise of their rights as citizens.
>
> [O]ur citizens have at least an abstract right to express their views on controversial issues of public importance. But freedom of speech does not exist in the abstract. On the contrary, the right to speak can flourish only if it is allowed to operate in an effective forum. . . . For in the absence of an effective means of communication, the right to speak would ring hollow indeed. . . . [T]he broadcast frequencies allotted to the various radio and television licensees constitute appropriate "forums" for the discussion of controversial issues of public importance.[12]

Recognizing the importance of ensuring effective forums of communication for those seeking to express their views on controversial issues of public importance (whether via powerful public or privately owned forums), Justice Brennan criticized the majority's curtailment of the state action doctrine and its refusal to subject the broadcasters' censorial actions to First Amendment scrutiny.

• • •

The court's contraction of the state action doctrine—coupled with the increasing privatization of communities in which individuals live and conduct their daily activities— means that an increasing amount of speech regulation is for all practical purposes outside the scope of First Amendment scrutiny.

State Answers to the State Action Problem

One potential recourse to address the curtailment of free speech rights is for state courts to interpret their own constitutions to grant broader rights for individuals against censorship by powerful private entities. Indeed, in response to the Supreme Court's contraction of the state action doctrine of the First Amendment, several state supreme courts have done just that.

In the case of *Robins* v. *Pruneyard Shopping Center*,[13] for example, the California Supreme Court interpreted the free speech protections in the California Constitution to apply to regulations imposed by private entities. In *Pruneyard,* several California high school students sought to protest a United Nations resolution opposing "Zionism" by distributing leaflets in a large shopping mall located in California. The case arose subsequent to the decision of *Lloyd* v. *Tanner,* in which the United States Supreme Court held that students protesting the Vietnam War had no First Amendment right to do so within the confines of a privately owned shopping center. While recognizing that the First Amendment, per the Supreme Court's decision in *Lloyd,* did not grant the activists the right to protest, the California Supreme Court held that the California Constitution's free speech clause granted the protestors this right. In weighing the shopping center's property and free speech rights to exclude against the free speech rights of the protestors, the court held that the protestors' rights outweighed those of the mall.

In reaching its decision, the *Robins* court relied on its decision in *In re Hoffman,*[14] in which it held that individuals seeking to protest the Vietnam War enjoyed the right to do so within a privately owned railroad depot that was generally open to the public and that served as the functional equivalent of a traditional public forum. That court struck down portions of a municipal ordinance that imposed criminal penalties on those who remain longer than reasonably necessary upon the grounds of a "common carrier," including a railway station, in order to exercise their right to free speech. Consistent with the ruling in *In re Hoffman,* the *Robins* court made clear that large shopping centers that were open to the public served the same functions as traditional public forums, and that the trend toward privatization of such places required an interpretation of the free speech guarantee to render it meaningful in the face of such privatization trends. The court also made clear that, like a government actor, the shopping center in *Pruneyard* enjoyed the right to impose time, place, and manner restrictions on the speech at issue, but did not enjoy the right to censor such speech in its entirety.

The shopping mall in *Pruneyard* claimed that the California Supreme Court's holding violated its First Amendment rights by forcing it to use its property as a forum for the speech of others. The United States Supreme Court rejected this challenge, and made clear that states were free to privilege the free speech rights of members of the public over the free speech rights of the shopping center. It explained, first, that because the private property owners had expressly thrown their property "open to the public to come and go as they please" and had not "limited [it] to the personal use of the appellants," the mall's free speech interests in this case were quite limited. Second, because the state supreme court's decision depended upon the fact that the mall was open to the public for expression generally, "no specific message is dictated by the State . . . [and] there consequently is no danger of governmental discrimination for or against a particular message."[15]

In effect, in *Pruneyard*, the United States Supreme Court invited state supreme courts to interpret the free speech protections in their state constitutions more broadly than the First Amendment, and made clear that states enjoyed the discretion to do so without fear of violating the constitutional rights of the owners of speech forums. In particular, the Court made clear that the First Amendment rights of the owners of large forums for expression such as shopping malls were quite limited and were not infringed by the state's decision to allow members of the public to engage in free speech on such property.

The California Supreme Court further championed the primacy of free speech rights over property rights in the Internet context in *Intel v. Hamidi*.[16] In that case, Hamidi, a disgruntled ex-employee of Intel, sent emails to Intel employees criticizing Intel's employment and labor practices. The California Supreme Court declined to construe Intel's property rights so broadly as to encompass the right to prohibit Hamidi from sending emails via Intel's email server, and recognized that extending property rights so broadly would hinder open Internet communication.

Several other states in addition to California have taken up the Supreme Court's invitation to interpret their constitutions' free speech clauses more broadly in accordance with the affirmative conception of the free speech guarantee. These courts have recognized their citizens' right to express themselves in forums owned by large corporations. In a context similar to those involved in *Lloyd* and *Pruneyard,* the Supreme Court of New Jersey held that a coalition of groups opposed to the (first) war with Iraq enjoyed the free speech right under the New Jersey Constitution[17] to hand out leaflets in areas of regional shopping centers that were open to the public.[18] Writing for the court, Chief Justice Robert Wilentz quoted the United States Supreme Court's mandate in *Marsh* that when courts assess the "constitutional rights of owners of property against those of people to enjoy freedom [of expression], we remain mindful of the fact that the latter occupy a preferred position." The Supreme Court of New Jersey held that leafleting and associated speech must be allowed in regional shopping centers because the expressional interests at issue were very strong and would not interfere with the private owner's use of the property. The court found that shopping centers today are the functional equivalent of downtown areas and indeed in some towns have completely replaced (government-owned) downtown areas as places of public gathering.[19] Given these circumstances, in weighing the mall's free speech and property interests against the leafletter's free speech interests, the court concluded,

> There is no doubt about the outcome of this balance. On one side, the weight of the private property owners' interest in controlling and limiting activities on their property has greatly diminished in view of the uses permitted and invited on that property. The private property owners in this case, the operators of regional and community malls, have intentionally transformed their property into a public square or market, a public gathering place, a downtown business district, a community; they have told this public in every possible way that the property is theirs . . . through the practically unlimited permitted public uses found and encouraged on their property. The sliding scale cannot slide any farther in the direction of public use and diminished private property interests.
>
> On the other side of the balance, the weight of plaintiff's free speech interest is the most substantial in our constitutional scheme. Those interests involve speech that is central to the purpose of our right of free speech. At these centers, free speech, such as leafletting, can be exercised without any discernible interference with the owners' profits or the shoppers' and non-shoppers' enjoyment. . . . If constitutional provisions of this magnitude should be interpreted in light of a changed society . . . the most important change is the emergence of these centers as the competitors . . . and to a great extent as the successors to the downtown business district.

The significance of the historical path of free speech is unmistakable and compelling: the parks, the squares, and the streets, traditionally the home of free speech, were succeeded by the downtown business districts, [which] have now been substantially displaced by these centers. If our State constitutional right of free speech has any substance, it must continue to follow that historic path. . . . [20]

Florida courts have similarly construed the free speech provisions of their constitution. In *Wood* v. *State*,[21] for example, the court held that Florida's constitution provides individuals with a right to engage in free speech in the form of political expression within privately owned shopping centers. That court reversed the trespass conviction of Kevin Wood, a candidate for public office who sought to collect signatures at Panama City Mall in order to get his name in the ballot. Wood was told by the Mall's security guards to leave or face arrest for trespass. When Wood refused to leave, he was arrested and found guilty of trespass. In reversing his conviction, the court explained that

> Free speech serves . . . as a means of securing participation by the members of society, including political decision-making, and as a means of maintaining the balance between stability and change in society.[22]

After citing approvingly to *Marsh* and *Pruneyard,* the *Wood* court held that, despite the fact that malls and shopping centers are private property, they take on a "quasi-public" character that limits their right to exclude and that entitles members of the public to engage in peaceful political activity on their property.

Massachusetts courts have followed a similar course of broadly construing their constitution to protect the right to engage in political expression on certain private property. In *Batchelder* v. *Allied Stores International,*[23] the Supreme Judicial Court of Massachusetts held that under the Commonwealth's constitution, a potential candidate enjoyed the right to engage in political speech—in the form of soliciting signatures and distributing associated material in a large, private shopping center—in support of his nomination for public office. The court recognized this right notwithstanding the fact that the candidate had alternative avenues available to him in which to engage in such speech. While expressly recognizing that there were alternative means to engage in such political expression—such as in downtown areas of municipalities or via door-to-door solicitation—the court observed that shopping centers are the "most favorable site" for such expressive activity and protected individuals' right of access to these most favorable sites. The court explained,

[S]hopping malls . . . function in many parts of this State much as the "downtown" area of a municipality did in recent years. [Because] the North Shore Shopping Center is the most favorable area in [the relevant] District to solicit signatures, [the candidate's] political activity . . . would be substantially impaired in the absence of access.[24]

Courts in other states, including Pennsylvania[25] and Washington,[26] have also interpreted their state constitutions' free speech and related provisions to extend to individuals expressive rights on privately owned property that serves as the functional equivalent of municipal public forums—places where the people can be found for purposes of reaching out for political and other expressive purposes. Indeed, as the *Batchelder* Court characterized this trend, "a majority of the state courts that have recently considered rights under state constitutions to engage in orderly free speech, free assembly, or electoral activity on private property held open to the public have recognized such a right."[27] Consistent with the recent trend among state courts considering this issue, states should interpret their own constitutions' free speech clauses to grant individuals the right to express themselves in forums for expression that are open to the public—in real space *and* in cyberspace.

The State Action Doctrine in Cyberspace

In recent years, individuals have unsuccessfully brought suit against various types of Internet speech regulators claiming that they were state actors for First Amendment purposes. First, individuals have claimed that conventional Internet service providers such as CompuServe and AOL were state actors and were constitutionally required not to discriminate against unsolicited commercial email. Second, individuals have claimed that those entities responsible for domain name registration, and domain name administration more generally, were state actors that were constitutionally required not to discriminate on the basis of content. Third, individuals have claimed that Google in the performance of its search engine function was a state actor and was therefore prohibited from unconstitutionally manipulating its search engine results. Each of these efforts to characterize private regulators of Internet speech as state actors for First Amendment purposes has been unsuccessful. In applying the state action analysis to these challenges, courts have ruled that these private regulators of Internet speech are not equivalent to state actors because (1) they do not perform "traditional" government functions, (2) there is no evidence of entanglement between the government and the actions of these regulators, (3) the government was not attempting to evade its responsibilities for these functions by delegating them to private entities in such cases.

The analysis of the state action doctrine in these cases is based on an antiquated and inadequate interpretation of the doctrine. Given the role that Internet speech regulators (such as broadband providers) serve in regulating and managing expression in this forum that is highly suited to the expression and exchange of ideas, regulators of Internet speech that exercise near-complete control and broad power over Internet expression should be conceptualized and regulated as state actors for First Amendment purposes.

First, the "traditionality" inquiry in the state action analysis—as in the public forum analysis[28]—disserves the protection of free speech in new and emerging mediums and should be jettisoned—or at least more broadly construed—by the courts. Absent a reworking of this factor, courts will continue to conclude that "the Internet is by no stretch of the imagination a traditional and exclusive public function,"[29] and will categorically exempt Internet speech regulation from the dictates of the First Amendment.

Courts should adopt a more functional interpretation of the traditionality prong of the state action doctrine, and should return to the principles articulated by the Supreme Court in its foundational state action free speech jurisprudence. In undertaking an analysis of whether a private Internet speech regulator is a state actor, courts should reach the threshold conclusion that the Internet itself is the functional equivalent of a traditional public forum—a forum for expression that, like public streets, sidewalks, and parks, has a broad speech-facilitating character and is a "natural and proper place for the dissemination of information and opinion."[30] As the courts have recognized, the Internet as a forum constitutes "the most participatory form of mass speech yet developed"[31] and is a "paradigmatic loc[us] of First Amendment values . . . because [it] permits speakers to communicate with a wide audience at a low cost."[32] Thus the regulation of speech in such a forum is tantamount to the regulation of a public forum for expression, which is a function traditionally performed by the government.

Second, in construing the state action doctrine in this context, courts should recognize the ways in which the U.S. government has sought to pass the mantle for the regulation of speech in this public forum to private entities and attempted to delegate responsibility for these functions to private entities. The Internet was created and developed by the U.S. government (under the aegis of the National Science Foundation, a U.S. government agency) primarily as a means to enable individuals to communicate and exchange information, initially via electronic mail.[33] With the expansive growth of this communications medium, as the Internet began to fulfill its promise of becoming an unprecedented vehicle for the exchange of information and ideas, the U.S. government chose to privatize the ownership and management of this forum for expression. Like the decision to delegate responsibility for managing a town and its erstwhile public forums to a private entity, the U.S. government's decision to turn over ownership and control of the Internet to private entities enabled it to delegate its responsibility for facilitating the free flow of information in this forum for expression. The "entanglement" prong of the state action doctrine should be recast and construed to take into account the many ways in which the U.S. government acted to turn over the mantle of speech regulation on the Internet to private entities.

In the late 1990s, the U.S. government undertook measures to turn over many aspects of the Internet to private entities. First, in its passage of the Communications Decency Act of 1996,[34] Congress advanced this end by explicitly encouraging Internet service providers to restrict their subscribers' speech—and subscribers' access to speech—even where the speech so restricted would be protected by the First Amendment if the government were to regulate it. In effect, Congress (among other things) encouraged private Internet actors to do what it could not constitutionally do itself—to censor "objectionable" (yet First Amendment protected) speech. The statute expressly insulates ISPs from liability for restricting access to expression that the ISPs deem inappropriate or objectionable, "whether or not such material is constitutionally protected."[35] In doing so, the government passed the mantle of speech regulation over to private entities and excised itself from the role of regulating and protecting free expression on the Internet.

In 1998, the U.S. government also ceded control of management of the Internet's infrastructure to a private entity, by privatizing management of the Domain Name System and repositing control over this system in the Internet Corporation for Assigned Names and Numbers (ICANN). ICANN is a private entity unaffiliated with any preexisting territorial government or international governance entity, to which the U.S. government conferred the power to establish policies regulating expression on the Internet.[36] Accordingly, ICANN and those it authorizes to regulate the Domain Name System enjoy substantial control over the infrastructure for expression, and for expression itself, on the Internet.

State governments have also attempted to turn over regulation of the Internet to private entities such as ISPs in attempting to combat child pornography on the Internet. Pennsylvania (unsuccessfully) sought to require ISPs themselves to be responsible for blocking websites that the state attorney general identified as child pornography.[37] Recently, the attorney general of New York entered into an arrangement with three of the world's largest ISPs—Verizon, Time Warner Cable, and Sprint—requiring them to prohibit access to newsgroups that allegedly have been used to facilitate child pornography and to purge their servers of all websites that are identified as child pornography by the National Center for Missing and Exploited Children—a private entity.[38]

Because the Internet constitutes an unprecedented forum for expression that was originally created for expressive purposes by the U.S. government, courts should conclude that the management and control of expression on the Internet in general constitutes a public function. Because the U.S. government sought to pass the mantle for regulation of this public forum for expression to private entities, courts should scrutinize carefully whether to subject such private entities' speech-regarding decisions to First Amendment scrutiny. In updating their state action jurisprudence and evaluating which private regulators of Internet speech should be considered state actors, courts should (1) assess the extent of the power that the actor exerts over the Internet expression at issue (including whether there are alternatives available for Internet speakers to escape such power) and (2) balance the competing free speech and other claims of the regulator against those of the would-be speaker.[39] In the following sections, I discuss how courts have analyzed, and should analyze, whether different types of regulators of Internet speech are state actors for First Amendment purposes.

Conventional ISPs and Email Providers

Entities have sought to hold conventional (nonfacilities based[40]) ISPs and email providers, such as CompuServe and AOL, to constitutional obligations not to discriminate against the expression they are charged with transmitting. I analyze these cases in two categories—first, in the context of spammers seeking to secure a right to transmit unsolicited commercial email messages, and second, in the context of individuals seeking to transmit noncommercial email messages.

In an example of the first category in cases brought against ISPs CompuServe and AOL, bulk commercial emailer Cyber Promotions argued that these ISPs were state actors because they were exercising exclusive government functions in facilitating electronic communications—in particular, in serving as postmaster—and were violating Cyber Promotions' First Amendment rights by refusing to deliver its email to the ISPs' subscribers. Cyber Promotions argued that much as the U.S. Post Office is responsible for facilitating the transmission of nonelectronic communications (and is regulated as a common carrier subject to nondiscrimination obligations), these ISPs were serving as postmaster and performing the traditional government function of managing a mail system, and therefore should be charged with First Amendment obligations not to discriminate in the performance of this function.

Consistent with the analysis I advocate, courts should first consider the amount and extent of power that the regulator in question enjoys over the speech (and relatedly, the would-be senders and recipients) in question. Courts should also inquire into the availability of alternative avenues of expression for the would-be speakers to reach their intended audience generally and their intended recipients specifically. In cases in which AOL or CompuServe serves as the exclusive gatekeeper for the electronic communications received by their email subscribers, this factor militates in favor of a finding of state action. On this point, Cyber Promotions had argued, citing *Logan Valley* and *Lloyd* v. *Tanner*, that AOL's provision of email service constituted a traditional, exclusive public function because there were no alternative avenues of communication available to Cyber Promotions to disseminate its message to AOL members via email. The court rejected this argument, finding that Cyber Promotions had other means available to reach AOL members, including U.S. mail, telemarketing, television, cable, newspapers, magazines, and leafleting. The court essentially concluded that the alternative avenues of expression for Cyber Promotions to reach its desired audience of AOL members were non-Internet-based ones. The Supreme Court recently rejected this approach and made clear that (at least when the government is regulating) the relevant inquiry is into whether the speech regulation at issue leaves open alternative avenues of expression *within the speaker's chosen medium of expression.* This issue was confronted by the Court in *ACLU* v. *Reno,*[41] in which the Court reviewed the constitutionality of a statute prohibiting "indecent" and "patently offensive" communications on the Internet. Part of the government's defense of the statute's constitutionality was that even though the statute proscribed certain types of speech *on the Internet,* there were ample *real space* avenues of communication available for speakers. The Supreme Court rejected this argument, explaining that such an analysis if accepted would foreclose an entire medium of communication from constitutional protection.

Accordingly, in assessing whether alternative avenues of expression exist for purposes of determining whether to subject private speech regulation to First Amendment scrutiny, courts should look to whether there are adequate alternative avenues of communication *within the Internet medium itself* for the speaker to communicate its message to its intended (and willing[42]) audience—both to specific targeted listeners and to a general audience. Because the *Cyber Promotions* court looked to non-Internet mediums in concluding that alternative avenues of expression existed for Cyber Promotions to reach its intended audience, this part of its analysis was flawed. Instead, courts should conclude that the exercise of such total power by a private actor over the channels of email communication militates in favor of a finding of state action.

Courts should then evaluate the free speech interests of the speaker versus the property and free speech interests of the speech regulator. In cases in which the communications involved attempting to send bulk unsolicited commercial emails that allegedly caused damage to the functioning of the ISP's email servers, the courts are justified in concluding—as they did in both *Cyber Promotions* cases—that the ISP's interest in avoiding damage to its email servers outweighed the bulk emailer's right to communicate. Although the ISPs exercise substantial control over the speech received by their subscribers, their right to be free from physical harm to their property predominates, and courts should not hold that the conventional ISPs or email providers are state actors.[43]

In cases in which the subject communications involved were not in the nature of unsolicited bulk email, the prospective speaker has a stronger argument. In *Intel* v. *Hamidi,* for example, Intel served as the "postmaster" for the email of its employees. On a handful of occasions, Hamidi, a disgruntled former employee, sent to Intel employees emails that were critical of Intel's labor practices, which Intel was unable to stop by technological means. Intel brought suit against Hamidi in order to stop these communications. In evaluating such a case, the court should first evaluate the extent of power exercised by Intel over the communications involved. Intel was the sole postmaster for the email accounts that it provided to its employees, and exercised substantial control over communications sent to and received by these employees. Yet Intel employees likely had other, non-work-related email accounts, so Hamidi might have had other electronic means of contracting those employees. In addition, Intel arguably has a legitimate interest in controlling the email system that it provided for its employees.

In evaluating the claims of Hamidi, the court should recognize that Hamidi enjoyed a strong claim to communicate via email to criticize the labor practices of Intel—much as he would enjoy the right to send non-electronic mail to Intel employees to criticize their employer. Unlike in the *Cyber Promotions* cases, in this case, Intel did not claim any harm to its computer servers; it merely claimed the right to prevent this concededly harmless interference with its computer servers and the right to control the messages its employees received. In these circumstances, Hamidi's interests in communicating with Intel employees (and the public interest in maintaining the free and open channels of email communication) were substantial. Indeed, under the reasoning of the Supreme Court's state action/property line of cases, there were no other alternative avenues of (electronic) expression for Hamidi to reach his intended audience on the subject of criticizing the labor practices of Intel itself. And, unlike the Cyber Promotions cases, Intel was not asserting that these emails interfered with the efficient functioning of its email servers. Nor could Intel plausibly claim that it had a First Amendment right *of its own* to control the free flow of information that was received by its employees via email.

On balance, the California Supreme Court was justified in concluding that Intel was a state actor, especially as it was applying the California constitution's more speech-protective analysis.[44] Yet in most cases, private employers should be permitted to enforce policies that limit the type and manner of communications that their employees can receive at the workplace. Indeed, the state as an employer is constitutionally permitted to regulate the speech of its employees to a greater extent than it can regulate the speech of the citizenry in general.[45]

Broadband Service and Email Providers

In a challenge to restrictions on Internet speech by a dominant broadband provider such as Comcast or Verizon, consistent with the state action analysis outlined in the preceding section, courts should first evaluate the power exercised by the provider over Internet communications and the alternatives available to the would-be speaker in light of such power. Next, courts should balance the free speech interests of those seeking to communicate against the property and free speech interests of the broadband and email providers. For example, in considering the incident in which Comcast blocked email from AfterDowningStreet for all Comcast email subscribers, courts should first consider the power that Comcast exercises over communication on the Internet. Broadband providers exercise substantial control over the communications in which their subscribers are able to engage. The market for residential broadband services is currently dominated by the cable-DSL duopoly, in which 95 percent of all residential broadband is provided either by cable companies such as Comcast or Cox or telephone companies such as Verizon DSL.[46] Given the absolute gatekeeper power that broadband providers exercise over the communications received by their subscribers, a would-be sender has no alternative avenues to communicate via email with the vast number of intended recipients who are Comcast subscribers. Accordingly, this factor militates strongly in favor of a holding that Comcast is a state actor.

Second, in balancing the free speech interests of the would-be senders and recipients of email communications against the property and free speech interests of the broadband providers, courts should readily find that the balance tips in favor of the former. Such a case does not involve any claim of interference with the efficient functioning of the providers' computer systems, nor does it involve the weightier interest of an employer in controlling the email use of its employees. Nor should the court give credence to the asserted free speech or property rights on the part of the broadband provider to control the content of the information flowing through its pipes.[47] Indeed, the arguments that Comcast and others have asserted for regulating the content of the information flowing through their pipes—including a desire to cater to the interests of the majority of their subscribers—show precisely why pipeline providers must be treated as state actors. Broadband providers have the incentive to cater to the interests of the majority of their subscribers, who may disfavor certain types of unpopular—yet constitutionally-protected—expression.[48] Upon receiving complaints about a particular type of content, broadband providers have the incentive to censor such content. For example, in the case of AfterDowningStreet's attempt to send email messages advocating impeachment of President Bush, Comcast justified its censorship on the grounds that it had received complaints about such emails.[49] This is precisely why broadband providers should be held to the constitutional obligation not to discriminate on the basis of content—to protect countermajoritarian and other unpopular expression from censorship by powerful private gatekeepers of Internet speech.

Furthermore, broadband providers have the ability not only to censor the content received by their email subscribers (those who actually use their jones@comcast.net accounts) but also to censor the content received and accessible by their subscribers in any capacity. Using deep packet inspection technology,[50] broadband providers have the ability to censor information based on the content in packets, and can implement such technologies to discover information about, and take action based on, the nature of any content found in those packets. Or if they know in advance which content they wish to censor, they can use other means to render such content inaccessible to their subscribers. As described in Chapter 1, AT&T did just that in 2007, when it censored a live cablecast of a concert performance by Pearl Jam, apparently believing that Eddie Vedder's lyrics critical of President Bush would be offensive to some subscribers.

Because broadband providers enjoy absolute gatekeeper control over the content received by their subscribers (whether via email or other forms of Internet communication), and because any interest they have in restricting speech based on its content is overwhelmingly outweighed by the interests of those seeking to communicate via their pipes, courts should find that broadband providers are state actors subject to the dictates of the First Amendment.

Control Over the Internet's Infrastructure— ICANN and Domain Name Registrars

In several recent cases, individuals have claimed that domain name registrars were state actors that were constitutionally required not to discriminate on the basis of content in the registration of domain names. Prospective domain

name registrants have claimed that domain name registrars unconstitutionally discriminated on the basis of content in refusing to grant them the exclusive right to their domain name of choice. Domain name registrars indeed
enjoy the power to determine whether to grant an individual the exclusive
right to his or her desired domain name, and in so doing, exercise the power
traditionally enjoyed by the state to confer (or withhold) exclusive rights in
terms and expressions. Domain name registrars have recently gone beyond
their traditional function of serving as initial gatekeeper in the domain name
registration process and have exercised the authority to terminate a domain
name holder's exclusive rights on the grounds that the content *to be made
available* on the website was objectionable or otherwise in violation of its
terms of service.[51] Individuals have also claimed that ICANN is a state actor.
Analysis of these claims requires an understanding of the government's relationship with the Internet's infrastructure in general and the Domain Name
System in particular. The details and evolution of this relationship are complex, but I provide the outlines as follows.

In 1993, the National Science Foundation entered into a cooperative agreement with Network Solutions Inc. (NSI) under which it transferred to NSI the
responsibility for managing the Domain Name System and for registering domain names, and provided NSI with government funding for the exercise of
these responsibilities. In 1998, the government ceded control of management
of the Internet's infrastructure to ICANN. As noted earlier, ICANN is a nominally private entity essentially unaffiliated with any government or international governance entity that enjoys the power to regulate the Internet's infrastructure and to establish policies restricting expression on the Internet.[52]
When the United States ceded control over the Internet's infrastructure to
ICANN, one of the most important functions it transferred was control over
the Domain Name System. ICANN's control over the Domain Name System,
in turn, encompasses the ability to enact policies regulating the acquisition
and maintenance of domain names and policies for resolving disputes between trademark owners and domain name holders. As such, ICANN exercises another power traditionally enjoyed by the state—the power to regulate
intellectual property rights. Furthermore, ICANN's control over the Domain
Name System translates into control over the acquisition and maintenance of
websites, which translates into control over speech on the Internet. Because
the ability to express oneself via a website constitutes one of the most power-

ful vehicles for expression available today, ICANN's control over the Domain Name System translates into control over expression in this important speech forum on the Internet.

ICANN's control over the Domain Name System also encompasses the power to control the resolution of disputes between intellectual property owners and domain name holders in ways that affect speech on the Internet. In one of its most significant exercises of policymaking authority, ICANN enacted a policy for resolving disputes between trademark owners and domain name holders that has an impact on the free speech rights of Internet users. ICANN's dispute resolution policy for resolving disputes between trademark owners and domain name registrants is binding on all domain name registrants throughout the world. Under ICANN's Uniform Domain Name Dispute Resolution Policy, ICANN requires that all domain name registrants—essentially everyone with a website—submit to mandatory arbitration by ICANN-selected panelists in the event that a trademark owner claims that a domain name is infringing. Under the policy, the domain name can be removed from the website owner and transferred to the domain name owner under circumstances specified by ICANN. ICANN thereby exerts power over Internet actors in the performance of a government-like function—promulgating rules and systems of dispute resolution.

Accordingly, ICANN and powerful domain name registrars such as NSI enjoy substantial control over the infrastructure for expression, and for expression itself, on the Internet. Because of the exclusive power that ICANN exercises over Internet expression, and because of the absence of alternatives available to individuals seeking to avoid ICANN's power, ICANN itself should be considered a state actor subject to First Amendment obligations.[53] Even under the traditional test for assessing state action, ICANN should be considered to be a state actor. As Michael Froomkin contends,

> Given that [the U.S. government] called for an ICANN to exist, clothed it with authority, persuaded other government contractors to enter into agreements with it (including the one with NSI that provides the bulk of ICANN's revenue), and has close and continuing contacts with ICANN, a strong . . . case can be made that ICANN is a state actor.[54]

Further, under the modified state action analysis outlined earlier, ICANN should also be deemed a state actor for First Amendment purposes. In what follows, I consider this analysis in the context of challenges to ICANN's and NSI's speech-restrictive policies and actions.

In the 2003 case of *McNeil* v. *Verisign,* Philip McNeil, a disgruntled former distributor of Stanley Works Mac Tools, sued ICANN and his domain name registrar for their roles in forcing him to relinquish domain names that he had registered in order to set up a website critical of his former employer Stanley Works. In particular, McNeil alleged that ICANN's role in promulgating universally applicable rules and policies for domain name administration and dispute resolution, pursuant to which his domain name was ultimately removed from him, constituted state action in violation of the First Amendment. McNeil asserted a First Amendment right in continuing to use his chosen domain name, and a violation of that right by the operation of ICANN's dispute resolution policy.

Under the modified state action analysis outlined earlier, courts should first examine the extent of power exercised by ICANN over the Domain Name System, and should then balance the rights of the speaker against those of the speech regulator. Because ICANN enjoys exclusive power to regulate the Domain Name System, and to establish a mandatory policy for resolving disputes regarding domain names, this factor weighs in favor of ICANN being considered as a state actor. Second, given the free speech interests of domain name registrants, and the absence of free speech interests on the part of ICANN, this balancing factor also militates in favor of holding ICANN to First Amendment obligations.[55]

Whether individual domain name registrars should be considered state actors is a closer question, and depends in part on the degree of power and control exercised over Internet speech by the domain name registrar in question. Prior to the government's transfer of control over the Domain Name System to ICANN, the National Science Foundation vested a single entity— NSI—with exclusive control over the registration of domain names in the .com, .net, and .org top-level domains. Subsequent to that transfer, ICANN authorized a host of companies to register domain names. During the period in which NSI was exclusively in control of registration, a strong case could have been made that NSI was a state actor with respect to its management of the Domain Name System.

In ruling in cases in which disappointed domain name registrants challenged domain name registrars' refusal to register the domain name of choice, courts should first inquire into the degree of power exercised by the speech regulator over the expressive activity of the would-be speaker, including whether there are alternatives available to the speaker to escape the power of that actor. Because ICANN's policies apply to all domain name registrars, courts should hold ICANN to be a state actor for purposes of the First Amendment. Similarly, when NSI was the only domain name registrar authorized to register domain names in the .com, .org, and .net top-level domain name spaces, it enjoyed absolute power over this forum for expression, and this factor should have militated in favor of NSI being considered a state actor.

In one such case, disappointed domain name registrant Island Online brought suit against NSI, challenging its refusal to register certain domain names during the period of time in which NSI was the only authorized domain name registrar.[56] Given the absolute control that NSI then exerted over the ability to register a domain name on the Internet, the court should have found that this factor militated in favor of a finding of state action. However, if and when substantial competition exists in the domain name registration market, then any given registrar cannot be said to exercise substantial control over the expression of a would-be domain name registrant, and this factor would militate against a finding of state action. Indeed, while the *Island Online* suit was pending, other domain name registrars became authorized to register domain names, and other individuals managed to secure registration of the domain names sought by Island Online through registrars that had less restrictive policies than NSI. The existence of alternative avenues for Island Online to secure the desired domain name then militated against a finding of state action.

Courts next should balance the free speech interests of the would-be speaker against those interests of the domain name registrar in determining whether to hold the domain name registrar to constitutional obligations. In the *Island Online* case, while neither side had particularly overwhelming free speech claims, those of the would-be domain name registrant, on balance, should have been held to predominate. Island Online, an adult Internet content provider, unsuccessfully sought to register certain sexually themed domain names in association with websites on which to make available its adult-oriented content. NSI refused, claiming that the requested domain names were "inappropriate" under its recently adopted policy (even though it had earlier agreed to register similarly inappropriate domain names).[57] In refusing to register Island Online's chosen domain names, NSI asserted that it enjoyed "a right founded in the First Amendment of the Constitution to refuse to register, and thereby publish, on the Internet registry of domain names words that it deems to be inappropriate." Courts should hold that NSI, and other domain name registrars, enjoy no such First Amendment right to elect which domain names to "publish" and should prioritize the would-be speaker's free speech rights to use these constitutionally protected terms over the rights of NSI to refuse them. Yet the ability of the speaker to escape the registrar's power—and the availability of alternative avenues for a disappointed domain name registrant to register his or her domain name of choice—militate in favor of a finding of no state action.

In summary, under a modified state action analysis, in the domain name context, the balance of free speech interests favors the would-be speaker over the speech regulator. However, the extent of power factor varies. While ICANN's broad (and inescapable) power renders it a state actor for First Amendment purposes, because of the competition that now exists among domain name registrars, the power enjoyed by any one registrar is not so extensive as to mandate a finding of state action.

Dominant Internet Search Engines

Individuals have also brought suit against dominant search engines such as Google, claiming that these entities should be considered state actors for First Amendment purposes. They have complained about Google's manipulation and censorship in the context of (1) its general search engine, (2) its provision of "sponsored links," and (3) its Google News search engine.

As discussed in Chapter 1, in an example of the first, SearchKing, a search engine optimization website, alleged that Google reduced its "PageRank" from high rank to zero—effectively banishing it from the universe of sites accessible via a Google search—because Google perceived SearchKing to be a competitor.[58] In an example of the second, political activist Christopher Langdon alleged that Google violated his First Amendment rights by refusing to allow him to secure sponsored links for www.ncjusticefraud.com and www. chinaisevil.com.[59] Google refused Langdon's request on the grounds that his requested links "advocate against any individual, group, or organization," in violation of Google's terms of service.[60] In an example of the third, Inner City

Press, a United Nations–focused media organization, claimed that Google News removed its website after it questioned Google regarding its failure to sign a human rights and anticensorship agreement.[61] Each complaint against Google explicitly or implicitly raises the issue that Google is a state actor for First Amendment purposes.[62]

The first type of claim requires us to consider whether Google should be deemed a state actor in connection with its function of serving as the dominant provider of a general search engine—and in manipulation and blocking of content in connection with this function. In the performance of this function, as just discussed, in the *SearchKing* case Google was charged with actively manipulating the rank of a competitor's website, on an individualized basis, from a high rank to "no rank"—thereby banishing the site to Google oblivion. In a similar case, Google was charged with actively manipulating its search results on an individualized basis to advance its position in an ongoing litigation. In *Google v. American Blinds and Window Factory, Inc.*[63] (in which American Blinds unsuccessfully contended that Google violated its trademark by selling advertising keyed to its trademarked term *American Blinds*), on the day that the district court was to hear arguments in that case, Google apparently surreptitiously manipulated its search results on an individualized basis before the court's and the litigants' very eyes:

> [As a] member of the American Blinds legal team . . . [attempted to] test the system, he brought up Google and entered what had become a habitual search query: "American Blinds." . . . Every [other] time someone entered "American Blinds" into Google's search field, competitors to American Blinds came up on the screen [evidencing the alleged trademark violation].
>
> Only this morning, for some reason, they did not.
>
> The lawyer suspected Google had changed its results, and called colleagues in other parts of the country. Sure enough, searches in other regions returned different results, including the [allegedly] infringing advertisements.[64]

In assessing whether such acts by Google of manipulating its search results on an individualized basis constitute state action in violation of the First Amendment, courts should first analyze the extent of power and control that Google exercises over Internet speech. Google's search engine enjoys between a 60 and 70 percent share of the six billion plus searches in the United States each month.[65] This leaves approximately 30 to 40 percent of the searches conducted by other search engines, including Yahoo!, Microsoft, and Ask.com. Accordingly, speakers do enjoy alternative avenues of expression besides Google's search engine to communicate with Internet users. Furthermore, although search engines are popular vehicles for accessing web content, they are not absolute gatekeepers of such content, since websites can be accessed without benefit of search engines by simply typing in the domain name for the website into one's web browser. Although Google enjoys substantial power and control over the search engine market, because there are alternative search engines and alternative means of accessing websites, the power factor of the modified state action analysis does not weigh in favor of considering Google as a state actor.

Second, courts should balance the free speech and other claims of the would-be speaker against the free speech and other claims asserted by Google. Speakers have a free speech interest in having their websites meaningfully accessible to their desired audience via Google's dominant search engine. This interest outweighs Google's asserted free speech interests in its search results. Google has claimed, in defending its right to manipulate its search engine results as it sees fit, that its search ranks constitute its subjective "opinions" about the relative importance of websites, which it enjoys a First Amendment right to determine and to manipulate however it chooses.[66] Indeed, Google has gone so far as to file motions under California's anti-SLAPP statute to strike complaints that challenge its manipulation of search results, contending that such lawsuits inhibit Google's exercise of its free speech rights in its search results. Under this statute, losing claimants are required to pay the winner's attorney fees. Google has used the statute to strong-arm challengers into dropping their suits for fear of having to pay Google's attorney fees if Google ultimately prevails.

Google's PageRanks are the product of an objective, mathematical algorithm, and Google therefore does not enjoy the sort of editorial discretion over such listings that would merit First Amendment protection (or that would outweigh speakers' interests in being heard). Google itself has conceded this point when it serves its interests. It steadfastly maintains that "[t]here is no human involvement or manipulation of [search] results, which is why users have come to trust Google as the source of objective information untainted by paid placement."[67] As Google attests further, in response to the public outcry over Google's ranking of an anti-Semitic website as the number one hit for the search term *Jew*:

If you recently used Google to search for the word "Jew," you may have seen results that were very disturbing. We assure you that the views expressed by the sites in your results are not in any way endorsed by Google. . . . *A site's ranking in Google's search results relies heavily on computer algorithms using thousands of factors to calculate a page's relevance to a given query. . . . The beliefs and preferences of those who work at Google . . . do not determine or impact our search results.* Individual citizens and public interest groups do periodically urge us to remove particular links or otherwise adjust search results. Although Google reserves the right to address such requests individually, Google views the comprehensiveness of our search results as an extremely important priority.[68]

Google apparently seeks to have it both ways—to claim a First Amendment right to its ranking of websites as a product of its editorial judgment and to claim that its search results are solely the product of objective computer algorithms with no human intervention on an individualized basis. While courts should readily recognize Google's intellectual property rights in its search engine algorithm, they should reject its claim of First Amendment rights in its search engine results, or at least hold that would-be speakers' free speech interests predominate over Google's free speech interests.[69]

Considering the extent of power currently enjoyed by Google over Internet communications, the availability to speakers of alternative avenues of expression, and the evaluation of competing interests, on balance courts probably should not hold that Google is a state actor in its function of providing a general search engine. And Google has a greater claim to not being considered a state actor in connection with its specialized search engines such as Google News and in connection with its policy for selling sponsored links. However, courts should not strongly weight Google's claims that its search rankings constitute its First Amendment protected speech. Indeed, legislative or other measures may be necessary to regulate Google to ensure that Internet users continue to enjoy appropriate and meaningful access rights to this important forum for expression. Google should not be permitted to have it both ways—to represent to the public that its search results are solely the product of objective computer algorithms without human intervention and to manipulate results on an individualized basis when it serves its interests—not when such important interests in communication are at stake.

• • •

In summary, the state action doctrine, as recently interpreted by the Supreme Court in the First Amendment context, fails to hold Internet speech regulators to the standards necessary to protect our free speech rights. Although the doctrine was inaugurated and initially construed to hold powerful private regulators of speech to meaningful scrutiny, in recent years the doctrine, consistent with the negative conception of the First Amendment, has failed to protect the free speech rights of individuals against censorship by dominant private actors. In particular, the doctrine's focus on whether the regulator performs "traditional" state functions effectively insulates Internet speech regulators from meaningful constitutional scrutiny. The doctrine should be recast to focus on the extent of the regulator's power over expression and to balance the legitimate interests of the regulator against those of the would-be speaker. Applying this analysis, broadband providers should be regulated as state actors when they censor the communications available to their subscribers. Similarly, ICANN should be considered a state actor when it adopts speech-regarding policies that are applicable down the line to all Internet users. Dominant Internet search engines like Google, on balance, should not be regarded as state actors. Yet because of the important speech-facilitating functions that Google serves and because of the representations Google makes to those of us who use its search engine billions of times each month, regulation may be necessary to ensure that Google is true to these representations.

6   Speech Conduits and Carriers

A S DESCRIBED IN PREVIOUS CHAPTERS, FROM THE EARLY YEARS of our nation, the state has imposed affirmative obligations on certain private entities engaged in transportation, communications, and other important public service functions to facilitate the free flow of information and commerce, free of censorship or discrimination. Through the common carriage doctrine, the state has bridged the gap between public and private entities and imposed affirmative duties on entities that provide important communication and transportation functions for the benefit of the public. Rather than granting private conduits of communication the discretion to regulate speech however they see fit, the common carriage doctrine countenances affirmative government intervention in this market for communication by imposing the obligation that such conduits not discriminate among communications and requiring that they carry all legal content on the same terms and conditions. This doctrine assures members of the public the right of nondiscriminatory access to communications providers.

The common carriage doctrine has played a critical role in regulating communications providers over the past several decades. The FCC's recent rejection of common carriage obligations for broadband providers has led to a state of affairs in which broadband providers will continue to enjoy the power to restrict Internet communications however they see fit.

The FCC made a fundamental misjudgment in removing common carriage nondiscrimination obligations from broadband providers. Until 2005, telephone companies providing Internet access via narrowband and via DSL were subject to common carriage obligations, while the common carriage status of cable broadband providers was the subject of debate within the courts. In 2005, in its *Brand X* decision, the Supreme Court held that the FCC enjoyed the discretion to decline to impose common carriage obligations on cable broadband providers. In this chapter I examine the underpinnings and the recent evolution of the doctrine. I argue that the FCC's removal of common carriage obligations from Internet broadband providers will have the result of encouraging restrictions on freedom of expression in the most important medium of expression in the twenty-first century.

The concept of common carriage and the obligations imposed by communications law on common carriers are elucidated by the Supreme Court's decision in *Sable Communications, Inc.* v. *F.C.C.*[1] In that case, the Supreme Court explained that common carriers are to serve as transparent conduits for all (legal) content originated by others. The role of a common carrier such as the telephone company is neither to generate content nor to make editorial or qualitative decisions regarding which content to carry and which to censor. Common carriers do not enjoy independent First Amendment rights to exercise editorial discretion. Accordingly, the Court held in *Sable* that a federal statute prohibiting telephone companies from providing adults with access to a certain category of messages that enjoyed protection under the First Amendment was inconsistent with telephone companies' obligations as common carriers not to discriminate against legal communications. The *Sable* decision accords with the traditional model of common carriers' obligations, under which they are prohibited from "mak[ing] individualized decisions, in particular cases, whether and on what terms to deal."[2] Common carriers are prohibited from making "any unjust or unreasonable discrimination in charges, practices, classifications, regulations, facilities, or services . . . or to make or give any undue or unreasonable preference or advantage to any particular person [or] class of persons . . . or to subject any particular person [or] class of persons . . . to any undue or unreasonable prejudice or disadvantage."[3] Accordingly, under the paradigm common carriage model, conduits for communication such as telecommunications providers do not themselves enjoy independent First Amendment rights; rather, they are made to facilitate the free speech interests of others, without discrimination.

Over the past thirty years, courts and policymakers have substantially curtailed the common carriage doctrine, by weakening the obligations owed by telephone companies to those they service and by exempting broadband providers from common carriage regulation.

Case Law Weakening Common Carriage

In a number of decisions in the 1980s, courts weakened the common carriage doctrine as applied to telephone companies by holding that such carriers enjoyed the right to exercise "business judgment" to refuse to carry unpopular (but lawful) content. For example, in *Carlin Communications v. Mountain States Telephone & Telegraph*,[4] a provider of (constitutionally protected) sexually themed messages sought to require the regional telephone company to carry its messages on its 976 network, through which users could pay a special fee in order to access such content. The district court held in *Carlin* that the telephone company, as a common carrier, was required to carry all legal content—however unpopular[5]—without discrimination.[6] But the Ninth Circuit reversed,[7] holding that the telephone company enjoyed the right to exercise its "business judgment about what messages, even lawful ones, it will carry."[8] Through the vehicle of the "business judgment" exception to common carriage requirements, telephone companies were permitted to discriminate against unpopular content and wrest themselves free from their obligations under the common carriage doctrine to facilitate the transmission of all legal content. In a similar case involving the same content provider, in *Carlin Communication v. Southern Bell Telephone and Telegraph*, the Eleventh Circuit also held that the regional telephone company could exercise its "business judgment" to refuse to carry Carlin's unpopular messages via its dial-it medium.[9]

These decisions allowing paradigmatic common carriers—telephone companies—to discriminate against unpopular but legal content turn the First Amendment on its head by essentially privileging the free speech rights (and commercial interests) of the conduits over the free speech rights of those seeking to communicate through their pipes. As Jerome Barron contends, anticipating the problems that arise in weakening common carriage obligations in the Internet realm,

> The business judgment exception to the nondiscrimination principle of common carrier law . . . opens the door to content discrimination. Instead of the carrier saying, "We don't like the content of your message," the carrier may simply say, "We don't wish to do business with you." Content discrimination, normally impossible for a telephone carrier, is thereby possible through the business judgment doctrine. These are troubling precedents as the telcos are about to commence the transmission of information services and video services. The

end result could be that the regional telco will not only control who enters the conduit but also what can be said on it.[10]

Furthermore, despite the fact that such regional telephone companies were heavily regulated by the government and enjoyed monopoly status within their region for these services, the courts refused to characterize them as "state actors" whose acts of censorship would be in violation of the First Amendment.[11]

The Common Carriage Doctrine and Computer Processes

In the Communications Act of 1934, Congress granted the FCC the authority to regulate telephone companies as common carriers under Title II of that act. In the 1970s, as telephone companies began offering value-added services in addition to their essential conduit services, the FCC sought to develop a regulatory framework that would distinguish between their conduit function and the value-added services. In a series of three "Computer Inquiry" decisions in the 1970s and 1980s, the FCC established essentially the following two categories of services: (1) basic services—those that "offer[ed] transmission capacity for the movement of information"[12]—which were regulated under traditional Title II common carrier concepts, and (2) "enhanced" or value-added services—those that "combin[ed] basic service with computer processing applications that act on the . . . subscriber's transmitted information, or provide the subscriber additional, different, or restructured information, or involve subscriber interaction with stored information"[13]—the provision of which were not regulated under traditional common carrier concepts and were subject only to the FCC's generic oversight authority under Title I of the Act. Under the Second Computer Inquiry, basic services, such as telephone and facsimile services, were those offering "a pure transmission capability over a communications path that is virtually transparent in terms of its interaction with customer supplied information."[14] By "pure" or "virtually transparent" transmission, the FCC meant "a communications path that enabled the consumer to transmit an ordinary-language message to another point. . . ."[15] "Enhanced" services, by contrast, were those in which "computer processing applications are used to act on the content, code, protocol, or other aspects of the subscriber's information."[16] Because of what it believed to be the "fast-moving, competitive market"[17] for these enhanced services, the Commission declined to impose common carriage regulations on them[18] and instead left decisions regarding the carriage of communications and content by enhanced services carriers to the market. The revised categorizations and attendant obligations set forth in the Second Computer Inquiry were limited to "traditional wireline services and facilities," and were never imposed by the FCC on cable facilities.[19]

The Telecommunications Act of 1996

In 1996, Congress passed a major amendment to the Communications Act of 1934. In its passage of the Telecommunications Act of 1996, Congress revisited the categorization of services subject to common carriage regulation that was established under the Computer Inquiries. Under the 1996 Act, "telecommunications" services were made subject to common carriage regulation (replacing the category of "basic services"), while "information services" were exempted from common carriage regulation (replacing the formerly exempt category of "enhanced services"). The Act maintained significant common carrier obligations on providers of "telecommunications services," while leaving "information services" providers subject to far less regulation.

The Act defined a "telecommunication service" as "the offering of telecommunications for a fee directly to the public . . . regardless of the facilities used."[20] The FCC has ruled that, despite the changes in nomenclature, the basic distinctions between these two categories remain the same. The 1996 Act changed the rights and responsibilities of common carriers by specifying more precisely the obligations that common carriers must assume. While the Act creates a presumption that telecommunications carriers will be treated as common carriers, it authorized the FCC to forbear from enforcing any provision of the Act if the FCC determines that such enforcement is unnecessary to guard against discrimination, to ensure just and reasonable services, to safeguard consumers, or to serve the public interest.[21]

Title II of the Communications Act sets forth a complex regulatory regime imposed upon common carriers, many aspects of which—such as rate supervision, construction, and so on—are not within the scope of my inquiry. Instead I focus on the duty imposed under the Communications Act upon common carriers not to discriminate in the offering of their services and, in particular, not to discriminate against certain types of content in serving as conduits for the transmission of such content.

In the passage and interpretation of the Telecommunications Act, a central issue confronting policymakers and courts was how, if at all, the provision of Internet access by cable providers (and the provision of broadband Internet access more generally) should be regulated. If regulated as "telecommunications services," then providers of broadband Internet access would be subject to common carriage regulation prohibiting them, among other things, from discriminating against any type of legal content (and requiring them to allow interconnection by unaffiliated ISPs).[22] If regulated instead as providing only "information services," then providers of broadband Internet access would be free of such common carriage obligations. To understand the regulatory issues regarding the provision of Internet access, an explanation of the different methods of accessing the Internet and the historical application of common carriage obligations applied to such methods will prove helpful.

Historically, users connected to the Internet by attaching a dial-up modem to a telephone line in order to connect with their choice of Internet service providers (ISPs). Providers of traditional telephone lines are regulated as "telecommunications services" under the Telecommunications Act of 1996[23] (and were similarly regulated as "basic" services under earlier regulatory schemes). As such, the providers of such telephone lines were subject to common carrier regulation prohibiting them from discriminating against content (and requiring them to grant all requesting ISPs access to their lines). This regulatory framework essentially gave birth to the Internet, by ensuring that networks remained open for a variety of content and services. As Vint Cerf, known by many as the "father of the Internet," explains, this common carriage regulatory framework enabled vast numbers of Internet users to "unleash their creative, innovative, and inspired . . . ideas . . . , without artificial barriers erected by the local telephone companies."[24] FCC commissioner Michael Copps described the regime governing the early years of the Internet's development as follows:

> In the dial-up world, there is something akin to consumer sovereignty. The consumer has jurisdiction over the applications that prevail, and what power that is! No network owner telling you where to go and what to do. You run the show. This freedom—this openness—has always been at the heart of what the Internet

community and its original innovators have celebrated. Anyone can access the Internet . . . and read or say what they want. No one can corner control of the Internet for their purposes.[25]

Over the past ten years, however, many Internet users have migrated from the dial-up, narrowband universe to broadband technologies that provide fifty to one hundred times faster Internet access. The predominant broadband technology used by residential Internet users is provided via high-speed cable modems.[26] In the 1990s, cable companies began to upgrade their systems to support two-way transmission of signals, over which users could access Internet content at much faster speeds. Internet users who live in certain locations also have the option (among others) of securing broadband Internet access from telephone companies over digital subscriber lines (DSL). Because such DSL broadband Internet access is provided via telephone lines, the provision of this service was initially regulated as a "telecommunications service" subject to common carriage nondiscrimination regulations. The regulation of broadband access via cable, however, proved to be a more complicated question. If cable broadband providers essentially served as pure conduits of Internet content originated by others—in the same way that narrowband telephone and DSL providers did—regulatory parity would dictate that they be subject to the same types of common carriage obligations not to discriminate as were dial-up and DSL providers. Certainly the unaffiliated ISPs seeking access thought so, and argued that the FCC should extend the same common carriage obligations that were applicable to DSL providers to cable companies' provision of broadband Internet access. Cable companies objected and claimed that their cable modem services were inextricably intertwined with their value-added Internet services and that neither the sum of such services nor the component parts should be regulated under a common carriage regime.

The FCC undertook an inquiry into the issues raised by cable companies' offering of broadband Internet access and their claims that they should be exempt from common carriage obligations. In its 2002 "Inquiry Concerning High-Speed Access to the Internet Over Cable and Other Facilities"[27] (hereinafter "Declaratory Ruling"), the FCC concluded that cable modem service was an "information service" with "no separate offering of 'telecommunications service,'"[28] the latter of which would have rendered such services subject to common carriage obligations. The Commission ruled that the provision of cable broadband service does not contain a separate telecommunications service because the transmission of the data is "part and parcel" of that service, and is integral to its capabilities.[29] As an "information service" with "no separate offering of telecommunications service," cable operators' provision of broadband Internet access is not subject to the common carrier regulations of Title II of the Communications Act. This ruling by the FCC is significant in that it reverses course on the history of the Commission's regulation of telecommunications services. Throughout the 1970s and 1980s, the FCC formulated and implemented a workable distinction between the underlying common carrier network, on the one hand, and the services and information made available over that network, on the other. The 2002 Declaratory Ruling collapsed this crucial speech-facilitating distinction and for the first time permitted network operators to discriminate against services and content transmitted over their networks.

The decision by the FCC to exempt cable broadband from common carriage obligations was challenged by unaffiliated ISPs who asserted the right to interconnect with cable providers' pipelines and sought a ruling that cable broadband should be regulated as the provision of a telecommunications service subject to common carriage obligations. In a case that FCC commissioner Michael Copps described as involving nothing less than the "future of the Internet,"[30] the Supreme Court in *Brand X* determined that the FCC enjoyed the discretion to interpret the Telecommunications Act as it had done in its Declaratory Ruling to decline to subject cable operators' provision of broadband Internet access—or the provision of any other type of broadband Internet access—to common carriage nondiscrimination obligations. The FCC's Declaratory Ruling, and the Supreme Court's decision upholding that ruling, have wrought fundamental changes in the nature of the Internet as a medium of communication. In the prophetic words of *Wired* magazine senior writer Charles Platt:

> Broadband will inflict major changes on its environment. It will destroy, once and for all, the egalitarian vision of the Internet.[31]

The "Future of the Internet": The Story Behind the *Brand X* Decision

In the early days of the deployment of cable broadband services, local governmental franchising authorities sought to exercise regulatory control over cable broadband to require (among other things) that such services provide "open access" to their cable broadband network for unaffiliated non-facilities-based ISPs (in other words, those ISPs that do not own the transmission facilities they use to connect end-users to the Internet). Cable companies, on the other hand, sought the exact opposite—they wished to preserve their exclusive relationships with their chosen ISPs and challenged the imposition of open access requirements on them. In an early dispute that figures prominently in the *Brand X* case, *AT&T v. City of Portland*,[32] the City of Portland sought to condition AT&T's acquisition of the Telecommunications Inc. (TCI) cable franchise on the provision of open access to its cable broadband network for competing ISPs. The City of Portland premised its regulatory authority on the position that cable modem services were "cable services" and that therefore the city's franchising authority under the Telecommunications Act extended to such services.[33] AT&T contended that the cable broadband service it offered was properly classified as an "information service" under the Act and that it was therefore not subject to franchising authorities' regulation as a "cable service"—or to common carriage requirements imposed upon "telecommunications services" under the Act.

In *AT&T v. Portland,* the Ninth Circuit ruled against both the city's and AT&T's interpretations of the Act, and held that cable broadband services were "telecommunications services" subject to common carrier obligations under the Act. In properly analyzing the functionality offered by broadband providers for purposes of the Telecommunications Act, the court explained,

> Internet access for most users consists of two separate services. A conventional dial-up ISP provides its subscribers access to the Internet at a "point of presence" assigned a unique Internet address, to which the subscribers connect through telephone lines. . . . The telephone service linking the user and the ISP is classic "telecommunications," which the Communications Act defines as "the transmission, between or among points specified by the user, of information of the user's choosing, without change in the form or content of the information as sent and received." A provider of telecommunications services is a "telecommunications carrier," which the Act treats as a common carrier to the extent that it provides telecommunications to the public, "regardless of the facilities used."
>
> By contrast, the F.C.C. considers the ISP as providing "information services" under the Act, defined as "the offering of a capability for generating, acquiring, storing, transforming, processing, retrieving, utilizing, or making available

information via telecommunications." As the definition suggests, ISPs are themselves users of telecommunications when they lease lines to transport data on
their own networks and beyond on the Internet backbone. However, in relation
to their subscribers, who are the "public" in terms of the statutory definition of
telecommunications service, they provide "information services," and therefore
are not subject to regulation as telecommunications carriers. . . .

Like other ISPs, [AT&T's cable broadband service] consists of two elements: a "pipeline" (cable broadband instead of telephone lines) and the Internet service transmitted through that pipeline. However, unlike other ISPs, [the
cable broadband provider] controls all of the transmission facilities between
its subscribers and the Internet. To the extent [a cable broadband provider] is
a conventional ISP [and provides Internet services], its activities are that of an
information service. *However, to the extent that [a cable broadband provider]
provides its subscribers Internet transmission over its cable broadband facility, it
is providing a telecommunications service as defined in the Communications Act
[and is therefore subject to the Act's common carriage requirements].*[34]

In summary, the Ninth Circuit held that in order to properly classify the
provision of cable broadband access under the Act, it must separate out the
functionality involved into (1) the transmission function over its pipeline,
which constituted a "telecommunications service" subject to common carrier
obligations, and (2) the value-added Internet services transmitted through
that pipeline, which constituted an "information service" that is not subject to
common carrier obligations.[35]

In response to this and other decisions involving the regulatory status of
cable broadband, the FCC undertook the Inquiry described earlier, in which
it ultimately concluded—in contrast to the Ninth Circuit—that broadband
Internet access provided by cable operators is properly classified as an information service exempt from common carriage requirements, and that no
separate offering of telecommunications service is made by cable broadband
providers. Under this Declaratory Ruling, cable operators providing broadband Internet access are not subject to common carriage obligations as providers of telecommunication services. Rather, as providers of "information
services," they are subject to less stringent regulation under the Act under
the FCC's Title I ancillary authority, under which the FCC enjoys the authority to impose requirements that are "reasonably ancillary to the effective
performance of [its] various responsibilities."[36] The Commission found that

cable broadband providers offer "a single, integrated service that enables the subscriber to utilize Internet access service . . . and to realize the benefits of a comprehensive service offering,"[37] and concluded that the integrated service provided was an "information service," without a separate "telecommunications service" component that would render the providers subject to common carriage regulation. The FCC grounded its decision, in part, on the policy judgment that "broadband service should exist in a minimal regulatory environment that promotes investment and innovation in a competitive market."[38]

Seven petitions for review of the Commission's ruling were filed, in three different Circuit Courts. Brand X, a non-facilities-based ISP, along with several other petitioners, contended that the FCC should have classified cable broadband not just as an "information service," but also as a "telecommunications service," and should have subjected the provision of that service to common carriage regulation.[39] The Judicial Panel on Multidistrict Litigation required the consolidation of the petitions before the Ninth Circuit.

In *Brand X* v. *Federal Communications Commission,*[40] the Ninth Circuit held that the FCC's interpretation of the Communications Act did not require it to revisit its earlier holding in *AT&T* v. *Portland*[41] that the provision of cable broadband constituted part "information service" and part "telecommunications service" and that the latter part was subject to common carriage regulation. The Supreme Court reversed. First, the Court explained that as a matter of administrative law, *Chevron*[42] deference applied to the FCC's Declaratory Ruling involving the regulatory classification of broadband cable Internet service. The Court concluded that the Ninth Circuit erred in declining to apply *Chevron* and in holding instead that the FCC's interpretation of the Act was foreclosed by the Ninth Circuit's earlier, conflicting construction of the Act. The Court explained that, under *Chevron,* if a statute is ambiguous, and if the agency's construction of the statute is reasonable, a federal court must accept the agency's construction of the statute, even if the agency's reading differs from what the federal court believes to be the best statutory interpretation. The Ninth Circuit would have been permitted to substitute its prior judicial construction of the statute for the FCC's construction only if it had concluded that its construction followed from the unambiguous terms of the statute, which left no room for agency discretion. Because the Ninth Circuit had concluded merely that its reading was the best reading—and not the only permissible reading— of the statute, the Supreme Court held that the Ninth Circuit's construction could not trump the FCC's construction of the statute.

The Supreme Court then explained that the FCC's construction of the statutory definition of "telecommunications service" to exclude cable companies' provision of cable modem service was a permissible reading of the Act. Given the ambiguous statutory language, it was permissible for the FCC to determine that the transmission component of cable modem service was sufficiently integrated with the complete service such that it was reasonable to describe the combination as a single, integrated offering and to classify that integrated offering as solely an "information service."

Applying *Chevron*'s second step, the Court concluded that the FCC's construction of the Act was a reasonable policy choice within the Commission's discretion. The Court rejected the argument that the construction was unreasonable because it would allow communications providers to evade common carriage regulation. It also rejected the argument that the FCC's interpretation was arbitrary and capricious because it left providers of broadband Internet access *via DSL* subject to common carriage requirements while removing such requirements from cable broadband providers. The Court held that the FCC enjoyed the discretion to alter telecommunications policy gradually in order to eventually exempt the provision of all broadband Internet access—via cable modem, DSL, or otherwise—from common carriage requirements. Although the Court explained that the FCC "remains free to impose special regulatory duties," it held that the FCC was not required to impose any obligations on broadband providers under its Title I ancillary jurisdiction.[43]

The Import of the *Brand X* Decision

The Supreme Court's decision to allow the FCC the discretion to roll back common carriage obligations on cable and other broadband providers heralds a substantial blow for free speech values as applied to Internet communications. After the *Brand X* decision, the FCC subsequently removed common carriage regulations from every other type of broadband provider. One month after the *Brand X* decision was handed down, the FCC ruled that DSL, like cable broadband, was also an "information service," and that therefore telephone companies' provision of broadband Internet access via DSL would no longer be subject to common carriage requirements.[44] The FCC subsequently ruled that all other types of broadband are likewise exempt from common carriage nondiscrimination regulations.[45] Accordingly, decisions about what speech to censor and what speech to facilitate are now left solely to the discretion of the companies providing broadband Internet access—in most cases, the cable-telephone duopoly.[46]

It is difficult to overstate the import of these developments. They herald a transition from an Internet that is governed by a nondiscrimination principle facilitating the free flow of information to an Internet that is subject to discrimination and bottleneck control by a small handful of network operators. In the powerful words of warning of FCC commissioner Michael Copps, lamenting the demise of the historically open, nondiscriminatory Internet:

> This Internet may be dying. It may be dying because entrenched interests are positioning themselves to control the Internet's chokepoints [and have successfully lobbied] the F.C.C. to aid and abet them. The founders' vision of the Internet is being exchanged for a constricted and distorted view of technology development, entrepreneurship and consumer preferences. [The F.C.C.] seems to be buying into a warped vision that open networks should be replaced by closed networks and that traditional user accessibility can be superseded by a new power to discriminate. Let this vision prevail and the winners will be entrenched interests with far greater power than they have today to design and control the Internet of the future. . . . Until now the big companies that control the bottlenecks have been unable to convert their reach into controlling power over the Internet. But now we face scenarios wherein those with bottleneck control may be able to discriminate against both users and content providers— users and content providers that they don't have commercial relationships with, don't share the same politics with, or just don't want to offer access to for any reason at all. . . . [O]ld attitudes favoring industry consolidation and limited access are again seeking to re-establish themselves. Free from the dynamic of competition, a favored few interests may try to set up shop as gatekeeper of the Internet. . . . [W]e could be witnessing the beginning of the end of the Internet as we know it.[47]

Given the current regulatory regime, we now find ourselves in a state in which expression in cyberspace is subject to the dictates of the private entities who serve as gatekeepers for Internet expression, and those private entities are not subject to any meaningful constraints on their ability to discriminate against expression, whether under telecommunications policy or First Amendment law.

The FCC's Piecemeal Regulation of Networks in the Wake of *Brand X*

Shortly after the *Brand X* decision, at the same time that it removed common carriage requirements from DSL providers, the FCC issued a policy statement on broadband access (hereafter "Broadband Policy Statement")—the legal force of which is subject to some uncertainty—setting forth four principles regarding consumers' access to the Internet:

1. Consumers are entitled to access the lawful Internet content of their choice

2. Consumers are entitled to run applications and use services of their choice, subject to the needs of law enforcement

3. Consumers are entitled to connect their choice of legal devices that do not harm the network

4. Consumers are entitled to competition among network providers, application and service providers, and content providers[48]

I focus on the first two principles, which implicate freedom of expression and the free flow of information (and leave to others the discussion and analysis of the latter two principles).[49]

In this policy statement, the Commission recognized that it has "the duty to preserve and provide the vibrant and open character of the Internet as the telecommunications marketplace enters the broadband age," and, in order to do so, promised to "incorporate the above principles into its ongoing policy-making activities."[50] The Commission, however, made clear that in adopting the policy statement, it was not adopting formal rules. The FCC also limited the effect of its adoption and approval of these principles by stating that these principles were "subject to reasonable network management."[51] Although these principles by their terms appear to embody important free speech goals prohibiting conduits from restricting access to Internet content, they currently have limited and uncertain legal force. As FCC chairman Kevin J. Martin explained when issuing the policy statement, "the policy statements do not establish rules nor are they enforceable documents."[52] Rather, Martin expressed his confidence, consistent with the FCC's recent trend toward the negative conception of the free speech guarantee, that the marketplace itself would ensure that these principles were upheld. The nonbinding legal status of the policy statement underscores the FCC's adoption of a conception of the

First Amendment in which it generally reposes its trust in the marketplace to determine which speech to facilitate and which speech to censor.

The FCC and other agencies have, however, taken limited, piecemeal steps to regulate some Internet conduits, in particular, in the context of several large mergers. For example, in response to the FTC's challenge to the proposed merger between AOL and Time Warner, the parties entered into a consent decree requiring the merged entity to open its cable system to competitor Internet service providers on a nondiscriminatory basis for all content and preventing the merged entity from interfering with the content of nonaffiliated ISPs.[53] Similarly, in 2006, as a condition of signing off on the $85 billion merger of AT&T and BellSouth, the FCC extracted a promise from the merged entity that it would not prioritize Internet traffic over its platform. In particular, AT&T/BellSouth was made to promise that, over the course of the ensuing two years (or until network neutrality legislation was passed), it would not "provide or sell to Internet content, application, or service providers, including those affiliated with AT&T/BellSouth, any service that privileges, degrades or prioritizes any packet transmitted over AT&T/BellSouth's wireline broadband Internet access service based on its source, ownership or destination."[54] Net neutrality commitments were also extracted from the parties as conditions on the SBC-AT&T merger[55] and the Verizon-MCI merger.[56]

Recently, the FCC has evidenced greater receptivity to the issue of net neutrality by voting to seek public comment on whether to add an explicit network neutrality principle to its Broadband Policy Statement of 2005. In opening a "Notice of Inquiry" into how broadband providers are managing and prioritizing their Internet traffic, FCC chairman Kevin Martin explained that "although we are not aware of any current blocking situations, the Commission remains vigilant in protecting consumers' access to content on the Internet."[57] The FCC issued a public notice in response to a petition filed in November 2007 by Vuze, Inc., the leading source of self-published video content online. Vuze requested that the FCC initiate a rulemaking to clarify what it meant by "reasonable network management" practices by broadband providers. In its petition, Vuze claimed that Comcast engages in "overbroad and clandestine attempts to interfere with traffic" that were not "reasonable"—including secretly degrading and blocking Vuze traffic. Vuze asked the FCC to establish that "reasonable network practices" do not include the ability to discriminate against lawful Internet content or applications.[58]

In January 2008, the FCC undertook an investigation into Comcast's and other broadband providers' network management practices. This investigation was prompted in part by a complaint and a petition for a declaratory ruling filed by a number of public interest groups alleging that Comcast was secretly degrading peer-to-peer file-sharing signals and blocking access to file-sharing applications, including BitTorrent trackers, using deep packet inspection technology.[59] In response to these allegations, Comcast acknowledged that it "purposely slows down some traffic on its network, including some music and movie downloads," but claims that it should be permitted to do so in order to direct traffic to prevent network clogs. Comcast asserted that, in doing so, it has engaged in "reasonable network management" and that its practices "are in accordance with the F.C.C.'s policy statement on the Internet where the Commission clearly recognized that reasonable network management is necessary for the good of all customers."[60]

In its August 1, 2008, action on this matter, the FCC pursued a middle course, finding that Comcast's selective degrading of peer-to-peer connections "interfered with Internet users' right to access the lawful Internet content and to use the applications of their choice" but refusing to impose fines on Comcast for this violation.[61] Ruling on the complaint and petition for declaratory ruling, the FCC found that Comcast's actions were discriminatory and not tailored to address Comcast's concerns about network congestion. It further observed that Comcast had an anti-competitive motive to engage in such discrimination, as the applications it discriminated against posed a competitive threat to Comcast's own video-on-demand service. The FCC also found that Comcast's level of disclosure to its subscribers regarding its discriminatory actions was inadequate, as its subscribers could not have reasonably known that such discrimination was occurring.

Although the FCC's decision appears to be an important step in the right direction, across-the-board regulation of broadband providers is still necessary to make clear that such discrimination is prohibited and to ensure that discrimination against content and application providers does not occur in the first place. In this case, Comcast's discriminatory actions occurred in October 2007, in a manner that was not at all transparent to its subscribers, and the FCC did not reach its decision reprimanding Comcast for such actions until ten months later. While after-the-fact reprimands are an important indication of the FCC's prevailing attitude toward net discrimination, they do not obviate the need for permanent, broadly applicable, ex ante regulation. As FCC commissioner Michael Copps colorfully remarked—in calling for the FCC to adopt an Internet policy explicitly prohibiting net discrimination—more is necessary to "make clear that the Commission is not having a one-night stand with net neutrality, but an affair of the heart and a commitment for life."[62]

On the related matter of content discrimination by mobile carriers, the FCC has also recently taken action, by sending letters of inquiry to Verizon Wireless asking it to clarify its network management practices in response to allegations that Verizon initially failed to provide NARAL ProChoice America with the means necessary for it to send text messages to its members.[63]

In summary, since the FCC removed common carriage obligations from broadband providers, it has been scrambling to pick up the pieces that resulted from this ill-founded policy decision. The FCC's current practice in response to net discrimination by broadband providers, which depends upon piecemeal, after-the-fact reactions and investigations, is insufficient to ensure that members of the public are secured the right to communicate on the Internet free from discrimination.

Proposed Net Neutrality Legislation

Free speech advocates and others concerned about the free flow of information on the Internet have pursued various solutions to the problem of discrimination against (or in favor of) Internet content. Some have lobbied for passage of federal (and state[64]) "net neutrality" legislation that would prohibit broadband providers from discriminating against any legal content or applications that they are charged with transmitting. Beginning in 2006, in the wake of *Brand X* and in response to the removal of common carriage nondiscrimination obligations from broadband providers, and to actual and threatened acts of censorship by broadband and other Internet providers,[65] free speech advocates prevailed upon members of Congress to introduce network neutrality legislation. The most speech-protective of the proposed legislation would prohibit broadband providers from blocking, impairing, degrading, or discriminating against the ability of any person to use a broadband connection to access the content or services available on broadband networks.[66] Certain provisions of the proposed legislation would also reimpose other common-carriage-type requirements on broadband providers, including interconnectivity obligations requiring broadband providers to allow interconnection with the facilities of other network providers on a reasonable and nondiscriminatory basis.[67] Other provisions would mandate that consumers have the option of purchasing a standalone broadband connection that is not bundled with cable, telephone, or VoIP service.[68] Alternative proposed legislation would not directly prohibit broadband providers from discriminating against content or applications, but would grant the FCC explicit authority to adjudicate consumer complaints regarding discrimination and to enforce the principles articulated in the Broadband Policy Statement.[69]

None of the federal network neutrality bills has been passed as of May 2009, but as the issue becomes increasingly more pressing and publicized, passage of such legislation has become a more realistic possibility. In January 2007, Senators Dorgan and Snowe introduced the Internet Freedom Preservation Act of 2007, which would amend the Communications Act of 1934 to make it unlawful for any broadband service to

> block, interfere with, discriminate against, impair, or degrade the ability of any person to use a broadband service to access, use, send, post, receive, or offer any lawful content, application or service made available via the Internet, [or to] charge on the basis of the type of content, applications, or services made available.

The Act would also require broadband services to

> enable any content, application, or service made available via the Internet to be offered, provided, or posted on a basis that is reasonable and nondiscriminatory, including with respect to quality of service, access, speed, and bandwidth, [and is] at least equivalent to the access, speed, quality of service, and bandwidth that such broadband provider offers to affiliated content, applications, or services. . . . [70]

As noted earlier, two months after the introduction of the Internet Freedom Preservation Act of 2007, the FCC evidenced some receptivity to the issue of net neutrality by voting to seek public comment on whether to add a network neutrality principle to its Broadband Policy Statement.[71] In response, the Department of Justice weighed in to oppose network neutrality legislation.[72] In addition, the Federal Trade Commission conducted an extensive public workshop on broadband connectivity competition policy to analyze the issue of net neutrality (while ultimately concluding that "lawmakers should be hesitant to enact new regulations in this area").[73] In early 2008, Representatives Markey and Pickering introduced The Internet Freedom Preservation Act of 2008, which would, among other things, (1) establish that it was the national broadband policy to maintain freedom to use broadband networks without unreasonable interference from or discrimination by network operators and to safeguard against unreasonable discrimination and degradation of content based on source, ownership, or destination and (2) require the FCC to assess broadband services and consumer rights via a series of public broadband summits, and report back to Congress on its findings.[74]

In summary, the FCC and the Supreme Court wrought havoc by removing from broadband providers the common carriage and nondiscrimination obligations that historically have been imposed on telecommunications providers. This has enabled broadband providers, who serve as the gatekeepers of Internet speech, to engage in discrimination against Internet content. Although the FCC and other agencies have engaged in limited, piecemeal efforts to repair the damage wrought by this ill-founded decision, to date these efforts have been insufficient. Those concerned about free speech rights in this medium have responded by advocating net neutrality regulation, which, not surprisingly, has been forcefully opposed by the gatekeepers themselves. The issue of net neutrality—and of discrimination by broadband providers—is now front and center in policymakers' and the public's eye. Legislation prohibiting broadband providers from censoring the flow of expression on the Internet is necessary to ensure that members of the public enjoy the right to communicate freely in the most important forum for communication ever created.

7 Protecting Free Speech in the Internet Age

T HE FCC'S DECISION, APPROVED BY THE SUPREME COURT, TO exempt broadband providers from the common carriage obligations traditionally imposed on telecommunications providers threatens free speech values. If the courts decline to hold that broadband providers are state actors subject to obligations under the First Amendment not to discriminate against content,[1] then Congress should regulate broadband providers to reimpose (or require the FCC to reimpose) nondiscrimination obligations on them. Such regulation would not violate broadband providers' First Amendment rights, and would advance important free speech values that the Supreme Court has traditionally recognized in its jurisprudence adopting an affirmative conception of the First Amendment. Although the regulation I advocate would encompass some of the provisions embodied in proposed net neutrality legislation, my argument focuses specifically on regulation prohibiting broadband providers from discriminating on the basis of content. Other types of gatekeepers of Internet communications beyond broadband providers also enjoy the power to threaten free speech in this medium and should be monitored to ensure that they respect free speech values. In particular, in light of the extensive control that dominant search engines such as Google exercise over information on the Internet, it may be necessary for Congress to enact legislation prohibiting dominant search engines from unfairly or deceptively manipulating search results on an individualized basis.

Regulation of Broadband Providers to Prohibit Content-Based Discrimination

The debate over regulation of broadband providers—whether before Congress, the agencies, or the public at large—generally assumes the following contours. On one side, favoring regulation, are certain content and applications providers, including non-facilities-based providers of Internet services (ISPs such as Brand X that are unaffiliated with broadband providers) and content providers such as Google, that wish to ensure they are accorded non-discriminatory treatment by broadband providers. These proponents claim that the current unregulated broadband market enables broadband providers to discriminate against disfavored content and applications and to transform the Internet from a free and open forum for communication into a "walled garden"—analogous to the cable television market—in which the only accessible content is that which is approved by the broadband provider or for which the content provider has paid the broadband provider's price. Opponents of regulation consist primarily of the dominant broadband providers themselves, who wish to avoid regulation. They contend that an unregulated market is necessary to advance their economic interests, which, they maintain, correspond with the public interest, and which require them to be able to innovate freely in offering their services, unrestricted by regulation.

The arguments for and against regulation of broadband providers are extensive, complex, and, in some cases, quite technical.[2] Many such arguments—especially with respect to prioritization and traffic shaping—are framed predominantly in economic terms. Christopher Yoo, for example, one of the most prominent voices in the net neutrality debate, advances his arguments against regulation primarily in economic terms and explicitly forgoes "any discussion of non-economic issues, such as network neutrality's implications for democratic deliberation or the First Amendment."[3] My emphasis and the thrust of my analysis are different: I focus on individuals' free speech interests in communicating within this unprecedented public forum, free from censorship by broadband providers and other powerful gatekeepers of Internet content such as dominant search engines. I have argued that courts should consider broadband providers to be state actors chargeable with First Amendment obligations that prohibit them from discriminating on the basis of content, both in their function as email providers and in their function as gatekeepers regarding the content accessible by their subscribers. I contend further that if courts decline to conceptualize broadband providers as state actors, they should be regulated as common carriers that are at least subject to nondiscrimination requirements. In this chapter I analyze the non-economic arguments for and against imposing nondiscrimination requirements on broadband providers, and conclude that the meaningful protection of free speech values on the Internet supports such regulation.

Broadband Service, Competition, and Free Speech

The Supreme Court has emphasized that each medium of expression requires its own First Amendment inquiry.[4] Accordingly, an exploration of some of the characteristics of the broadband market is helpful in evaluating the free speech implications of regulating broadband providers to limit their discretion to discriminate on the basis of content.

The opposing sides of the debate over regulation disagree about the relevant characteristics of the market for broadband service. Essentially, opponents of regulation contend that the market for residential broadband is (or may become) a robust one and that intervention into this market is therefore unjustified and unwarranted. They claim that this market has the *potential* to be characterized by robust competition—buoyed by such possible entrants as mobile wireless, fiber, satellite, fixed wireless, and broadband over power lines,[5] and that regulation will discourage the investment necessary for such competition to develop and flourish.

Proponents of regulation, on the other hand, emphasize that the current *actual* market for residential broadband is in fact dominated by the cable-telephone duopoly, in which, according to the most recent FCC statistics, 95 percent of all residential broadband is provided either by cable companies such as Comcast or Cox or by telephone companies such as Verizon DSL.[6] While alternatives to the duopoly are available in some markets, proponents of regulation contend that such alternatives are few and far between and do not constitute effective substitutes. The greater such concentration of power, the greater the control such conduits exercise over individuals' speech. Such concentration of power over the free flow of communications has been a significant factor militating in favor of upholding regulation in the Supreme Court's evaluation of the constitutionality of legislation regulating conduits for expression. As the Supreme Court made clear in *Turner*, even if the regulated conduit for expression does not enjoy absolute gatekeeper control over all speech within that medium, the extent of the power it does enjoy is an important factor supporting the legislation in question. The importance of preserving nondiscriminatory access to information from a wide variety of sources trumps the gatekeepers' economic interests and its editorial interests in selecting which information to make available. Because of the central role they serve as conduits for expression, broadband providers can and should be regulated to prohibit them from discriminating against any and all legal content they are charged with transmitting, notwithstanding the economic benefits to providers that may accrue under the current unregulated environment. The First Amendment permits such regulation, and the meaningful protection of free speech values in the Internet context requires such regulation.

The FCC's fundamental misstep in removing common carriage nondiscrimination obligations from broadband providers (later approved by the Supreme Court in *Brand X*) was its determination that cable operators providing broadband Internet access were not—in whole or in part—offering "telecommunications services" and were therefore not subject to regulation as common carriers or pure communications conduits.[7] The Commission erred by prioritizing the very limited editorial role of cable broadband providers (for example, in selecting material to be available on the Comcast home page) over the much weightier free speech interests of members of the public who necessarily rely on broadband providers to serve as conduits for their expression. Courts that have prioritized broadband providers' editorial function and free speech interests over the public's interest in the free flow of information[8] have made the same fundamental misjudgment.[9]

The proper analysis of the respective free speech interests of broadband providers and members of the public was undertaken by the Ninth Circuit in *AT&T* v. *City of Portland*.[10] That court recognized that cable broadband providers predominately serve as conduits for the expression of others and therefore should be subject to nondiscrimination obligations imposed under communications law. As the Ninth Circuit correctly held, broadband providers function essentially and primarily as conduits of the expression—the content and applications—of others. Like the telephone company and the postal service, these providers primarily serve to facilitate the communication and transmission of the content sought to be disseminated by members of the public. And like telegraph companies of old,[11] and like telephone companies and the postal service today,[12] broadband providers' minimal free speech interests are outweighed by the free speech interests of those who seek to communicate via their pipes.

These general free speech principles have been recognized by the Supreme Court over the years in instances in which conduits for expression such as telephone companies, the postal service, and broadcasters sought to censor disfavored speech. In those cases, the Supreme Court made clear that such conduits for expression do not enjoy First Amendment (or other) interests that trump the rights of those whom they serve (if they enjoy any First Amendment rights at all). As the Court made clear in *Sable*, telephone companies do not enjoy free speech rights that trump the rights of those who seek to communicate via their pipes. Nor does the postal service enjoy an independent free speech right to censor content of which it disapproves, as the court made clear in *Lamont*.[13] And, as the Court explained in *Red Lion*,[14] even broadcasters—who enjoy much greater claims to independent First Amendment rights than broadband providers—do not enjoy free speech rights that trump the free speech rights of members of the public to access a broad range of content from a multiplicity of sources. And, while in *Turner*[15] the Court recognized that cable network operators enjoyed limited free speech interests in selecting which content to make available on which channels, it nonetheless emphasized that the important First Amendment goal of protecting the dissemination of information and ideas from a multiplicity of sources outweighed the cable operators' interest in selecting which information and ideas to facilitate via their pipes.

The only type of speech "conduit" for which the Supreme Court reached a different conclusion is the newspaper publisher, but the difference between newspaper publishers and broadband providers proves the point. The newspaper publisher enjoys far greater claim to its own right to freedom of expression than do conduits for expression such as telephone, telegraph, and broadband providers. In the *Tornillo* case,[16] the Supreme Court was unwilling to allow the free speech interests of members of the public to trump the First Amendment editorial rights of newspapers to determine which content to publish. Regulation that would require newspaper publishers to grant a right of reply to political candidates was held impermissibly to conflict with the free speech interests of newspaper publishers in the exercise of their editorial discretion to determine which speech to include and which to exclude from their papers.

Further, such a requirement would force the newspaper to be associated with content not of its own choosing.

When we analyze where on the First Amendment spectrum—pure conduit versus pure editor—broadband providers fall, it becomes clear that the functions broadband providers essentially provide place them much nearer to the pure conduit end than the pure editor end. Decisions prioritizing broadband providers' free speech interests over the free speech interests of those whose content they are charged with transmitting are misguided.[17] Although a Comcast or Verizon exercises minimal editorial discretion (in determining which content to make available via its home page, for example), the predominant function that broadband providers actually provide is that of serving as a conduit for the expression of Internet users. Furthermore, unlike in the *Tornillo* scenario, there is virtually no risk that the content made available via a broadband provider's pipes would be attributed to the broadband provider itself.[18] The predominant free speech interests in the broadband context are those of members of the public—content providers and end users—to uncensored transmission of the expression they seek to send and receive, not those of the broadband providers that facilitate the public's access to the Internet. The public's free speech interests outweigh whatever minimal editorial rights might be asserted by broadband providers. Accordingly, Congress enjoys the power to regulate—or to require the FCC to regulate—broadband providers to subject them to the obligation not to discriminate on the basis of content.

Furthermore, even assuming that broadband providers enjoyed a protectible First Amendment interest in the editorial functions they perform, regulation that prohibits them from engaging in discrimination on the basis of content in the exercise of their conduit function would be analyzed as a content-neutral regulation of speech subject to intermediate scrutiny. Courts should readily hold that such regulation advances the substantial government interest of protecting the public's access to the wide dissemination of information from a multiplicity of sources, and so long as the regulation was carefully crafted and appropriately tailored to advance this interest, it would readily withstand First Amendment scrutiny.[19] Following the Supreme Court's analysis in *Turner*, in which the Court recognized the limited First Amendment editorial rights of the cable companies while upholding regulations requiring them to carry content that was not of their choosing in order to ensure that "the public has access to a multiplicity of information sources," regulation of broadband providers of the kind outlined here should be held to comport with the First Amendment's protections. Thus, even if broadband providers were able to convince a court that their First Amendment interests were compromised by such regulation, *Turner* would counsel in favor of holding that such interests were outweighed by the countervailing public interest in "the widest possible dissemination of information from diverse and antagonistic sources" and in "public discussion and informed deliberation [that] . . . democratic government presupposes and the First Amendment seeks to achieve."[20] Accordingly, the free speech interests of broadband providers do not render the imposition of nondiscrimination obligations upon them unconstitutional. On the contrary, such regulation is consistent with the protection of the important free speech values and policies recognized by the Supreme Court and embodied in the affirmative conception of the First Amendment.

Having shown that regulation of broadband providers would be constitutional, I now turn to why such regulation is essential in order to preserve nondiscriminatory access to the predominant forum for free speech in the twenty-first century.

In regulating broadband providers consistently with free speech policies, Congress and the FCC should look to the principle underlying modern communications law that liberal democracies require a well-informed citizenry, which in turn requires that citizens enjoy the freedom to communicate and to access communications from a multiplicity of sources. The same principles that justify regulating telephone and telegraph operators and the postal service as common carriers subject to nondiscrimination requirements—in order to "protect ordinary citizens in their right to communicate"[21]—are valid today with regard to Internet communications.

This fundamental free speech and communications policy of protecting the public's right to communicate and to access a broad range of expression that was embodied in the early regulation of telecommunications providers was carried over, in a modified form, to the broadcast realm. Under the fairness doctrine, broadcasters—although not considered common carriers—were charged with the obligation of ensuring public access to a broad array of content from diverse and antagonistic sources on matters of public importance. This obligation was then carried over, in a modified form, to the regulation of cable television, under which the FCC and the Supreme Court recognized the importance of imposing limitations on the discretion of cable companies to select which content to make available to the public. In *Turner I* and *II*, the Court recognized that the discretion of conduits of speech that exercise control over critical pathways of communication can constitutionally be held in check by regulations that protect "the free flow of information and ideas."[22] From the *Associated Press* decision in 1945 to the *Red Lion* decision in 1969 up through *Turner II* in 1997, the Supreme Court has emphasized that members of the public must enjoy the freedom to communicate and to access communications from a multiplicity of sources in order to advance the free speech values of facilitating deliberation and debate on matters of public importance.

The recent regulatory state of affairs in the Internet context, which allows broadband providers to discriminate against whatever content or applications they choose for whatever reasons they choose, is inconsistent with the historical progression of according individuals protection in their freedom to communicate. By allowing broadband providers to restrict the free flow of information and ideas, the current regime allows these private gatekeepers of speech to obstruct the "dissemination of information from diverse and antagonistic sources"[23] and to thwart the "public discussion and informed deliberation that . . . democratic government presupposes and the First Amendment seeks to achieve."[24] Absent regulation, broadband providers will continue to enjoy the discretion to discriminate against the content or applications of their choosing. Under such a regime, the citizenry is not guaranteed access to a multiplicity of uncensored viewpoints from diverse and antagonistic sources, and is instead limited to expression that is approved (or not disapproved) by the one or two broadband providers who serve as gatekeepers for essentially all Internet communications.

Given the importance for the protection of free speech values of regulating broadband providers, the arguments of opponents that it may be economically inefficient to do so[25] carry little weight. Just as it may be economically inefficient for the government to be required to maintain a public forum,[26] or for cable companies to be required to carry local broadcast or educational television signals instead of to exclusively carry their own preferred content,[27] so too it may be economically inefficient for broadband providers to be prohibited from discriminating against disfavored content or applications. The protection of free speech values has never been perfectly aligned with the economic interests of conduits for expression. Yet in its foundational free speech decisions, the Supreme Court has recognized the preeminent importance of free speech rights over private economic interests. As the Court explained in *Marsh* v. *Alabama*, "[w]hen we balance the constitutional rights of owners of property against those of the people to enjoy freedom [of expression], we remain mindful of the fact that the latter occupy a preferred position."[28]

Opponents of regulation of broadband providers also contend that such regulation offers a "solution in search of a problem" and will bring needless regulation and complexity to the current state of affairs.[29] They claim that there have been only a few, insignificant instances of network discrimination, and that these instances were appropriately dealt with by the FCC under the current regulatory regime. They also claim that broadband providers have every incentive to act as "good stewards" by facilitating the delivery of all legal content and applications through their networks, and that providers have little incentive to discriminate against content or applications.[30] They point to the Madison River/Vonage incident[31] as the only significant example of such discrimination, and contend that the FCC had the authority to censure such conduct.

In contrast, the most powerful argument in support of regulation is the fact that under the current unregulated regime, broadband providers have recently engaged in acts of blocking disfavored applications and content, notwithstanding the fact that they are under close scrutiny, as Congress and the public evaluate the necessity of net neutrality regulation. As I described in Chapter 1, for example, Comcast has blocked its subscribers' ability to receive email on politically charged subjects such as the impeachment of the president and the war in Iraq. AT&T, for its part, has censored a cablecast of a Pearl Jam concert in which the lead singer expressed mild criticisms of the president. Other instances of discrimination against content and applications by broadband providers have been identified.

Opponents of regulating broadband providers maintain that the government should let the market decide whether such content restrictions are allowed to prevail. They contend that Internet users can appropriately discipline providers that restrict or censor content, if they care, by switching to a less censorial provider.[32]

There are several problems with relying on Internet users to impose meaningful checks on censorship by broadband providers. First, as discussed previously, such censorship is frequently not readily transparent to the Internet users whose actions the opponents of regulation would rely upon to discipline the market. When Comcast blocked AfterDowningStreet's emails, for example, it took several days for the senders and intended recipients to determine that Comcast engaged in and was responsible for this blocking.[33] Similarly, when Comcast blocked and degraded its subscribers' use of file-sharing applications, it did so in a clandestine manner.[34] If the problem is not visible to those who are to be charged with remedying the problem, then "consumers' preferences [opposing discrimination] might not be enough to motivate the market" and the market discipline solution will not be viable.[35] As Seth Kreimer explains in a related context:

> Even where an exit to competing [ISPs] is available, if the target does not know about the censorship . . . , theoretically available market discipline may be at most a small check on overzealous censorship. This condition is likely to be common, for the easiest way [for an ISP] to avoid customer backlash and potential liability simultaneously is by censoring the flow of information without alerting either the sender or the receiver. The challenge of ferreting out [the details and] terms of censorship may be well beyond the capacity of all but the most sophisticated [Internet users].[36]

Second, even assuming that Internet users and others concerned are sufficiently aware of the details of such censorship to attempt to respond to it, users may have insufficient alternatives to which to switch their patronage. As discussed earlier, 95 percent of all residential users have only one or two choices for broadband providers[37]—a cable modem provider (such as Comcast) or a DSL provider (such as Verizon or AT&T)—all of which have already engaged in various acts of blocking disfavored Internet content and applications. For most residential Internet users, there is simply nowhere to turn.[38]

Third, opponents of regulation are simply wrong to claim that broadband providers have no incentive to censor content and have every incentive to be "good stewards" facilitating the free flow of all manner of content through their pipes. Indeed, broadband providers have an economic incentive to censor a great deal of content and applications that conflict with their economic interests. As Jerome Saltzer, co-author of the "end-to-end" argument, explains, each broadband provider has the incentive to "find a technical or political excuse to filter out services that compete with the . . . Internet services it also offers."[39] Similarly, as Tim Wu puts it,

> In general, a Bell or cable company has some interest in giving you as broadly useful a network as possible. . . . But that interest in neutrality holds true only to a point. If a product being offered over the network, say Internet voice ("VoIP") for $5 a month, competes with an established revenue source (telephone service, offered at $30 a month), the temptation to block is strong.[40]

Fourth, and most important, the current unregulated state of affairs fails adequately to protect the singular most important aspect of the free speech guarantee—the right to engage in unpopular and countermajoritarian expression—even if such expression is the subject of complaints from other users, even if such expression is unpopular or "objectionable." Absent regulation, broadband providers have the incentive to cater to majoritarian interests. The majority of a broadband provider's subscribers may disapprove of certain types of unpopular—yet constitutionally protected—expression. Upon receiving (or anticipating) complaints about a particular type of content, broadband providers have the incentive to censor such content so as to cater to the interests of the majority of their customers. For example, in the case of After-DowningStreet's attempt to send email messages advocating impeachment of the president, Comcast justified its censorship of such communication on the grounds that it had received complaints about such emails. Similarly, Verizon Wireless initially sought to restrict NARAL's pro-choice text messages on the grounds that such messages "may be seen as controversial or unsavory to any of our users."[41] Broadband providers' incentive to cater to the majoritarian interests of the market is *precisely* the reason why nondiscrimination obligations should be imposed upon them—in order to protect countermajoritarian and other unpopular expression from censorship by these powerful gatekeepers of Internet speech. Just as the state has the incentive to censor speech that is critical of it or that is disfavored by the majority, so too do powerful conduits of expression such as broadband providers. And so too should broadband providers' incentive to censor such speech be held in check by regulation to advance and protect free speech values.

Broadband providers might respond that they need to be able to block content such as sexually themed expression in order to better serve their users. To be sure, regulation should not prohibit providers from offering tools to their subscribers to enable the *end users themselves* to effectively filter out content that is undesirable to the users. Just as the U.S. Postal Service provides individuals with a mechanism for declining to receive junk mail, and the FTC allows individuals to decline to receive unsolicited telephone calls via the National Do Not Call Registry, broadband providers should be permitted to provide their subscribers with tools to restrict unwanted (but constitutionally protected) sexually themed expression, spam, and other speech that the user does not wish to receive. What the broadband provider should *not* be permitted to do is to exercise its own discretion to block legally protected expression that it is charged with transmitting to end users.[42]

Broadband providers might also respond that they need to be able to block applications that physically harm their network, such as viruses, worms, Trojan horses, applications threatening network security, or other malware. Indeed, providers should not be prohibited from blocking such applications that are harmful to the network so long as such blocking is done in a manner that is transparent to users. Just as telephone companies, consistent with their common carriage nondiscrimination obligations, have been allowed to prohibit the attachment of equipment that harms the operation of the network,[43] so too should broadband providers be permitted to block applications and equipment that physically harm their network.

Any regulation prohibiting broadband providers from blocking legal content should also mandate *transparency* in any such blocking of allegedly illegal content, requiring broadband providers to inform subscribers of any content or applications that were blocked and the reasons for such blocking (for example, the provider claims that the content was illegal obscenity, child pornography, or physically harmful malware). Mandating transparency in blocking will enable users to impose meaningful checks on the blocking decisions of broadband providers and ensure that such blocking does not mask the provider's unlawful discrimination on the basis of content. Under the current unregulated state of affairs—as was evident in the case of Comcast's discriminatory blocking and degrading—it is quite difficult if not impossible for users to discern whether content or applications have been blocked. Indeed, lack of transparency in connection with a broadband provider's acts of blocking (or degrading) content or applications will only compound the discrimination—because users will attribute the difficulties in access to the blocked content or applications themselves instead of placing the blame where it belongs—with their broadband provider.

Because of the importance of protecting countermajoritarian speech within liberal democracies, mandating transparency alone—without a prohibition on blocking legal content—will not suffice to fully protect free speech values. A requirement that broadband providers merely act transparently in blocking or discriminating against unpopular speech may help to advance the majority's free speech interests, but will not secure individuals' right to engage in unpopular, dissident, or other countermajoritarian expression. To protect this aspect of the free speech guarantee, broadband providers must be prohibited from blocking any and all legal content.

In summary, broadband providers should be subject to regulation—whether imposed by new legislation or by enforceable FCC rules—that require them to assume at least the nondiscrimination obligations that historically have been imposed upon common carriers—the duty to facilitate and transmit in a nondiscriminatory manner any and all legal content and applications that do not harm the network, and to engage in any blocking of illegal content or applications in a transparent manner that is meaningfully subject to checks by Internet users.

Prioritization (and Degradation)

Opponents of regulation claim that network operators should be permitted to prioritize or degrade the flow of whatever content or applications they choose. They claim that freedom from regulation on this front will bring about a state of "network diversity" in which broadband providers will be free to explore different prioritization methods and Internet users will be able to choose among broadband providers with different prioritization policies.[44] They suggest that, under such a scenario, some broadband providers would voluntarily employ neutral criteria for prioritizing data flows while others would prioritize the transmission of affiliated content or applications, and Internet users would enjoy the discretion to choose among these options.

For example, under the scenario contemplated by opponents of regulation, Comcast could enter into a deal with Yahoo! in which Yahoo! pays for the privilege of having its search engine load and process requests faster than Google's.[45] Comcast subscribers then either would forgo use of the Google applications or would have the incentive to switch to another broadband provider that employed neutral criteria for processing data flows or that prioritized Google applications (if one were available). Under this scenario, by choosing Comcast as their broadband provider, users would be opting against maximizing Google's efficiency, and regulators would leave to the market—such as it is—decisions about which content and applications would be favored and which would be disfavored (subject only to antitrust checks[46]).

Alternatively, broadband providers might opt to prioritize content in a less discriminatory and more neutral manner by giving priority to applications that inherently require such prioritization for their efficient functioning. Under this scenario, broadband providers might give priority to latency-sensitive applications such as Voice over Internet Protocol or delay- and jitter-sensitive applications over applications such as email that are not similarly sensitive to network prioritization.

Opponents of regulation claim that, because there are some neutral and objectively desirable types of prioritization—such as those just described for latency-sensitive applications—regulation is unwarranted. Christopher Yoo, for example, contends that regulation restricting prioritization is unwarranted and unwise because it would prohibit broadband providers from successfully satisfying the "increasingly intense and heterogeneous demands imposed by end users . . . by giv[ing] a higher priority to traffic associated with truly sensitive applications."[47] A carefully crafted set of regulations prohibiting the first type of prioritizing described above (which I will call discriminatory prioritization), while allowing the second type, would protect Internet users' access to the unbiased, free flow of information on the Internet while preserving providers' discretion neutrally and efficiently to manage the flow of content over their networks.[48] As FCC commissioner Michael Copps puts it, "the trick is to find the fine line between reasonable network management techniques that allow the Net to flourish and unreasonable practices that distort and deny its potential."[49]

Network operators should be permitted to grant priority to types of traffic that inherently require high bandwidth without discriminating within and among those types of applications. They should be permitted to engage in uniform application-based prioritizing, in which all applications of a certain type are accorded the same priority of delivery.[50] Under such regulation, broadband providers should not be prohibited from according higher priority to all VoIP packets, because such packets are latency-sensitive.[51] However, broadband providers should be prohibited from prioritizing *within* such types of applications so as to favor their affiliated VoIP applications over those of a rival (as providers have been accused of doing in discriminating against VoIP provider Vonage while prioritizing and favoring their own VoIP applications[52]). Whatever incentive the network operator has to be a "good steward" of the applications for which it serves as a conduit,[53] that incentive is likely outweighed by the operator's incentive to maximize its own financial interests, by prioritizing affiliated applications or content. To protect the free flow of information, such discriminatory prioritization should be prohibited.

This is especially true if the broadband provider can engage in discriminatory prioritization in a manner that is not readily detectable by its subscribers.[54] As discussed earlier, because broadband providers can discriminate against content and applications—by outright blocking them or degrading their transmission—in a manner that is not transparent to Internet users, users cannot effectively "discipline" these actions in any case. Accordingly, broadband providers should be barred from entering into deals with content or application providers in which the latter pay for priority of delivery—resulting in the relegation of nonpaying applications and services to degraded transmission speeds. As conduits for information in this public forum for expression, broadband providers should be prohibited from engaging in bias and allowing dominant content or applications providers to lock in their dominant positions and lock out disfavored content or applications.

If, for example, in 2000, Comcast had been permitted to enter into a deal with AltaVista to prioritize its search engine application to the exclusion of others, then a market entrant such as Google would not have enjoyed a fair and equal chance to compete on the merits. Of even greater concern from a First Amendment perspective, if Comcast had been permitted in 2000 to enter into an exclusive arrangement with the *Wall Street Journal*'s news service to the exclusion of competing news services and to prioritize the delivery of the *Journal*'s content over all other news content, then Comcast subscribers would have been deprived of access to a multiplicity of news services (and many would have had no other meaningful alternatives to secure broadband Internet access). While broadband providers should be permitted to engage in nondiscriminatory prioritization and content-neutral network management practices in which they offer different levels of priority to categories of applications that inherently require network prioritization, they should be prohibited from offering preferential treatment within such categories.[55]

In summary, Congress should pass legislation prohibiting (or requiring the FCC to prohibit) broadband providers from blocking legal content or applications and from engaging in discriminatory prioritization or degradation of such content or applications. Such legislation should also mandate transparency in blocking or degrading, requiring broadband providers to inform end users in a meaningful way of any content or applications that were blocked or degraded and the reasons therefor, so that end users will be able to impose meaningful checks on these decisions of broadband providers and ensure that such actions do not mask the provider's unlawful discrimination.

Regulation of Dominant Search Engines

Dominant search engines, while not state actors under current or proposed First Amendment analysis,[56] nevertheless exercise tremendous control over Internet communications—over the billions of Internet searches conducted in the United States each month. Because of the important role they serve in facilitating Internet expression, and because of the representations they make to the public regarding their services, dominant general search engines such as Google should be prohibited from acting in a manner inconsistent with such representations.

Google apparently seeks to have it both ways in terms of its responsibility for the search results it makes available. On the one hand, it claims that the rank it assigns to a particular website is the purely objective result of the application of its highly valued computer algorithms, and represents that it assumes a purely hands-off approach with respect to such rankings. Google maintains that "[t]here is no human involvement or manipulation of [search] results"[57] and that "[t]he beliefs and preferences of those who work at Google . . . do not determine or impact our search results."[58] On the other hand, in cases in which Google seeks to defend its manipulation of search results—for example, its demoting a disfavored website from its former high rank to "no rank"— Google claims that its rankings constitute its subjective opinions that it is allowed to manipulate however it chooses and that such subjective opinions are entitled to First Amendment protection and are exempt from any type of regulation or scrutiny.

Google's own expression in connection with the performance of its general search engine function is so minimal and its impact on the ability of others to communicate is so great that regulation is warranted to protect free speech values in this forum. Such regulation should prohibit dominant general search engines such as Google from deliberately manipulating their search results on an individualized basis to block or degrade the rank of websites that it indexes. Millions of Internet users rely upon Google's implicit and explicit representations that its search engine operates objectively and without bias and presents relevant information to users based on their search queries. Google should be prohibited from deliberately skewing such results on an individualized basis and interfering with users' justifiable expectations and free speech interests. As Frank Pasquale argues,

> Search engines . . . are poised to become the chief organizer and forum for research, public discussion and commercial competition among Internet users. . . . Rather than hiding behind the mechanical application of First Amendment protections, new public fora like search engines should promote the First Amendment goal of open public forums.[59]

Even if Google enjoys some minimal First Amendment interest in its search results, this interest is outweighed by the free speech interests of the public in accessing "information from diverse and antagonistic sources [that] is essential to the welfare of the public."[60] As the Supreme Court held in *Turner,* in upholding must carry regulations imposed upon cable systems operators, although the operators enjoyed some First Amendment editorial rights in deciding what content to carry, these rights were outweighed by the free speech interests of members of the public in the "widest possible dissemination of information from diverse and antagonistic sources."[61] Furthermore, Congress can constitutionally regulate dominant search engine providers, not only to require that they provide access to such content but also to require that they provide *meaningful* access to such content. The Cable Act upheld in *Turner* required cable systems operators not just to carry broadcast stations, but to carry them in a manner in which they would be meaningfully accessible by members of the public. Similarly, Congress enjoys the power to authorize the regulation of dominant search engines to require that they provide meaningful access to content, free from deliberate manipulation of the ranking of these websites by the search engine providers.

Congress also has the power to authorize the regulation of the provision of advertising by dominant search engine providers—much as it did in the statute involved in *C.B.S. v. F.C.C.*—to ensure that members of the public have meaningful access to information necessary for the effective operation of the democratic process. If dominant search engines were to prohibit political candidates from securing sponsored links to enable them to present information necessary to the effective operation of the democratic process, Congress has the authority to regulate such providers to ensure that they provide rights of access in this forum. Indeed, Google has been roundly criticized for the aspect of its sponsored link policy that prevents individuals from securing a link that "advocates against an individual, group, or organization,"[62] which Google has employed to prohibit a substantial amount of political discussion and debate.[63] Whatever right to editorial discretion is enjoyed by the dominant search engines to control their advertising, in balancing these free speech interests against the free speech interests of the political candidates and the electorate, the Supreme Court has made clear in a related context that "[i]t is the right of the viewers and listeners, not the right of the broadcasters [or search engines], which is paramount."[64] As in *C.B.S.* v. *F.C.C.*, a limited, statutory right of access for political candidates in this context would make "a significant contribution to freedom of expression by enhancing the ability of candidates to present, and the public to receive, information necessary for the effective operation of the democratic process."[65] Further, such a right of access would be consistent with ensuring that such an "important resource . . . will be used in the public interest."[66]

· · ·

In summary, Congress should pass legislation prohibiting (or requiring the FCC to prohibit) broadband providers from blocking legal content or applications and from engaging in discriminatory prioritization or degradation of such content or applications. Such legislation should also mandate transparency in blocking or degrading. It may also be necessary for Congress to enact legislation authorizing the regulation of dominant search engines (such as Google in today's market) to prohibit them from manipulating search results on an individualized basis and to require them to provide political candidates with meaningful, uncensored access to forums for communicating with the public.

Conclusion

THIS BOOK HAS EXAMINED THE CONSEQUENCES THAT FLOW from the fact that expression on the Internet is ultimately controlled by a handful of powerful private entities. The pipelines and forums for Internet speech are now owned by a handful of private corporations, and those owners are no longer regulated in their ability to facilitate or thwart the transmission of such expression on the Internet. I have explored how free speech doctrine and policy have evolved to the point where the companies who own the pipelines and forums for Internet expression now have the power to decide which expression is and which expression is not communicated via their pipelines and forums and how they exercise that power in ways that threaten free speech values. As a result of such privatization and concentration of power, and of actions taken by the FCC and the courts to immunize these Internet actors from regulation, we may indeed be "witnessing the beginning of the end of the Internet as we know it."[1]

When the government privatized the Internet's infrastructure, the conduits that were responsible for facilitating the transmission of expression—providers of narrowband Internet access—were still regulated as common carriers and were obligated not to discriminate against content or applications. Then, in 2002, the FCC—influenced by a negative conception of the First Amendment—began to remove nondiscrimination obligations from broadband providers. Abandoning this nation's long history of regulating telecommunications providers (such as mail, telegraph, and telephone providers) to charge them with obligations not to discriminate against content, the FCC chose instead to entrust the protection of Internet users' free speech interests to the market (such as it is). And the Supreme Court approved of this course of events in 2005 in the *Brand X* decision, which further encouraged the FCC to continue its course of deregulating broadband providers.

Under the current legal regime, broadband providers and other Internet conduits for expression are now essentially free to censor and otherwise discriminate against whatever content or applications they choose. Given this freedom, these actors have indeed discriminated against content and applications in a variety of ways—including against political expression and other speech that is highly valued within our constitutional scheme. It should come as no surprise that they would do so. As unregulated market actors, these private speech regulators have various incentives to discriminate against expression—expression that they believe is unpopular or disfavored by their subscribers or expression that conflicts with their own political, economic, or other interests. The prevailing negative conception of the First Amendment maintains that private actors—including powerful regulators of Internet speech such as broadband providers and dominant search engines—should enjoy this freedom to regulate speech on (and through) their property however they see fit. Under an affirmative conception of the First Amendment, however, such powerful private Internet actors could constitutionally be regulated, and should be regulated, to prohibit them from discriminating against expression. Indeed, in its foundational free speech jurisprudence, the Supreme Court embodied an affirmative conception of the First Amendment in various important doctrines, under which powerful private actors are charged with obligations to facilitate and not discriminate against expression.

The Supreme Court and the FCC's earlier adoption of the affirmative conception of the First Amendment is most clearly evidenced in the state action doctrine, the fairness doctrine, the common carriage doctrine, and must carry regulations, each of which imposes on dominant private regulators of speech the obligation to facilitate and not discriminate against the speech of others. In the past, the Court has evidenced its strong approval of the imposition of these obligations upon powerful private conduits, in order to uphold First Amendment values, which ultimately provide the foundation for our system of democratic self-government. As the Court explained in *Turner,* such obligations advance our national communications policy of securing "the widest possible dissemination of information from diverse and antagonistic sources." Further, regulation of powerful private speech regulators, pursuant to this national communications and free speech policy, "seeks to facilitate the public discussion and informed deliberation, which, as Justice Brandeis pointed out many years ago, democratic government presupposes and the First Amendment seeks to achieve. . . . [A]ssuring that the public has access to a multiplicity of information sources is a governmental purpose of the highest order, for it promotes values central to the First Amendment."[2]

So, how should we begin to protect freedom of expression in the Internet age? First, the Supreme Court and the FCC should revive the affirmative conception of the First Amendment in order to impose nondiscrimination obligations on powerful conduits of Internet expression. The Court should update and recast its state action jurisprudence, to abandon its reliance on whether the actor in question performs "traditional" functions of the government, because such an antiquated analysis will forever preclude Internet actors from being considered state actors chargeable with First Amendment duties. Following the lead of state courts in interpreting the free speech guarantees of their constitutions, federal courts should update their interpretation of the "traditional government function" and other prongs of the state action doctrine, and should return to the principles articulated by the Supreme Court in its foundational state action free speech jurisprudence to impose constitutional obligations on powerful private regulators of speech.

In applying the state action doctrine within the Internet context, courts should reach the conclusion that the Internet itself is the functional equivalent of a public forum—a forum for expression that, like public streets, sidewalks, and parks, has a broadly speech-facilitating character, is a "natural and proper place for the dissemination of information and opinion,"[3] and is today one of the "paradigmatic loci of First Amendment values because it permits speakers to communicate with a wide audience at a low cost."[4] The regulation of speech on the Internet by powerful private regulators therefore constitutes the regulation of speech within a public forum for expression. In evaluating which private regulators of Internet speech should be considered state actors, courts should (1) assess the extent of the power that the actor exerts over the Internet expression at issue (including an assessment of the availability of alternatives for the Internet speaker to escape such power) and (2) balance the competing free speech and other claims of the regulator against those of the would-be speaker. Applying this updated interpretation of the state action doctrine, courts should conclude that at least two types of Internet speech regulators—broadband providers and the Internet Corporation for Assigned Names and

Numbers—are state actors chargeable with the same First Amendment obligations as is the government.

Under the Supreme Court's foundational First Amendment jurisprudence, the government itself, of course, is charged with the obligation to facilitate and not discriminate against expression—most important, in forums that are especially suited to the communication and exchange of ideas and information. The public forum doctrine mandates that the government make available public property that is well-suited for such communication for the "uninhibited, robust, and wide-open" discussion of and debate on matters of public and societal importance. But the public forum doctrine, like other doctrines embodying the affirmative conception of the First Amendment, has also been substantially weakened in recent years. As a result of the courts' contraction of the public forum doctrine, we find ourselves in a situation in which not only dominant private regulators but also the rare *public* regulators of Internet forums are increasingly immune from meaningful First Amendment scrutiny. Indeed, the Supreme Court recently held that public libraries' provision of Internet access to their patrons did not constitute a public forum—despite the acknowledgment by the libraries that they provided Internet access to their patrons precisely to create a public forum for the exchange of information and ideas on all manner of subjects. As a result, the Supreme Court went on to hold that libraries' content-based restrictions on their patrons' Internet access were not subject to meaningful First Amendment scrutiny (and were not in violation of the First Amendment). Other courts have followed suit and have declined to subject government actors to meaningful First Amendment scrutiny in their actions discriminating against Internet content. Like the other First Amendment doctrines embodying an affirmative conception of the free speech guarantee, the public forum doctrine should be reinvigorated by the courts to impose meaningful scrutiny of Internet speech regulations.

In summary, the Supreme Court should reinvigorate the various First Amendment doctrines that incorporate the affirmative conception of the free speech guarantee and should apply these doctrines within the Internet realm. Government actors should be held to meaningful First Amendment scrutiny when they restrict expression on the Internet, as should powerful private actors such as broadband providers and ICANN.

In the alternative, if judicial relief is unavailing, Congress should step in to enact legislation to remedy the problems wrought by the FCC's decision to immunize broadband providers from common carriage obligations, and should reimpose—or require the FCC to reimpose—on broadband providers the nondiscrimination obligations historically imposed on conduits for communication under common carriage law. Contrary to the contentions of broadband providers, such legislation would not violate providers' First Amendment rights. Congress enjoys the power to enact such regulation and should do so in order to advance important free speech values. In particular, Congress should pass legislation prohibiting broadband providers from blocking or discriminating against legal content or applications. Such legislation should also mandate transparency in blocking or degrading, requiring broadband providers to inform end users in a meaningful way of any content or applications that were blocked or degraded and the reasons therefor. This transparency requirement will enable end users to impose meaningful checks on broadband providers' determinations that the content or applications that were blocked were illegal, and will help to ensure that such actions do not mask the provider's unlawful discrimination on the basis of content.

In addition, given the enormous, unchecked power that dominant search engines such as Google exercise over forums for Internet expression, Congress should enact legislation authorizing the regulation of such dominant search engines to require that they provide meaningful, uncensored access to Internet content (as they in fact promise to do) and to prohibit them from deliberately manipulating search results on an individualized basis. Such legislation would not violate the First Amendment rights of dominant search engines, and would advance important free speech goals by ensuring that the public has meaningful, unbiased access to the universe of Internet content and applications.

· · ·

To fulfill the Internet's promise of being "the most participatory marketplace of mass speech that this country—and indeed the world—has yet seen,"[5] those few companies that serve as the gatekeepers for expression on the Internet should be regulated to ensure that they act as good stewards within this marketplace—free of discrimination and censorship, and true to the free speech values that are necessary to facilitate the public discussion and informed deliberation that democratic government presupposes and the First Amendment requires.

REFERENCE MATTER

Notes

Introduction

1. See, *e.g.,* Andrew Keen, Google in the Garden of Good and Evil: How the Search Engine Giant Moved Beyond Mere Morality, *Daily Standard,* May 3, 2006, http://www .WeeklyStandard.com/Content/Public/Articles/ 000/000/012/176wtlbv.asp (explaining that "[e]verything that the Chinese government blocks, Google also blocks"); John Leyden, Skype Uses Peer Pressure Defense to Explain China Text Censorship, *The Register,* Apr. 20, 2006, http://www.theregister.co.uk/2006/04/20/skype_China_ censorship_row/ (to comply with local censorship laws, VoIP firm Skype's Chinese partner filters instant messages sent using its software); Glenn Kessler, Cisco File Raises Censorship Concerns, *The Washington Post,* May 20, 2008 (Senate Judiciary Committee on the Global Internet Freedom Act considers Cisco internal documents suggesting that Cisco was willing to assist the Chinese government in combating the "Falun Gong evil cult and other hostile elements").

Chapter 1

1. See Management of Internet Names and Addresses, 63 Fed. Reg. 31,741 n. 5 (1998), available at http://www.ntia.doc.gov/ntiahome/ domainname/domainhome.htm (explaining that in 1992 the United States Congress granted the National Science Foundation the statutory authority to allow commercial activity on what was to become the Internet).

2. See, *e.g., American Civil Liberties Union v. Reno,* 929 F. Supp. 824, 831 (E.D. Pa. 1996), aff'd, 521 U.S. 844 (1997).

3. See 929 F. Supp. at 844.

4. See, *e.g.*, David J. Goldstone, A Funny Thing Happened on the Way to the Cyber Forum: Public vs. Private in Cyberspace Speech, 69 *U. Colo. L. Rev.* 1, 6 (1998) (setting forth consideration of how public forum doctrine applies to cyberspace communication); David J. Goldstone, The Public Forum Doctrine in the Age of the Information Superhighway (Where Are the Public Forums on the Information Superhighway?), 46 *Hastings L. J.* 335 (1995) (providing analytical framework for identifying public forums on the Internet); Steven G. Gey, Reopening the Public Forum—From Sidewalks to Cyberspace, 58 *Ohio St. L. J.* 1535, 1610–18 (1998) (public forum doctrine should apply in online contexts).

5. *Turner Broadcasting System, Inc. v. F.C.C.* [hereinafter Turner I], 512 U.S. 622, 657 (1994).

6. *Id.*

7. Pub. L. No. 104-104, 110 Stat. 133 (codified as amended at 47 U.S.C. § 223 (2000)). Section 230(c)(2) of the CDA states

> No provider . . . of an interactive computer service shall be held liable on account of any action voluntarily taken in good faith to restrict access to or availability of material that the provider . . . considers to be obscene, lewd, lascivious, filthy, excessively violent, harassing, *or otherwise objectionable, whether or not such material is constitutionally protected.* 47 U.S.C. Section 230 [emphasis added].

8. Pub. L. No. 416, 48 Stat. 1064 (codified, as amended, at 47 U.S.C.A. Sec. 227 (2000)).

9. *ACLU v. Reno*, 929 F. Supp. 824, 883 (E.D. Pa. 1996), (Dalzell, J., concurring), aff'd, 521 U.S. 844 (1997).

10. Remarks of Michael J. Copps, FCC Commissioner, The Beginning of the End of the Internet? Discrimination, Closed Networks, and the Future of Cyberspace, New America Foundation, Washington, D.C., Oct. 9, 2003.

11. *Brand X v. Federal Communications Commission*, 545 U.S. 967 (2005), discussed in Chapter 6.

12. Postal Reorganization Act, 39 U.S.C.A. Sec. 101 *et seq.*

13. 47 U.S.C.A. Sec. 202 (a) *et seq.*

14. See discussion of the cable-DSL duopoly in Chapter 7.

15. See AT&T Worldnet, AT&T DSL Subscriber Agreement, http://worldnet.att.net/general-info/terms-dsl-data.html.

16. See Chapter 7 for a discussion of residential broadband providers' market share and the argument that we should trust the market and market discipline as a response to censorial actions by ISPs.

17. Kevin Graham, Protest Draws Attention to Memo, *St. Petersburg Times,* June 3, 2005.

18. See Comcast Kills Email from "AfterDowningStreet" Coalition! The Bradblog, July 15, 2005, http://www.bradblog.com/?p=1603.

19. Telephone conference with David Swanson, co-founder of AfterDowningStreet.

20. Reprinted by permission from Seth F. Kreimer, Censorship by Proxy: The First Amendment, Internet Intermediaries, and the Problem of the Weakest Link, 155 *U. Pa. L. Rev.* 11, 28 (2006).

21. This incident drew the attention of the FCC, which undertook an inquiry into Comcast's censorship of AfterDowningStreet's communications and other discrimination on the basis of content in connection with its review of Comcast and Time Warner's bid to buy Adelphia Systems. See F.C.C. Seeks Wide Range of Cable, Web Details in Adelphia Data Request, *Comm. Daily,* Dec. 7, 2005.

22. See Censoring Again: Comcast Blocks Emails Linking to Cindy Sheehan Website! The Bradblog, August 17, 2005, http://www.bradblog.com/?p=1721.

23. G. Robert Dieckmann, The Collapse of American Culture, *The Conservative Voice,* May 20, 2007, http://www.theconservativevoice.com/article/24785.html.

24. See Jim Kouri, Internet Providers Censoring Conservative News E-Mail, News with Views.com, April 26, 2007, http://www.newswithviews.com/NWVexclusive/exclusive114.htm. Apparently SBC Global directed these emails to its subscribers' bulk mail folders, while EarthLink directed these emails to their "Known Spam" folders. As of November 2006, Comcast was also blocking email newsletters and alerts from conservative websites such as NewsWithViews.com. NewsWithViews columnist Deanna Spingola reported in November 2006 that she had not received any email from News-WithViews for the past year and a half and that her efforts to remedy this issue with Comcast had failed. At first, Comcast told her that it did not block any emails and that any such blocking must have been caused by her email program. However, when Spingola went to Comcast's site directly and sought to access email using Comcast's email service, she was also prevented from accessing NewsWithViews' email newsletters and alerts. *Id.*

25. Mark Glaser, Internet Has Its Own Brand of War Censorship, Mar. 27, 2003, http://www.ojr.org/ojr/glaser/1048784333.php.

26. See Slashdot, Google Censors Abu Ghraib Images, Nov. 7, 2004, http://yro.slashdot.org/article.pl?sid=04/11/07/1442217. ("Try searching Google Images for Abu Ghraib [or for similar relevant search terms] and note how you don't get any pictures of U.S. soldiers torturing Iraqi prisoners of war.")

27. Terrorism Rears Its Anti-U.S. Message on the Net, *Milwaukee J. Sentinel,* Sept. 25, 2001, at M2.

28. See censored and uncensored video at http://blog.wired.com/music/2007/08/video-pearl-jam.html.

29. See Nate Anderson, Pearl Jam Censored by AT&T, Calls for Neutral Net, *Ars Technical,* Aug. 9, 2007, at http://arstechnica.com/old/content/2007/08/pearl-jam-censored-by-att-calls-for-a-neutral-net.ars.

30. See discussion of the role of domain name registrars in Chapter 5.

31. See Brian Krebs on Computer Security, Network Solutions Pre-Censors Anti-Islam Site, http://voices.washingtonpost.com/securityfix/2008/03/networksolutions_precensors_an.html.

32. See John Oates, Network Solutions Pulls Anti-Koran Website, Mar. 25, 2008, http://www.theregister.co.uk/2008/03/25/anti_koran_website.

33. See www.fitnathemovie.com (which in April 2008 had the Network Solutions' message, "This site has been suspended while Network Solutions is investigating whether the site's content is in violation of the Network Solutions Acceptable Use Policy. Network Solutions has received a number of complaints regarding this site that are under investigation.").

34. See Network Solutions, Acceptable Use Policy Version 1.5, http://www.network solutions.com/legal/aup.jsp.

35. See Adam Liptak, Verizon Rejects Text Messages from an Abortion Rights Group, *New York Times,* Sept. 27, 2007, at A1.

36. See Adam Liptak, In Reversal, Verizon Says It Will Allow Group's Texts, *New York Times,* Sept. 28, 2007; In the Matter of the Petition of Public Knowledge *et al.* for a Declaratory Ruling Stating That Text Messages and Short Codes Are Title II Services or Are Title I Services Subject to Section 202 Nondiscrimination Rules, Mar. 14, 2008.

37. See Chais Gaither & Joseph Menn, AOL Blocks Critics' E-Mails, *Los Angeles Times,* Apr. 14, 2006.

38. Larry Seltzer, Goodmail, One Year Later, *eWeek,* Feb. 1, 2007; Chloe Albanesius, Four ISPs Join Anti-Spam, E-Mail Delivery Program, *PC Magazine,* June 7, 2007.

39. See Michael Geist, Telecommunications Policy Review Submission 5-6 (2005), http://www.telecomreview.ca/eic/site/tprp-gecrt.nsf/eng/rx00043.html.

40. See, *e.g.,* Dawn C. Nunziato, Technology and Pornography, 2007 *B.Y.U. L. Rev.* 1535, for a discussion of ports and port-blocking technology.

41. Jonathan Krim, Phone Company Settles in Blocking of Internet Calls, *Washington Post,* Mar. 4, 2005. In response, the FCC investigated such actions, and the FCC and Madison River entered into a Consent Decree in which the latter agreed to pay a fine of $15,000 and to stop blocking ports used by VoIP applications. In the Matter of Madison River Communications, File No. EB-05-IH-0110, DA 05-543. While some have argued that the FCC's actions in this instance establish that the FCC has sufficient authority under the current regime to prohibit such discrimination, in fact this matter arose before the FCC issued its Wireline Broadband Order removing common carriage requirements from DSL broadband providers such as Madison River.

42. See Ben Charny, Vonage Says Its Calls Are Still Being Blocked, Cnet News, Mar. 21, 2005, http://news.cnet.com/Vonage-says-its-calls-are-still-being-blocked/2100-7352_3-5628564.html.

43. David Lazarus, Free Speech Could Lead to Online Disconnect, *Los Angeles Times,* Oct. 10, 2007, at C1.

44. See Written Statement of Michele Combs, Vice President of Communications of the Christian Coalition of America, Hearing on Net Neutrality and Free Speech on the Internet Before the Committee on the Judiciary, Task Force on Competition Policy and Antitrust Laws, U.S. House of Representatives, March 11, 2008.

45. In the Matter of Vuze, Inc., Petition to Establish Rules Governing Network Management Practices by Broadband Network Operators, Petition for Rule-Making, November 14, 2007.

46. Peter Svensson, Comcast Blocks Some Internet Traffic, MSNBC, October 19, 2007, available at http://www.msnbc.msn.com/id/21376597/.

47. Mark Hachman, BellSouth Says It's Not Blocking MySpace, *PC Magazine,* June 2, 2006.

48. Jonathan Krim, Verizon's Spam Policy Criticized, *Washington Post,* Jan. 19, 2005.

49. CNNMoney.com, Comcast Outage Blocks Google, YouTube, Sep. 27, 2006, http://money.cnn.com/blogs/browser/2006/09/comcast-outage-blocks-google-you tube.html.

50. See Charles B. Goldfarb, Access to Broadband Networks: Congressional Research Service Report to Congress (2006), at 10–11, 17–18.

51. See Internet Freedom and Innovation at Risk: Why Congress Must Restore Strong Net Neutrality Protection, http://www.aclu.org/ freespeech/Internet/26829res20060922 .html.

52. Turner I, 512 U.S. at 657.

53. According to the latest figures, Google's search engine enjoys between a 60 and 70 percent share of searches in the United States. See Danny Sullivan, Rating Service Faceoff: Search Share Compared, June 2007 to March 2008, *Search Engine Land,* Apr. 21, 2008, searchengineland.com/080421-205242.php.

54. *Id.*

55. See http://www.google.com/support/news/bin/answer.py?answer=40213&topic =8851.

56. *Id.*

57. See Jon Newton, New Google Censorship Accusation, p2pnet, Feb. 19, 2008, http://www.p2pnet.net/story/15027.

58. See Paul Joseph Watson, Google Caught Censoring Charlie Sheen 9/11 Story, Mar. 24, 2006, available at http://www.prisonplanet.com/articles/march2006/230306 googlecensoring.htm.

59. Internet Censorship: The Warning Signs Were Not Hidden, Dec. 9, 2005, http://www.worldproutassembly.org/archives/2005/12/internet censor.html.

60. See Kouri, Internet Providers Censoring Conservative News E-Mail.

61. See *SearchKing v. Google Technology,* 2003 WL 21464568 (W.D. Okla., 2003).

62. See http://adwords.google.com/support/bin/static.py?page=guidelines .cs&topic=9271&subtopic=9279.

63. *Id.*

64. Verne Kopytoff, Google's Ad Rule Complex, Controversial, *San Francisco Chronicle,* August 9, 2004.

65. See Google Builds World's Largest Advertising and Search Monetization Program, Mar. 4, 2003, http://www.google.com/press/pressrel/advertising.html.

66. *Id.*

67. Kopytoff, *supra* note 64.

68. Simon Caldwell, Christian Group Sues Google After Search Engine Refuses to Take Its Anti-Abortion Adverts, *Daily Mail,* Apr. 9, 2008, http://www.dailymail.co.uk/news/article-558177/Christian-group-sues-Google-search-engine-refuses-anti-abortion-adverts.html.

69. Kopytoff, *supra* note 64.

70. See W. Frederick Zimmerman, *Guantanamo/Abu Ghraib Ads Banned by Google,* Nimble Books, at http://www.wfzimmerman.com/index.php?page=3 (last visited Mar. 16, 2005).

71. Robert Cox, Google Bans Anti-MoveOn.org Ads, *The Examiner,* October 11, 2007, at http://www.examiner.com/a-983100~Robert_Cox__Google_bans_anti_MoveOn_org_ads.html.

72. See Google's Gag Order, Perrspectives, June 20, 2004, http://www.perrspectives.com/articles/art_gagorder01.htm.

73. See *Langdon v. Google, Inc.,* 474 F. Supp. 2d 622 (D. Del. 2007) (rejecting Langdon's First Amendment claims).

74. See note 62.

75. See Amy Harmon, Is a Do-Gooder Company a Good Thing? *New York Times,* May 2, 2004.

76. See discussion of fairness doctrine in Chapter 3.

77. See Google Refuses Our Ad, Unknown News, Mar. 17, 2003, http://www.unknownnews.net/google.html.

78. Kopytoff, *supra* note 64.

79. Sullivan, *supra* note 53.

80. See *Religious Technology Center v. Netcom On-Line Communications Services,* 907 F. Supp. 1361 (N.D. Cal. 1995). (Of course, prior to the enactment of the Digital Millennium Copyright Act, service providers might have been found liable for contributory or vicarious copyright infringement, and thus had some incentive even pre-DMCA to remove allegedly infringing content.)

81. 17 U.S.C. Sec. 512 (2000).   82. 17 U.S.C. Sec. 512 (c)(1)(c).

83. 17 U.S.C. Sec. 512 (c) (3).   84. 17 U.S.C. Sec. 512 (g) (3) (c).

85. See text accompanying note 88.   86. See 17 U.S.C. Sec. 512 (c)(1)(c).

87. Kreimer, *supra* note 20, at 32–33.

88. See Declan McCullough, Google Yanks Anti-Church Sites, *Wired,* Mar. 21, 2002, http://www.wired.com/politics/law/news/2002/03/51233. Google now passes along the notice and take-down requests it receives to ChillingEffects.org. See Jennifer M. Urban and Laura Quilter, Efficient Process or "Chilling Effects"? Takedown Notices Under Section 512 of the Digital Millennium Copyright Act, Summary Report, at http://mylaw.usc.edu/documents/512Rep.

89. See *Online Policy Group v. Diebold, Inc.,* 337 F. Supp. 2d 1195, 1204–05 (N.D. Cal. 2004); Press Release, Elec. Frontier Foundation, ISP Rejects Diebold Copyright

Claims Against News Website: EFF Defends Rights to Publish Links to Electronic Voting Memos, Oct. 16, 2003, http://w2.eff.org/legal/ISP_liability/20031016_eff_pr.php (although ISP Online Policy Group resisted Diebold's take-down demands, dozens of other ISPs readily acceded to Diebold's demands).

90. Daniel Lyons, Attack of the Blogs, *Forbes,* Nov. 14, 2005, at 128, 132, cited in Kreimer, *supra* note 20, at 33 n. 65.

91. See Urban and Quilter, *supra* note 88 (summarizing their detailed empirical analysis of DMCA takedown notices, with full report published in 22 *Santa Clara Computer and High Tech L.J.* 621 (2006)). Because the suggested revision of the Copyright Act is beyond the scope of this book, I leave to others a more detailed discussion of ways in which the take-down provisions of Section 512 should be modified to better protect Internet users' free speech and fair use rights. I raise this issue as another instance of ISPs enjoying the incentive and the discretion to block Internet users' expression.

92. This brief summary tracks the in-depth treatment of this issue provided in the recent FTC Staff Report, Broadband Connectivity and Competition Policy, June 2007 [hereinafter, FTC Broadband Policy Report]. See also Barry M. Leiner *et al.,* A Brief History of the Internet, http://www.isoc.org/internet/history/brief.shtml.

93. FTC Broadband Policy Report at 14.

94. *Id.* at 14–15.   95. *Id.* at 15.

96. *Id.* at 16.   97. *Id.* at 17.

98. *Id.* at 18.   99. *Id.* at 18.

100. *Id.* at 19.

101. As Lawrence Lessig characterizes it, "[T]hese networks [that constitute the Internet] connect over wires. All of these wires, and the machines linked by them, are controlled by someone. The vast majority are owned by private parties. . . ." Lawrence Lessig, *The Future of Ideas* 26 (2001).

102. See Jon M. Peha, The Benefits and Risks of Mandating Network Neutrality and the Quest for a Balanced Policy, 34th Research Conference on Communication, Information, & Internet Policy 3 (2006), https://www.dpacket.org/articles/benefits-and-risks-mandating-network-neutrality-and-quest-balanced-policy.

103. *Id.* at 4–5.

104. See, *e.g.,* David Clark *et al., New Arch. Future Generation Internet Architecture: Final Technical Report* (2003).

105. See Peha, *supra* note 102, at 4–6.   106. *Id.*

107. *Id.* at 6.   108. Lessig, *supra* note 101, at 159–60.

109. A packet sniffer is computer software or hardware that can intercept and analyze data packets passing over a network. See, *e.g.,* What Is a Packet Sniffer?, tech-FAQ, n.d., http://www.tech-faq.com/packet-sniffer.shtml.

110. See, *e.g.,* Dawn C. Nunziato, Toward a Constitutional Regulation of Minors' Access to Harmful Internet Speech, 79 *Chi.-Kent L. Rev.* 121 (2004).

111. See discussion of filtering software in Chapter 4.

112. See discussion of cable-DSL duopoly in Chapter 7.

Chapter 2

1. See generally Isaiah Berlin, *Liberty* (2002).

2. John Milton, *Areopagitica*, 58 (Jebb ed., 1918).

3. John Stuart Mill, *Utilitarianism, Liberty and Representative Government*, 104 (Lindsay, ed., 1957).

4. 250 U.S. 616 (1919). Abrams involved the prosecution of five Russians for violating the Espionage Act for encouraging resistance to the United States in the war against Germany in World War I.

5. *Id.* (emphasis added) (Holmes, J., dissenting). Holmes adopts in this passage a skeptical theory of ultimate truth—one in which ultimate "truth" cannot be known or identified, but merely consists in whatever emerges as the winner in the competition in the marketplace of ideas.

6. The marketplace of ideas metaphor has, however, been cited in support of restricting nongovernmental actors from censoring speech. In *Red Lion Broadcasting Co. v. F.C.C.,* 395 U.S. 367 (1969), for example, the Supreme Court quoted Mill's theory to support its decision upholding the fairness doctrine, which imposed requirements on broadcasters to provide equal time for competing political viewpoints. See 395 U.S. at 392 n. 18.

7. Donald M. Gillmor, Jerome A. Barron, and Todd F. Simon, *Mass Communication Law* (7th ed. 1998).

8. Cass R. Sunstein, The First Amendment in Cyberspace, 104 *Yale L. J.* 1757 (1995) (describing but not espousing this conception).

9. See Owen Fiss, Why The State? reprinted in *Democracy and the Mass Media* (Judith Lichtenberg, ed., 1990) [hereinafter, *Democracy and the Mass Media*] 140 (describing but not adopting this view).

10. See Cass R. Sunstein, *Democracy and the Problem of Free Speech* 18 (1993) (describing but not espousing this view).

11. Reprinted with permission from Jerome Barron, Access to the Press—A New First Amendment Right, published in 80 *Harv. L. Rev.* 1641 (1967).

12. See generally *Access to the Media—1967 to 2007 and Beyond: A Symposium Honoring Jerome A. Barron's Path-Breaking Article,* 76 Geo. Wash. Univ. L. Rev. 2008.

13. Access to Internet markets for expression is generally far easier to secure than access to the non-Internet mass media. However, both mediums ultimately present problems of censorship by powerful private speech regulators, as discussed further on. See generally *id.*

14. See Scott Powe, Scholarship and Markets, 56 *Geo. Wash. L. Rev.* 172, 181 (1987) ("For Barron, access was a way to add voices and ideas to the marketplace.")

15. Reprinted with permission from Cass R. Sunstein, *Democracy and the Problem of Free Speech* 18 (1993), at 18–19.

16. Alexander Meiklejohn, *Political Freedom* 27–28 (1960).

17. *Id.*

18. According to Meiklejohn, "the guarantee given by the First Amendment is not, then, assured to all speaking. It is assured only to speech which bears, directly

or indirectly, upon issues with which voters have to deal—only, therefore, to the consideration of matters of public interest. Private speech . . . has no claim whatever to the protection of the First Amendment." *Id.* at 79–80. Rather, Meiklejohn contended that "private" speech merited protection under the Due Process Clause of the Fifth Amendment. *Id.*

19. Sunstein, *supra* note 10, at 20–21.

20. *Id.* at 57–58.

21. Lee Bollinger, The Rationale of Public Regulation of the Media, reprinted in *Democracy and the Mass Media,* 366–67.

22. *Id.*

23. See, *e.g.,* Judith Lichtenberg, Foundations and Limits of Freedom of the Press, in *Democracy and the Mass Media,* at 104.

24. Fiss, *supra* note 9.

25. See William P. Marshall, Diluting Constitutional Rights: Rethinking "Rethinking State Action," 80 *Nw. U. L. Rev.* 558 (1985). The state action doctrine is also understood as a vehicle for limiting the reach of federal power and preserving a zone of state sovereignty. See *Lugar v. Edmondson Oil Co.,* 457 U.S. 922, 936 (1982).

26. See Robert Mnookin, The Public/Private Dichotomy: Political Disagreement and Academic Repudiation, 130 *U. Pa. L. Rev.* 1429, 1429 (1982) ("The distinction between public and private connects with a central tenet of liberal thought . . . ").

27. The Supreme Court has accorded special solicitude for the right to express oneself on one's own property. See *City of Ladue v. Gilleo,* 512 U.S. 43, 58 (1994) (invalidating a municipal ordinance restricting certain residential signs and explaining that "a special respect for individual liberty in the home has long been a part of our culture and our law; that principle has special resonance when the government seeks to constrain a person's ability to speak there").

28. See Marion Schwarzchild, Value Pluralism and the Constitution: In Defense of the State Action Doctrine, 1988 *Sup. Ct. Rev.* 129.

29. See Julian N. Eule & Jonathan D. Varat, Transporting First Amendment Norms to the Private Sector: With Every Wish There Comes a Curse, 45 *UCLA L. Rev.* 1537 (1998).

30. See, *e.g.,* Charles L. Black Jr., Foreword: "State Action," Equal Protection, and California's Proposition 14, 81 *Harv. L. Rev.* 69, 108 (1967); Frank Goodman, Professor Brest on State Action and Liberal Theory and a Postscript to Professor Stone, 130 *U. Pa. L. Rev.* 1331, 1340 (1982); Louis Henkin, *Shelly v. Kraemer:* Notes for a Revised Opinion, 110 *U. Pa. L. Rev.* 473 (1962). Louis Henkin contended that, for example, in construing the state action doctrine in the context of the Equal Protection Clause, courts should compare the various affected parties' interests to determine the consequences of prioritizing one over the other. In the context of rendering meaningful the equal protection guarantee in the face of claims that the state action doctrine insulates "private" action from constitutional scrutiny, Henkin considers two different scenarios: the first involving a racist host of a private dinner who excludes African-Americans from his home and the second involving a racist shopkeeper who excludes

African-Americans from his shop. In both cases, the racist parties seek to rely on the state law of trespass to protect their interests. In construing the state action doctrine in the first context, Henkin claims, courts should subordinate guests' equality interests in favor of the host's property and privacy interests because the host's interest is insular and does not substantially influence community affairs. Furthermore, the racist dinner host has stronger privacy and autonomy interests in choosing his companions than does the shopkeeper in choosing his customers. *Id.* In the second context, however, Henkin argues that courts should reach the opposite conclusion and should value the patrons' equality and access interests over the shopkeeper's property and privacy interests because the latter's discrimination "is public, and widespread; [and] the inequality and indignity therefore notorious and widespread, with important commercial consequences." *Id.* at 499. Accordingly, a balancing of the privacy and property interests against the equality and access interests at stake in each case enables courts to engage in a meaningful substantive inquiry instead of a formalistic one, and to insulate "private" regulation from constitutional norms in some cases but not in others.

31. *Marsh v. Alabama,* 326 U.S., 501, 509 (1946).

32. See Gregory P. Magarian, The First Amendment, the Public-Private Distinction, and Nongovernmental Suppression of Wartime Political Debate, 73 *Geo. Wash. L. Rev.* 101 (2004) (espousing a "public rights" theory of expressive freedom under which courts should invoke the First Amendment to enjoin nongovernmental exclusions of political speakers from expressive opportunities and reprisals against wartime dissenters).

33. See, *e.g., Lloyd v. Tanner,* discussed in Chapter 5.

34. See discussion of *Robins v. Pruneyard Shopping Center in* Chapter 5.

35. Compare the FCC's fairness doctrine, discussed in Chapter 3.

36. See *CBS v. DNC,* discussed in Chapter 5.

37. See discussion of censorship of political emails in Chapter 1.

38. See discussion of censorship of cablecasts in Chapter 1.

39. Onora O'Neill, Practices of Toleration, reprinted in *Democracy and the Mass Media,* 177.

40. Sunstein, *supra* note 10, at 37.

41. *Id.*

42. See discussion of fairness doctrine in Chapter 3.

Chapter 3

1. This famous characterization comes from *New York Times v. Sullivan,* 376 U.S. 254 (1964), in which Justice Brennan for the Court described our "profound national commitment to the principles that debate on public issues should be uninhibited, robust, and wide-open."

2. *Hague v. CIO,* 307 U.S. 494 (1939).

3. See discussion of state action doctrine below and in Chapter 5.

4. See *Hague v. CIO*, 307 U.S. 494 (1939).

5. *Id.*

6. See discussion of privatization of the Internet in Chapter 1.

7. *Hague v. CIO*, 307 U.S. 494 (1939).

8. *Commonwealth v. Davis*, 39 N.E.113 (1895), aff'd sub nom. *Davis v. Commonwealth of Massachusetts*, 167 U.S. 43 (1897).

9. 39 N.E. 113 (1895). See also Geoffrey R. Stone, Fora Americana: Speech in Public Places, 1974 *Sup. Ct. Rev.* 233, 237 (explaining that, under the reasoning of *Davis*, "the state possessed the power absolutely to prohibit the exercise of First Amendment rights [on] public property simply by asserting the prerogatives traditionally associated with the private ownership of land").

10. *Davis v. Massachusetts*, 167 U.S. 43, 47 (1897).

11. *Hague v. CIO*, 307 U.S. 496, 513 (internal quotations omitted).

12. *Id.* at 515–16.

13. The Court's reasoning in *Hague* rested in part on a "prescriptive easement" rationale, under which the public, because of its traditional, historical, continuous use of such public places, came to enjoy a right to continue to use such places for free speech purposes. This line of reasoning essentially works from within the private property conception of *Davis*, but limits the state property owner's rights under the property law doctrine of prescriptive easements. Although this limitation on the state's property rights provides a foundation for the public's right to use places that traditionally or historically have been used for communicative purposes, it will prove problematic within new forums for expression—such as Internet forums—that do not enjoy such a historical pedigree.

14. 308 U.S. 147 (1939).

15. *Id.* at 163 (emphasis added).

16. 308 U.S. 147 (1939) (emphasis added). See also *Jamison v. Texas*, 318 U.S. 413 (1943) (also invalidating a city ordinance prohibiting the dissemination of leaflets).

17. Richard Posner, Free Speech in an Economic Perspective, 20 *Suff. U. L. Rev.* 52 (1986).

18. Schneider, 308 U.S. at 163

19. In particular, authoritarian government forums, such as prisons, military bases, and schools, are generally considered nonpublic forums. See, *e.g.*, *Adderley v. Florida*, 385 U.S. 39 (1966) (county jail not a public forum); *Greer v. Spock*, 424 U.S. 828 (1976) (military base not a public forum); *Perry Educ. Ass'n v. Perry Local Educs. Ass'n*, 460 U.S. 37 (1983) (public school's interschool mail system not a public forum).

20. Within a designated public forum devoted to particular subjects, however, the government may impose restrictions limiting expression to the particular subject matter(s) for which the forum is designated.

21. See *Perry Educ. Ass'n v. Perry Local Educs' Ass'n*, 460 U.S. 37 (1983).

22. See, *e.g.*, *Burson v. Freeman*, 504 U.S. 191 (1992).

23. Steven G. Gey, Reopening the Public Forum—From Sidewalks to Cyberspace, 58 *Ohio St. L.J.* 1535, 1538–39 (1998).

24. See discussion of *ISKCON v. Lee* in Chapter 4.

25. See discussion of state action doctrine, in Chapter 5 and later in this chapter.

26. See discussion of privatization of the Internet in Chapter 1.

27. *American Library Association v. United States,* 539 U.S. 194 (2003).

28. 326 U.S. 501 (1946).

29. See Erwin Chemerinsky, Constitutional Law, 514–17 2006.

30. 513 U.S. 374, 396 (1995) (holding that Amtrak, a government-created and government-controlled corporation, was a state actor for First Amendment purposes, but declining to determine whether its speech restrictions were constitutional).

31. *National A-1 Advertising v. Network Solutions, Inc.,* 121 F. Supp. 2d 156 (D.N.H. 2000).

32. 326 U.S. 501 (1946).   33. *Id.*

34. *Id.* at 502.   35. *Id.* at 503.

36. See discussion of *Hague v. CIO* above.

37. As such, this case involved not only the First Amendment right to free speech but also the First Amendment right to free exercise of religion.

38. 326 U.S. at 505.   39. *Id.* at 506.

40. *Id.;* emphasis added.   41. *Id.*

42. 391 U.S. 308 (1968).   43. *Id.*

44. 227 A. 2d 874 (Pa. 1967).   45. 391 U.S. 308.

46. *Id.* at 315.   47. *Id.* at 324–25.

48. See Gregory P. Magarian, The First Amendment, the Public-Private Distinction, and Nongovernmental Suppression of Wartime Political Debate, 73 *Geo. Wash. L. Rev.* 101, 156 (2004).

49. See, *e.g., Lloyd v. Tanner,* 407 U.S. 551 (1972) and progeny, discussed in Chapter 5.

50. See Editorialization by Broadcast Licensees, Report of the Commission, 13. F.C.C. R. 1246, 1249 par.6 (1949).

51. 395 U.S. 367 (1969).   52. *Id.*

53. *Id.* at 386.   54. *Id.* at 389.

55. *Id.*   56. *Id.* at 390.

57. *Id.* at 392.   58. *Id.*

59. *Id.* at 394.   60. *Id.*

61. *Id.*

62. *Id.* at 390 (quoting *Garrison v. Louisiana,* 379 U.S. 64).

63. Stephen Holmes, Liberal Constraints on Private Power? Reflections on the Origins and Rationale of Access Regulation, reprinted in *Democracy and the Mass Media,* (Judith Lichtenberg, ed., 1990) [hereinafter, *Democracy and the Mass Media*], 44–45.

64. 453 U.S. 367 (1981).   65. *Id.*

66. *Id.* (quoting *Red Lion*).   67. *Id.* at 396.

68. *Id.* at 397.

69. See *Syracuse Peace Council v. Television Station WTVH,* 2 F.C.C.R. 5043, 5045–55 (1987).

70. 512 U.S. 622 (1994).

71. *Id.*

72. *Id.* at 630. Section 4 of the Act imposed must carry obligations with respect to "local commercial television stations" and required cable systems with more than twelve active channels and more than three hundred available channels to set aside up to one-third of their channels for commercial broadcast stations requesting carriage. Section 5 of the Act imposed must carry obligations with respect to noncommercial educational television stations.

73. *Id.* at x.

74. *Id.* at 640.

75. 418 U.S. 241 (1974).

76. 512 U.S. at 657; emphasis added.

77. *Id.* at 662–63.

78. *Id.* at 624.

79. *Id.* at 663.

80. *Id.* at 663–64.

81. *Id.* at 657.

82. *Id.* at 680 (O'Connor, J., dissenting).

83. *Turner Broadcasting System, Inc. v. F.C.C.,* 520 U.S. 301 (1997) [hereinafter, Turner II].

84. 520 U.S. at 194.

85. 520 U.S. at 226.

86. 520 U.S. at 226–27 (Breyer, J., concurring); emphasis added.

87. *Id.* at 227.

88. *Id.*

89. *Denver Area Educational Telecommunications Consortium v. F.C.C.,* 518 U.S. 727, 798–99 (1996) (Kennedy, J., concurring).

90. See, *e.g.,* Ithiel de Sola Pool, Technologies of Freedom 71–107 (1983).

91. *Id.* at 106.

92. Jerome A. Barron, The Telco, the Common Carrier Model, and the First Amendment—The "Dial-A-Porn" Precedent, 19 *Rutgers Computer & Tech. L. J.* 371 (1993).

93. *Id.* at 383.

94. See James B. Speta, A Common Carrier Approach to Internet Interconnection, 54 *Fed. Comm. L. J.* 225 (2002).

95. de Sola Pool, *supra* note 90, at 98.

96. *Primrose v. Western Union Telegraph Co.,* 154 U.S. 1 (1893). Common carriage obligations were also imposed on transportation providers. The Interstate Commerce Act of 1887 imposed affirmative common carriage obligations on railroads, requiring them to serve the public and to connect their tracks to one another, and prohibiting them from engaging in price discrimination.

97. Speta, *supra* note 94, at 261–63.

98. 47 U.S.C. §151 (1934).

99. See *Am. Tel. & Tel. Co. v. U.S.,* 299 U.S. 232 (1936). Under the Communications Act of 1934, common carriage obligations were imposed on "any person [or entity] engaged as a common carrier for hire in interstate or foreign communication by wire or radio." The Act's definition of common carrier looked to "whether the carrier holds itself out indiscriminately to a class of persons for service," regardless of whether the entity enjoyed monopoly power.

100. *Sable Communications, Inc. v. F.C.C.*, 492 U.S. 115 (1989).

101. *National Association of Regulatory Utility Commissioners v. F.C.C.*, 525 F. 2d 630, 641 (D.C. Cir. 1976).

102. See Daniel Brenner, Telephone Company Entry into Video Services: A First Amendment Analysis, 67 *Notre Dame L. Rev.* 97, 106 n. 24 (1983).

103. See, *e.g.,* Barron, *supra* note 92, at 377, 389 (explicating the dichotomy between the publisher-broadcaster model and the common carrier model).

104. See Chapter 6 for a fuller discussion of classifications under the Computer Inquiries.

Chapter 4

1. Portions of Chapters 4 and 5 were originally published in the *Berkeley Technology Law Journal,* Volume 20 (2005).

2. *Denver Area Educational Telecomm. Consortium, Inc. v. F.C.C.*, 518 U.S. 727, 802–3 (1996) (Kennedy, J., concurring in part, concurring in the judgment in part, and dissenting in part).

3. 593 U.S. 194 (2003).

4. *Hague v. CIO*, 307 U.S. at 515.

5. See *Perry Educ. Ass'n v. Perry Local Educs. Ass'n*, 460 U.S. 37 (1983).

6. *City of Madison Joint School Dist. v. Wisc. Employment Relations Comm'n*, 429 U.S. 167 (1976).

7. *Widmar v. Vincent*, 454 U.S. 263 (1981).

8. *Southeastern Promotions Ltd. v. Conrad*, 420 U.S. 546 (1975).

9. See *Int'l Soc'y for Krishna Consciousness v. Lee*, 505 U.S. 672 (1992).

10. See, *e.g., Rosenberger v. Rectors and Visitors of the University of Virginia*, 515 U.S. 819 (1995).

11. See, *e.g., Arkansas Educ. Television Comm'n v. Forbes*, 523 U.S. 666 (1998) (suggesting that if televised political debate had an "open-microphone format," it would constitute a designated public forum).

12. See, *e.g., Denver Area Educational Telecomm. Consortium, Inc. v. F.C.C.*, 518 U.S. 727 (1996) (Kennedy, concurring).

13. See, *e.g.,* Lee Bollinger and Geoffrey Stone, Eternally Vigilant: Free Speech in the Modern Era 288 (2002).

14. *Int'l Soc'y for Krishna Consciousness v. Lee*, 505 U.S. 672 (1992).

15. *Id.*

16. *Id.* at 680 (internal quotations omitted).

17. *Id.* at 680–81.

18. *Id.* at 695 (Kennedy, J., concurring).

19. *Id.*

20. *Id.* at 697.

21. *Id.* at 700.

22. *Id.* at 694.

23. *Id.* at 698.

24. *Id.* at 695–97; emphasis added.

25. 518 U.S. 727 (1996). In *Denver Area,* both the plurality (Justices Breyer, Stevens, O'Connor, and Souter) and the dissent (Justices Thomas and Scalia and Chief Justice Rehnquist) refused to characterize the forum at issue as a public forum.

26. *Id.* at 791 (Kennedy, J., joined by Ginsburg, J., concurring in part, concurring in the judgment in part, and dissenting in part).

27. *Id.* at 792.

28. *Id.* at 793–94.

29. *Id.* at 802–803 (citations omitted).

30. See, *e.g.,* Robert Post, Between Governance and Management: The History and Theory of the Public Forum, 34 *UCLA L. Rev.* 1713 (1987); David Goldberger, Judicial Scrutiny in Public Forum Cases: Misplaced Trust in the Judgment of Public Officials, 32 *Buff. L. Rev.* 175 (1983).

31. 539 U.S. 194 (2003).

32. 201 F. Supp. 2d at 406–7.

33. 47 U.S.C. § 254(h)(5)(B) (2000). While the terms *obscene* and *child pornography* are given their (constitutionally acceptable) standard meanings, CIPA defines material that is "harmful to minors" as any picture, image, graphic image file, or other visual depiction that

> (i) taken as a whole and with respect to minors, appeals to a prurient interest in nudity, sex, or excretion; (ii) depicts, describes, or represents, in a patently offensive way with respect to what is suitable for minors, an actual or simulated sexual act or sexual contact, actual or simulated normal or perverted sexual acts, or a lewd exhibition of the genitals; and (iii) taken as a whole, lacks serious literary, artistic, political, or scientific value as to minors.

34. *Id.*

35. *American Library Association, Inc. v. United States,* 201 F. Supp. 2d 401, 448 (E.D. Pa. 2002), rev'd., 539 U.S. 194 (2003).

36. *Id.* at 449.   37. *Id.* at 475.

38. *Id.* at 448.   39. *Id.* at 476–77.

40. *Id.* at 489.   41. *Id.* at 427.

42. *Id.*   43. *Id.*

44. *Id.* at 489.

45. See discussion of categorization of forums above.

46. 201 F. Supp. 2d at 454–55.

47. *Id.*

48. *Id.* at 457.

49. In its conclusion that the provision of Internet access in a public library constituted a designated public forum, the *American Library Association* court reached the same conclusion as the court in *Mainstream Loudoun v. Board of Trustees County Library,* 24 F. Supp. 2d 552 (E.D. Va. 1998). In that case, the court reviewed a challenge to a public library's restrictions on access to sexually explicit Internet sites that

mandated the use of filtering software. In determining whether public libraries' provision of Internet access constituted a designated public forum, the *Loudoun* court first observed that the library system had recently adopted a resolution declaring that its "primary objective [is] that the people have access to all avenues of ideas" and that the public interest requires "offering the widest possible diversity of views and expressions." *Id.* at 563. In light of the library's statement of its mission, the court concluded that the defendant "intended to designate the Loudoun County libraries as public fora for the limited purposes of the expressive activities they provide, including the receipt of communication and information through the Internet." *Id.*

50. *Id.* at 458 (quoting *Rust v. Sullivan,* 500 U.S. 173, 194 (1991)).

51. *Id.* at 460.   52. 515 U.S. 819 (1995).

53. *Id.* at 461.   54. *Id.* at 462.

55. *Id.*   56. *Id.*

57. 539 U.S. 194 (2003).

58. On this point, Rehnquist explained that "[w]e require the Government to employ the least restrictive means only when the forum is a public one and strict scrutiny applies." 539 U.S. at 207 n. 3.

59. *Id.* at 205–6 (internal quotation marks omitted).

60. *Id.* at 206.

61. See *id.* at 237 (Souter, J., joined by Ginsburg, J., dissenting) (observing that "the plurality's conception of a public library's mission has been rejected by the libraries themselves").

62. *Id.* at 206.

63. *Id.* at 207 n. 3 (internal quotation marks omitted).

64. *Id.* at 208 ("[I]t is entirely reasonable for public libraries to . . . exclude certain categories of content, without making individualized judgments that everything they do make available has requisite and appropriate quality.") This holding, in turn, was the predicate for the Supreme Court's ultimate holding that CIPA was a valid exercise of Congress's spending power and imposed no unconstitutional conditions upon libraries: "Because public libraries' use of Internet filtering software does not violate their patrons' First Amendment rights, CIPA does not induce libraries to violate the Constitution, and is a valid exercise of Congress' spending power. Nor does CIPA impose an unconstitutional condition on public libraries." *Id.* at 214.

65. 2007 U.S. Dist. LEXIS 23843, U.S. District Court for the Eastern District of Kentucky, Central Division (Mar. 30, 2007).

66. *Id.*

67. *Id.* at *15–16.

68. *Cf. Putman Pit, Inc. v. City of Cookeville, Tenn.* 221 F. 3d 834 (6th Cir. 2000) (while the city's web page was held to be a nonpublic forum, the city's refusal to allow a particular link from its web page may have constituted discrimination based on viewpoint in violation of the First Amendment).

69. 201 F. Supp. 2d 401 (E.D. Pa. 2002).

70. *Bidbay.com, Inc. v. Spry,* Cal. Ct. App., 2d App. Dist., No. B160126.

71. Cal. Civ. Proc. Code. § 425.16. In passing this legislation, California joined a number of other states that have also passed anti-SLAPP laws. See California Anti-SLAPP Project, available at http://www.casp.net/statutes/menstate.html (listing states that have passed and are considering passage of anti-SLAPP legislation).

72. *Id.*

73. *Id.*

74. 2004 WL 214330 (Cal. App. 2 Dist., 2004).

75. 93 Cal. App. 4th 993 (2001) (Internet message boards constitute public forums).

76. Cal. Ct. App., 2d App. Dist., No. B160126.

77. *Id.*

Chapter 5

1. 407 U.S. 551 (1972).   2. *Id.*

3. *Id.*   4. *Id.* at 557 (emphasis added).

5. Indeed, the Supreme Court made clear in *Hudgens v. National Labor Relations Board,* 424 U.S. 507 (1976), that *Lloyd* had sounded the death knell for the version of the state action doctrine adopted in *Logan Valley.*

6. *Tanner v. Lloyd Corp.,* 308 F. Supp. 128, 131 (D. Ore. 1970).

7. 407 U.S. at 586 (Marshall, J., dissenting).

8. 412 U.S. 94 (1973).   9. *Id.* at 97–99.

10. *Id.* at 172.   11. *Id.* at 181.

12. *Id.* at 183–94 (quotations and citations omitted).

13. 592 P. 2d 341 (Cal. 1979).

14. 434 P. 2d 353 (Cal. 1967).

15. The shopping mall also claimed that the state court ruling deprived it of its property without just compensation in violation of the Fifth and Fourteenth Amendments. The Supreme Court rejected this constitutional challenge as well, holding that California enjoyed the power to interpret its state constitution's free speech provisions more broadly than the First Amendment (and that so doing did not effect a taking of property without just compensation). The Court explained, "[o]ur reasoning in *Lloyd* does not limit the authority of the state to exercise its police power or its sovereign right to adopt in its own Constitution individual liberties more expansive than those conferred by the Federal Constitution." *Id.* at 80.

16. 1 Cal. Rptr. 3d 32 (2003).

17. New Jersey's constitution, which articulates a right of free speech more broadly and more in accordance with the affirmative conception of the free speech guarantee, provides that "[e]very person may freely speak, write, and publish his sentiments on all subjects, being responsible for the abuse of that right. No law shall be passed to restrain or abridge the liberty of speech or of the press." N.J. const. art. I, ¶ 6.

18. *New Jersey Coalition Against War in the Middle East v. J.M.B. Realty Corp.*, 650 A. 2d 757 (N.J. 1994).

19. *Id.*

20. *Id.* at 776–78. See also *Green Party of New Jersey v. Hartz Mountain Industries, Inc.*, 752 A. 2d 315 (N.J. 2000) (extending such free speech rights to those seeking to exercise them in smaller community shopping centers).

21. 2003 WL 1955433 (Fla. Cir. Ct. 2003).

22. *Id.* at *1 (quotations omitted; citing Thomas I. Emerson, Toward a General Theory of the First Amendment 3 (1963)).

23. 445 N.E. 2d 590 (Mass. 1983).

24. *Id.*

25. *Commonwealth v. Tate*, 432 A.2d 1382 (Pa. 1981).

26. *Alderwood Associates v. Washington Environmental Council*, 635 P. 2d 108 (Wash. 1981).

27. 445 N.E. 2d at 594.

28. See discussion of public forum doctrine in Chapter 4.

29. 119 F. Supp. 2d at 282.

30. *Schneider v. State*, 308 U.S. at 163.

31. *ACLU v. Reno*, 929 F. Supp. 824 (E.D. Pa. 1996).

32. 201 F. Supp. 2d at 467, rev'd., 539 U.S. 194 (2003).

33. See discussion of the Internet's origins in Chapter 1.

34. Pub. L. No. 104-104,110 Stat. 133 (codified as amended at 47 U.S.C. § 223 (2000)). Section 230(c)(2) of the CDA states

> No provider . . . of an interactive computer service shall be held liable on account of any action voluntarily taken in good faith to restrict access to or availability of material that the provider . . . considers to be obscene, lewd, lascivious, filthy, excessively violent, harassing, or otherwise objectionable, whether or not such material is constitutionally protected. 47 U.S.C. Section 230 (emphasis added).

35. *Id.*

36. When the United States ceded control over the Internet's infrastructure to ICANN, one of the most important functions it transferred was control over the Domain Name System. ICANN's control over the Domain Name System, in turn, encompasses the ability to enact policies regulating the acquisition and maintenance of domain names and hence the acquisition and maintenance of websites. Accordingly, such control over the Domain Name System translates into control over the ability to express oneself via a website, one of the most powerful vehicles for expression available today. ICANN's control over the Domain Name System also encompasses the power to establish policies for resolving disputes between intellectual property owners and domain name holders in ways that affect speech on the Internet. See generally Dawn C. Nunziato, Freedom of Expression, Democratic Norms, and Internet Governance, 52 *Emory L. J.* 187 (2003).

37. See *Center for Democracy and Technology v. Pappert*, 337 F. Supp. 2d 606 (E.D. Pa. 2004) (state law requiring ISPs to block access to websites that allegedly host child pornography violates the First Amendment because complying ISPs had been forced to block thousands of legal sites that shared domain names or IP addresses with those identified by the Pennsylvania attorney general as containing child pornography.)

38. See Press Release, Office of the New York State Attorney General Andrew M. Cuomo, Attorney General Cuomo Announces Unprecedented Deal with Nation's Largest Internet Service Providers to Block Major Sources of Child Pornography, June 10, 2008.

39. State action theorists such as Charles Black, Frank Goodman, and Louis Henkin advocate such a balancing of these competing claims in interpreting the state action doctrine, as discussed in Chapter 2.

40. See Chapter 6 for a discussion of facilities- versus nonfacilities-based ISPs.

41. 521 U.S. 844 (1997).

42. The Supreme Court has recognized that mailers do not have a constitutional right to continue to communicate with individuals who have made clear that they no longer wish to receive such communications. See *Rowan v. U.S. Post Office Dept.*, 397 U.S. 728, 736–37 (1970) (holding that the First Amendment did not forbid federal legislation that allowed addressees to remove themselves from mailing lists and stop all future mailings, and stating that the "mailer's right to communicate must stop at the mailbox of an unreceptive addressee. . . . To hold less would be to license a form of trespass[.]")

43. Indeed, holding conventional ISPs liable for restricting the transmission of such emails might run afoul of Section 230(c) of the CDA, discussed in Chapter 5, which arguably insulates ISPs from liability for exercising such editorial functions.

44. In the actual case, Intel was technically unable to prevent Hamidi from sending email to its employees via their Intel email addresses, and went to court seeking an injunction—an exercise of the state court's power to protect what Intel claimed were its rights to exclude with respect to its private property. The lower court agreed with Intel, and granted the injunction Intel sought, prohibiting Hamidi from sending further email to Intel employees. On appeal, the California Supreme Court rejected Intel's trespass to chattels claim, and suggested that Intel was a state actor. In so doing, it looked to the fact that Intel had invoked the state's power in enforcing its right to exclude, and found that, under the (much-criticized) state action analysis set forth in *Shelley v. Kraemer*, Intel should be considered a state actor charged with First Amendment obligations. Disagreeing with the characterization of this case as involving only "a private entity seeking to enforce private trespass rights," the California Supreme Court found that

> The injunction here was issued by a state court. While a private refusal to transmit another's electronic speech generally does not implicate the First Amendment, because no governmental action is involved . . . , the use of government

power, whether in enforcement of a statute or ordinance or by an award of damages or an injunction in a private lawsuit, is state action that must comply with First Amendment limits. *Intel Corp. v. Hamidi*, 71 P.3d 296, 311 (Cal. 2003).

The court concluded that Hamidi enjoyed the right to send such emails, as against Intel's claims that such emails violated its property rights, and held that to allow Intel's property rights to outweigh Hamidi's right to free expression would raise "concerns about control over the flow of information and views." *Id.* at 310 n. 7.

The court's invocation of the state action analysis in *Shelley* is questionable, as it would seem to convert any private trespass action into state action merely by the protection of a private party's property rights by a state court.

45. See *Pickering v. Board of Education*, 391 U.S. 563 (1968) (State's interests as an employer in regulating the speech of its employees "differ significantly from those it possesses in connection with regulation of the speech of the citizenry in general").

46. See FCC Wireline Competition Bureau, Industry Analysis and Technology Division, High-Speed Services for Internet Access: Status as of December 31, 2006, at Table 3, chart 6 (October 2007).

47. *Cf. Comcast Cablevision of Broward County v. Broward County,* discussed in Chapter 7, in which a cable broadband provider successfully challenged the constitutionality of a county open access ordinance, by claiming a First Amendment interest in controlling the information flowing through (and equipment attached to) its pipes. In that case, the court erroneously credited the broadband provider's arguments, among others, that it did not wish to be associated with objectionable content that might be provided by unaffiliated ISPs.

48. See discussion in Chapter 7 of broadband providers' incentives.

49. See Chapter 1.

50. See description in Chapter 1.

51. As discussed in Chapter 1, in March 2008, NSI suspended the domain name registration and website of Dutch lawmaker Geert Wilders because NSI believed that the website was going to be used to make available a short film critical of Islam. See discussion in Chapter 1.

52. See generally Dawn C. Nunziato, Freedom of Expression, Democratic Norms, and Internet Governance, 52 *Emory L. J.* 187 (2003), for a more detailed discussion of ICANN's power to regulate speech on the Internet.

53. *Cf. McNeil v. VeriSign, Inc.,* 2005 WL 741939 (9th Cir. Apr. 1, 2005) (unpublished opinion holding that ICANN is not a state actor).

54. Michael Froomkin, Wrong Turn in Cyberspace: Using ICANN to Route Around the APA and the Constitution, 50 *Duke L. J.* 17 (2000).

55. In the actual case, the court found that, because McNeil was a Canadian resident, and not a citizen or resident alien of the United States, he enjoyed no First Amendment rights to assert in any case. *McNeil v. Verisign*, 2005 WL 741939 (9th Cir. Apr. 1, 2005). Given that factor, the court had little patience for McNeil's claim that

ICANN was a state actor charged with protecting his First Amendment rights, and concluded that it was not.

56. *Island Online, Inc., v. Network Solutions, Inc.*, F. Supp. 2d 289 (E.D. N.Y. 2000).

57. The requested domain names included "fuckme.com," "fuckyou.com," "cock suckers.com," "fuck.net," "cocksucker.com," and "cunt.com." While these domain names may indeed seem "inappropriate," Island Online alleged that NSI had already consented to register the similarly inappropriate domain names "fucker.com," "fucking .com," "assfuck.com," "fuck.net," and "pricklicker.com." *Id.*

58. See *SearchKing v. Google Technology*, 2003 WL 21464568 (W. D. Okla., 2003).

59. See *Langdon v. Google, Inc.*, 474 F. Supp. 2d 622 (D. Del. 2007) (rejecting Langdon's First Amendment claims); and discussion in Chapter 1.

60. http://adwords.google.com/support/bin/static.py?page=guidelines.cs&topic= 9271&subtopic=9279.

61. See Jon Newton, New Google Censorship Accusation, p2pnet, Feb. 19, 2008, http://www.p2pnet.net/story/15027.

62. For example, although Search King grounded its claim against Google on tortious interference with contractual relations, the court recognized that the case involved "the interrelationship between Internet search engines and Internet advertising, and their collective connection to the First Amendment." See 2003 WL 21464568 at *1.

63. *Google Inc. v. American Blinds & Window Factory, Inc.*, No. 03-5340 JF (RS) (N.D. Cal., Apr. 18, 2007).

64. See John Battelle, How Google and Its Rivals Rewrote the Rules of Business and Transformed Our Culture 184 (2005).

65. Danny Sullivan, Rating Service Faceoff: Search Share Compared, June 2007 to March 2008, Search Engine Land, Apr. 21, 2008, searchengineland.com/080421 -205242.php.

66. See *SearchKing v. Google Technology*, 2003 WL 21464568.

67. See *Kinderstart.com LLC v. Google, Inc.*, No. 06-2057, slip op. at 2 (N.D. Cal. Mar. 16, 2007).

68. See An Explanation of Our Search Results, Google, n.d., http://www.google .com/explanation.html (commenting on the popularity of the anti-Semitic site www .jewwatch.com as a Google search result for the term *Jew*.).

69. Consistent with this analysis, the SearchKing court erred when it concluded that Google's search results constituted its First Amendment–protected opinions. See 2003 WL 21464568 at *4.

Chapter 6

1. 492 U.S. 115 (1989).

2. *National Association of Regulatory Utility Commissioners v. F.C.C.*, 525 F. 2d 630, 641 (D.C. Cir. 1976).

3. 47 U.S.C.A. §202(a).

4. 827 F. 2d 1291 (9th Cir. 1987), cert. denied, 485 U.S. 1029 (1988).

5. See Jerome A. Barron, The Telco, the Common Carrier Model, and the First Amendment—The "Dial-A-Porn" Precedent, 19 *Rutgers Computer & Tech. L. J.* 371 (1993) at 384 nn. 34–36 (describing the unpopularity of Carlin's messages).

6. 827 F. 2d at 1293.

7. *Id.*

8. *Id.* at 1294.

9. 802 F. 2d 1352 (11th Cir. 1986). See also *Network Communications v. Michigan Bell Telephone Co.,* 703 F. Supp. 1267 (E.D. Mich. 1989) (citing with approval circuit court decisions creating exception to common carriage obligations and permitting telephone companies to exercise "business discretion and judgment" to decline to carry legal, sexually themed messages).

10. Reprinted with permission from Jerome A. Barron, The Telco, the Common Carrier Model, and the First Amendment—The "Dial-A-Porn" Precedent, published in 19 *Rutgers Computer & Tech. L. J.* 371, at 386–87, 403.

11. See Barron, *supra* note 5, at 391–97 (criticizing courts' refusal to characterize telcos as state actors).

12. See Amendment of Section 64.702 of the Commission's Rules & Regulations (Second Computer Inquiry), Final Decision, 77 F.C.C. 2d 384, par. 5 (1980) [hereinafter, Computer II].

13. *Id.*   14. *Id.*

15. *Id.*   16. *Id.* at 976–77.

17. *Id.* at 977.

18. In Computer II, the FCC determined that only AT&T and GTE were significant monopolies, and only they had to "form separate subsidiaries" if ordered to offer enhanced services. Other carriers were removed from Computer I restrictions, and could offer basic and enhanced services through the same facilities. See In the Matters of Appropriate Framework for Broadband Access to the Internet Over Wireline Facilities, paragraph 24. The public's increasing dependence on electronic communications and the burgeoning commercial use of the Internet prompted the FCC to further modify its regulation of electronic communications mediums a few short years later. In 1986, the FCC issued its Third Computer Inquiry (Computer III), which has limited relevance for our purposes and was noteworthy primarily for removing the special limitations imposed on AT&T and GTE in Computer II.

19. See *Brand X v. Federal Communications Commission,* 545 U.S. 967 (2005) [hereinafter, Brand X]. Similarly, in *F.C.C. v. Midwest Video Corp.,* 440 U.S. 689, 701 (1979), the Supreme Court held that common carriage obligations could not be imposed on cable television systems because these systems are not engaged in making a "public offering to provide [communications facilities] whereby all members of the public who choose to employ such facilities may communicate or transmit intelligence of their own design and choosing." Because cable television systems could not be regulated

as common carriers, the Court rejected the FCC's attempts to impose public access requirements on these systems.

20. Communications Act of 1934, Section 3(44), as amended and codified at 47 U.S.C.A. Section 153(44) (West 1991).

21. See *Brand X*, 545 U.S. at 975–76.

22. The Act provides that common carriers must furnish service upon reasonable request and must establish reasonable charges, practices, classifications, and regulations regarding service. This section also imposes obligations upon common carriers to interconnect with the facilities and services of other carriers and end users, and sets out the terms and conditions under which incumbent carriers must interconnect with newcomer carriers. *Id.*

23. Pub. L. 104-104, 110 Stat. 56.

24. Letter from Vinton G. Cerf, Senior Vice President, WorldCom, Inc., to The Honorable Donald Evans, Secretary, U.S. Dep't of Commerce, and the Honorable Michael Powell, Chairman, F.C.C., CC Docket Nos. 02-33, 01-338 (May 20, 2002).

25. Remarks of Michael J. Copps, FCC Commissioner, The Beginning of the End of the Internet? Discrimination, Closed Networks, and the Future of Cyberspace, New America Foundation, Washington, D.C., Oct. 9, 2003.

26. See, *e.g.*, Internet World Stats, USA Broadband Market—Cable Modem & DSL—Analysis, Statistics & Forecasts, at http://www.internetworldstats.com/am/us.htm.

27. 17 F.C.C.R. 4798 (2002).

28. *Id.*

29. *Id.*

30. See Remarks of FCC Commissioner Michael Copps, *supra* note 25.

31. Charles Platt, The Future Will Be Fast But Not Free, *Wired,* May 2001, http://www.wired.com/wired/archive/9.05/broadband_pr.html.

32. 216 F. 3d 871 (9th Cir. 2000).

33. *Id.* at 876.

34. *Id.* at 1128–29 (emphasis added) (citations omitted).

35. *Id.* at 1132.

36. Inquiry Concerning High-Speed Access to the Internet Over Cable and Other Facilities, Internet Over Cable Declaratory Ruling, 17 F.C.C.R. 4798 (2002), subsequent history omitted.

37. *Id.*

38. *Id.* See Brand X, at 978 (citations omitted).

39. See Brand X, at 1001 (citations omitted).

40. 345 F. 3d 1120 (9th Cir. 2003), rev'd., 545 U.S. 967 (2005).

41. 216 F. 3d 871 (9th Cir. 2000).

42. *Chevron U.S.A. Inc. v. Natural Resources Defense Council, Inc.,* 467 U.S. 837 (1984) (holding that if a statute is ambiguous and the implementing agency's construction is reasonable, a federal court must accept the agency's construction even if it differs from what the court believes is the best statutory interpretation).

43. 545 U.S. at 996.

44. For transition purposes, the Wireline Broadband Order required that DSL providers continue to provide existing wireline broadband Internet access transmission offerings on a grandfathered basis to unaffiliated ISPs for one year after the date of the order's publication of September 25, 2005. See Wireline Broadband Order, 5-6, at 14858–59.

45. See, e.g., Rob Frieden, Neither Fish Nor Fowl: New Strategies for Selective Regulation of Information Services, 6 *J. Telecomm. & High Tech. L.* 373 (2008).

46. As discussed in Chapter 5, 95 percent of all residential broadband is provided by the cable-telephone duopoly.

47. Remarks of FCC Commissioner Michael J. Copps, *supra* note 25.

48. In Re Appropriate Framework for Broadband Access to the Internet Over Wireline Facilities, Policy Statement, 20 F.C.C.R. 14986 (2005).

49. See, e.g., Tim Wu, The Broadband Debate, A User's Guide, 3 *J. Telecomm. & High Tech. L.* 69, 88–89 (2004) (discussing broadband users' right to attach any non-harmful, legal equipment to their network).

50. In Re Appropriate Framework, supra note 48.

51. *Id.* at n. 15.

52. See Chairman Kevin J. Martin, Comments on Commission Policy Statement, Aug. 5, 2005), available at http://hraunfoss.fcc.gov/edocs_public/attachmatch/DOC-260435A2.pdf. Others have criticized the procedures (or lack thereof) through which these principles were adopted, and have questioned the FCC's statutory authority to adopt such principles. See Moran Yemini, Mandated Network Neutrality and the First Amendment: Lessons from Turner and a New Approach, Social Science Research Network, May 21, 2007, http://ssrn.com/abstract=984271, at 12–13.

53. Am. Online, Inc. & Time Warner, Inc., FTC Dkt. No. C-3989 (Apr. 17, 2001) (consent order), available at http://www.ftc.gov/os/2001/04/aoltwdo.pdf.

54. See AT&T Inc. and BellSouth Corp. Application for Transfer of Control, News Release, WC Docket No. de-74 (Dec. 29, 2006); merger conditions available at http://hraunfoss.fcc.gov/edocs_public/attachmatch/DOC-269275A1.pdf.

55. See SBC Communications, Inc. and AT&T Corp. Applications for Approval of Transfer of Control, Memorandum Opinion and Order, 20 F.C.C.R. 18290 (2005).

56. See Verizon Communications, Inc., and MCI, Inc., Applications for Approval of Transfer of Control, Memorandum Opinion and Order, 20 F.C.C.R. 18433 (2005). Both the SBC-AT&T merger and the Verizon-MCI merger are discussed in greater detail in Christopher Yoo, Net Neutrality and the Economics of Congestion, 94 *Geo. L. J.* 1847 (2006).

57. See Roy Mark, FCC Begins Net Neutrality Inquiry, internet news.com, Mar. 23, 2007, http://www.Internetnews.com/infra/article.php/3667481.

58. In the Matter of Vuze, Inc., Petition to Establish Rules Governing Network Management Practices by Broadband Network Operators, Petition for Rule-Making, November 14, 2007. See also Cheryl Bolen, F.C.C. Opens Inquiries into Concerns About Network Management Policies, *BNA Electronic Commerce & Law,* Jan. 23, 2008.

59. The complaint, filed on November 1, 2007, alleged that Comcast "secretly degrad[ed] innovative protocols used for transporting and sharing large files, like high-quality television programming and movies." See Formal Complaint before the Federal Communications Commission, Nov. 1, 2007, available at http://www .freepress.net/docs/fp_pk_comcast_complaint.pdf. In addition, consumer groups in California have filed a class-action suit against Comcast for fraud and breach of contract under the California Consumer Legal Remedies Act. See *Hart v. Comcast,* No. 07355993 (Cal. Sup. Ct., Nov. 13, 2007) (Alameda Co.); complaint available online at http://blog.wired.com/27bstroke6/files/hart_v_comcast.pdf. The complaint alleges that Comcast promises "unfettered access to all the internet has to offer," and that Comcast's alleged practice of blocking and degrading peer-to-peer file-sharing signals is an "unlawful, unfair, and fraudulent business practice . . . and false and misleading advertising." *Id.* at ¶¶ 2, 3.

60. Ryan Paul, FCC to Investigate Comcast BitTorrent Blocking, Ars Technica, Jan. 8, 2008, http://arstechnica.com/news.ars/post/20080108-fcc-to-investigate-com-cast-bittorrent-blocking.html.

61. See F.C.C. News, Commission Orders Comcast to End Discriminatory Network Management Practices, August 1, 2008.

62. Statement of Commissioner Michael J. Copps, Approving, Re Formal Complaint of Free Press and Public Knowledge Against Comcast Corporation for Secretly Degrading Peer-to-Peer Applications, File No. EB-08-IH-1518; Broadband Industry Practices, Petition of Free Press *et al.* for Declaratory Ruling That Degrading an Internet Application Violates the FCC's Internet Policy Statement and Does Not Meet an Exception for "Reasonable Network Management," WC Docket No. 07-52; Memorandum Opinion and Order, FCC 08-183 (Aug. 1, 2008).

63. See, *e.g.,* Phillip Weiser, The Next Frontier for Net Neutrality, 60 *Admin. L. Rev.* 273 (2008).

64. Maine recently enacted net neutrality legislation. See Me. Rev. Stat. Ann. Tit. 35-A, § 7109 (1988 & Supp. 2008). Although telecommunications regulation has historically been reserved for the federal government, Maine's law purports to provide broad net neutrality regulation. It requires all Internet service providers to "enable any content, application or service made available on the Internet, while prohibiting "block[ing], impair[ing] degrad[ing] or interfer[ing]" with any "lawful content." Maine's law has limited exceptions, which allow ISPs to block spam, prevent abuse of its terms of service, or protect a user's identity or computer security.

65. See Chapter 1.

66. See Markey Amendment, H.R. 5273, 109th Cong. (2006), to the Communications Opportunity, Promotion and Enhancement Act of 2006 ("H. 5252" or "COPE Act"); Internet Freedom and Nondiscrimination Act of 2006 (H. 5417) (prohibiting broadband Internet providers from interfering with users' ability to choose the lawful content, services, and applications they wish to access).

67. See, *e.g.,* the Internet Freedom and Nondiscrimination Act of 2006, H.R. 5417, 109th Cong. (2006).

68. See Internet Freedom Preservation Act, s. 2917, 109th Cong. (2006), Section 12(a).

69. The Communications Opportunity, Promotion and Enhancement (COPE) Act of 2006, H.R. 5252, 109th Cong. (2006).

70. *Id.*

71. See note 57.

72. In the Matter of Broadband Industry Practices, Ex Parte Filing, U.S. Dept. of Justice (2007).

73. See FTC Staff Report, Broadband Connectivity and Competition Policy, June 2007.

74. See Internet Freedom Preservation Act, H.R. 5353, 110th Cong. (2008).

Chapter 7

1. See Chapter 5 for further discussion.

2. See, *e.g.,* Cybertelecom Federal Internet Law & Policy, Net Neutrality Reference, available at http://www.cybertelecom.org/ci/neutralref.htm#pepper.

3. See Christopher Yoo, Network Neutrality and the Economics of Congestion, 94 *Geo. L. J.* 1847 n. 13.

4. See, *e.g., Red Lion Broadcasting v. F.C.C.,* 395 U.S. at 386.

5. See, *e.g.,* J. Gregory Sidak, A Consumer-Welfare Approach to Network Neutrality Regulation of the Internet, 2 *J. Competition L. & Econ.* 349, 399 (2006).

6. See FCC Wireline Competition Bureau, Industry Analysis and Technology Division, High-Speed Services for Internet Access: Status as of December 31, 2006, at Table 3, chart 6 (October 2007).

7. See discussion in Chapter 7.

8. See, *e.g., Comcast Cablevision of Broward County v. Broward County,* 124 F. Supp. 2d 685 (S.D. Fla. 2000) (County's imposition of open access requirements violates cable company's First Amendment rights).

9. *Cf.* Moran Yemini, Mandated Network Neutrality and the First Amendment: Lessons from *Turner* and a New Approach, Social Science Research Network, May 21, 2007, http://ssrn.com/abstract=984271 (arguing that broadband providers' First Amendment editorial and expressive interests should not be readily disregarded).

10. 216 F. 3d 871 (9th Cir. 2000).

11. See discussion of common carriers in Chapter 6.

12. See *id.*

13. *Lamont v. Postmaster General,* 381 U.S. 301 (1965).

14. See discussion of *Red Lion* in Chapter 3.

15. *Cf.* Yemini, *supra* note 9.

16. See Tim Wu & Lawrence Lessig, Letter to the F.C.C., Ex Parte Submission in CS Docket No. 02-52.

17. In *Comcast Cablevision of Broward County v. Broward County,* 124 F. Supp. 2d 685 (S.D. Fla. 2000), for example, the court erred in prioritizing cable broadband

providers' free speech interests and subjecting open access requirements to strict scrutiny. In that case, cable broadband providers claimed that the First Amendment prohibited the local government from imposing open access requirements on them. Broward County, Florida, had passed an open access ordinance requiring cable broadband providers to "provide any requesting Internet Service Provider with access to its Broadband Internet access transport services (unbundled from the provision of content) on rates, terms, and conditions that are at least as favorable as those on which it provides such access to itself, to its affiliates, or to any other person." *Id.* Plaintiffs TCI and Media One, which provided high-speed interactive cable modem services to their cable subscribers and each of which had exclusive arrangements with Internet service providers to provide content, challenged the ordinance's open access requirements on First Amendment grounds, among others. The cable operators further contended that the open access requirements impermissibly infringed on their editorial discretion regarding which content to make available through their choice of Internet service provider to be bundled with their provision of broadband access. TCI had formed a company called Excite@Home to develop content (such as news programming) to be made available via its cable modem services. The cable operators contended that, just as cable operators choose certain television programming to make available to their subscribers, they also choose to make certain Internet content available and to market their chosen Internet content provider as an integral part of their overall programming. The cable operators contended that, just like newspaper editors, they enjoyed a First Amendment right to choose which content to provide and which content to refuse to provide. Broward County, in contrast, defended its open access requirements by contending that the various functions provided by cable broadband operators—the pure transmission-conduit function and the editorial function—were severable, and could be regulated separately.

The court disagreed, and held that cable operators' provision of broadband Internet access was an integrated service, the sum of which was analogous to the editorial service provided by newspapers. Accordingly, the court held that the provision of broadband Internet access by cable operators was subject to similar protection against the state's efforts to intervene in their editorial decisions. It held that the ordinance "intrudes upon the ability of the cable operator to choose the content of the cable system, . . . penalizes expression, and forces the cable operators to alter their content to conform to an agenda they do not set." *Id.* at 11. The court found no justification for reducing the level of scrutiny applicable to the ordinance. Comparing the case to the circumstances of regulation at issue in *Turner,* the court found no special characteristics that would reduce the level of scrutiny applicable to the state intervention in the market under consideration. While in *Turner* the Supreme Court found that cable operators enjoyed "bottleneck" or "gatekeeper" control over the television programming channeled into subscribers' homes, the *Comcast* court found that cable broadband operators exercised no such bottleneck control (resting its finding in part on the fact that most Internet customers access the Internet via telephone, which is subject to common carriage requirements). Finding no reason to subject the ordinance's open access requirements to anything less than strict scrutiny, the court held that the ordinance unconstitutionally infringed the cable broadband providers' free speech rights.

In contrast, in *AT&T v. City of Portland,* 43 F. Supp. 2d 1146 (D. Or. 1999)—which figured prominently in the Ninth Circuit's *Brand X* decision—the court correctly concluded that the open access provisions imposed on AT&T did not violate its First Amendment rights. The open access provisions imposed by the City of Portland required AT&T to allow unaffiliated ISPs to connect their equipment directly to AT&T's cable modem platform and to bypass AT&T's proprietary cable ISP@Home. In rejecting AT&T's First Amendment argument, the court drew an analogy to the *Pruneyard* case, discussed earlier, in which the Supreme Court held that a state's regulation of shopping centers requiring them to provide open access to members of the public for free speech purposes did not violate the center's First Amendment rights. Because the center was "open to the public," the opinions and views expressed by members of the public "[would] not likely be identified as those of the [shopping center] owner." *Pruneyard Shopping Center v. Robins,* 447 U.S. 74, 87 (1980). Similarly, the district court held, any views expressed by unaffiliated ISPs would not likely be identified with AT&T, so the open access requirement did not violate AT&T's First Amendment rights. 43 F. Supp. 2d at 1154.

18. See discussion in Chapter 5 of the Supreme Court's rejection of shopping malls' First Amendment arguments in *Pruneyard.*

19. See Wu & Lessig, *supra* note 16.

20. See *Turner Broadcasting System, Inc., v. F.C.C.,* 520 U.S. at 227 [hereinafter *Turner II*] (Breyer, J., concurring) (quoting *Whitney v. California,* 274 U.S. 357, 375–76 (1927) (concurring opinion).

21. Ithiel de Sola Pool, Technologies of Freedom 106 (1983).

22. *Turner Broadcasting System, Inc. v. F.C.C.,* 512 U.S., [hereinafter, *Turner I*], at 655.

23. *Id.* at 192.

24. *Id.*

25. See Christopher S. Yoo, Beyond Net Neutrality, 19 *Harv. J. L. & Tech.* 1, 20–25 (2005).

26. See *Schneider v. State,* 308 U.S. 147 (1939).

27. See discussion of *Turner* in Chapter 3.

28. *Marsh v. Alabama,* 326 U.S. 501, 509 (1946).

29. See, *e.g.,* Bruce M. Owen & Gregory L. Rosston, Local Broadband Access: Primum Non Nocere or Primum Processi? A Property Right Approach (Stanford Law and Economics Olin Working Paper No. 263), Social Science Research Network, Nov. 10, 2003, http://ssrn.com/abstract=431620.

30. See, *e.g.,* Joseph Farrell & Philip J. Weiser, Modularity, Vertical Integration, and Open Access Policies: Toward a Convergence of Antitrust and Regulation in the Internet Age, 17 *Harv. J. L. & Tech.* 85, 104 (2003) (claiming that "the platform monopolist has an incentive to be a good steward of the applications sector of the platform"); James B. Speta, Handicapping the Race for the Last Mile? A Critique of Open Access

Rules for Broadband Platforms, 17 *Yale J. on Reg.* 39 (2000) (claiming that broadband operators have an incentive to maximize the value of their product to users and therefore will provide broad, unrestricted access to content and applications); Tim Wu & Christopher S. Yoo, Keeping the Internet Neutral? Tim Wu and Christopher Yoo Debate, 59 *Fed. Comm. L. J.* 575 (2007) [hereinafter Wu v. Yoo], at 580 (in which Christopher Yoo states that "[o]ne of the central insights of competition policy is that network owners have powerful incentives to maximize the value of applications and content delivered through their networks").

31. See Chapter 1.

32. Douglas Lichtman, for example, claims that "Internet subscribers can discipline service providers that disable content needlessly . . . by changing providers." Douglas Lichtman, How the Law Responds to Self-Help 56-57 (University of Chicago Law and Economics Olin Working Paper No. 232,Social Science Research Network, May 9, 2004, http://ssrn.com/abstract=629287.

33. See Chapter 1.

34. See discussion in Chapters 1 and 6.

35. See, *e.g.,* Lawrence Lessig, *The Future of Ideas* (2001), at 159–60 (setting forth reasons to be skeptical of a market solution to the problem of broadband censorship, including the fact that users will likely attribute ISPs' acts of degradation or blocking to network congestion generally: "[C]ustomers don't notice that they are living within a closed system. If a travel site comes up slowly because it is not a favored site, the user is likely to consider this as congestion.").

36. Reprinted with permission from Seth F. Kreimer, Censorship by Proxy: The First Amendment, Internet Intermediaries, and the Problem of the Weakest Link, 155 *U. Pa. L. Rev.* (2006), at 34–36.

37. See FCC Wireline Competition Bureau, Industry Analysis and Technology Division, High-Speed Services for Internet Access: Status as of December 31, 2006, at Table 3, chart 6 (Oct. 2007).

38. Further, those who access the Internet at their places of employment enjoy little or no control over the ISP through which they access the Internet in any case. See Paul Harwood & Lee Rainie, Pew Internet & Am. Life Project, People Who Use the Internet Away from Home and Work 2 (Mar. 2004), http://www.pewinternet.org/pdfs/PIP_Other_Places.pdf. (40 percent of those connecting to the Internet on a typical day log on from work).

39. Jerome Saltzer, "Open Access" Is Just the Tip of the Iceberg, Oct. 22, 1999, http://web.mit.edu/Saltzer/www/publications/openaccess.html, quoted in Lessig, *supra* note 35, at 157 and 307, n. 20.

40. Wu v. Yoo, *supra* note 30, at 577–78. Moreover, as Tim Wu points out, discrimination by broadband providers, like discrimination by employers, may not always be rational. Tim Wu, Net Neutrality, Broadband Discrimination, 2 *J. Telecomm. & High Tech. L.* 141, 155 (2003) (noting that "broadband providers may simply disfavor uses of their network for irrational reasons").

41. See Chapter 1.

42. *Cf. Lamont v. Postmaster General,* 381 U.S. 301, 307 (1965) (holding that the U.S. Postal Service had an obligation to deliver all constitutionally protected content and finding unconstitutional a requirement that willing recipients of Communist literature notify the Post Office that they wish to continue to receive such literature); *Bolger v. Youngs Drug Products Corp.,* 463 U.S. 60, 72 (1983) (government may not act on behalf of all addressees by generally prohibiting mailing of materials related to contraception, where those recipients who may be offended can simply ignore and discard the materials).

43. See, *e.g.,* John Windhausen Jr., Good Fences Make Bad Broadband: Preserving an Open Internet Through Net Neutrality, A Public Knowledge White Paper (Feb. 6, 2006).

44. See, *e.g.,* Wu v. Yoo, *supra* note 30 (in which Christopher Yoo claims that "[t]here would be little danger in allowing one of [three available broadband providers] to experiment with exclusivity arrangements" with a search engine, such as Google, for example).

45. See, *e.g.,* Wu v. Yoo, *supra* note 30, at 582.

46. Wu v. Yoo, *supra* note 30, in which Christopher Yoo argues that antitrust law's rule of reason should apply to evaluate whether such "net diversity" approaches undertaken by broadband providers harm competition.

47. Wu v. Yoo, *supra* note 30, at 575.

48. *Cf.* Tim Wu, Network Neutrality, Broadband Discrimination, 2 *J. on Telecomm. and High Tech. Law* 144, (discussing good and bad types of discrimination by broadband providers and outlining proposed forbidden and permissible grounds for discrimination in broadband usage restrictions).

49. Statement of Commissioner Michael J. Copps, Approving, Re: Formal Complaint of Free Press and Public Knowledge Against Comcast Corporation for Secretly Degrading Peer-to-Peer Applications, File No. EB-08-IH-1518; Broadband Industry Practices, Petition of Free Press *et al.* for Declaratory Ruling That Degrading an Internet Application Violates the FCC's Internet Policy Statement and Does Not Meet an Exception for "Reasonable Network Management," WC Docket No. 07-52; Memorandum Opinion and Order, FCC 08-183 (Aug. 1, 2008).

50. See FTC Staff Report, Broadband Connectivity Competition Policy, June 2007, at 88.

51. By employing packet marking, "preferential treatment can be given to latency-sensitive applications during periods of increased network congestion," and "[p]acket marking based on application classification . . . enables routers upstream or downstream . . . to prioritize traffic based on individual application requirements and address congestion at relevant network points." See Cisco Systems, Cisco Service Control: A Guide to Sustained Broadband Profitability 4-5 (2005), available at http://www.democraticmedia.org/files/CiscoBroadbandProfit.pdf, quoted in FTC Staff Report, at 89 n. 410.

52. See discussion of Madison River incident in Chapter 1.

53. *Cf.* Farrell & Weiser, *supra* note 30.

54. See, *e.g.,* discussion of censorship of AfterDowningStreet's messages in Chapter 1.

55. Opponents of regulation also criticize regulation prohibiting prioritization on the grounds that such regulations could prohibit providers from granting different tiers of service to their *subscribers*—greater access speeds and bandwidth for heavy users willing to pay more, reduced access speeds and bandwidth for less demanding users at a reduced rate. A carefully crafted regulation that prohibited discriminatory prioritization could nevertheless allow providers to offer *end users* different packages of services. Subscribers who are proportionately greater bandwidth consumers and who are interested in greater bandwidth consumption and the fastest access could be charged higher rates than those who are happy with average access speeds. Broadband operators that are concerned about high bandwidth consumption from online gaming or video use, for example, should be prohibited from undertaking measures to block or degrade such gaming or video traffic but should be permitted to address their network management needs by offering interested end-users the opportunity to purchase the requisite amount of bandwidth to optimize such uses. See, *e.g.,* Tim Wu, Network Neutrality, *supra* note 48, at 168–69.

56. See Chapter 5.

57. See *Kinderstart.com LLC v. Google, Inc.,* No. 06-2057, slip op. at 2 (N.D. Cal. Mar. 16, 2007.)

58. See An Explanation of Our Search Results, Google, n.d., http://www.google.com/explanation.html (commenting on the popularity of the anti-Semitic site www.jewwatch.com as a Google search result for the term *Jew.*).

59. Frank Pasquale, Rankings, Reductionism, and Responsibility, 54 *Cleve. St. L. Rev.* 115 (2006).

60. 512 U.S. at 663–64.

61. *Turner I,* supra note 22, at 663–64.

62. See http://adwords.google.com/support/bin/static.py?page=guidelines.cs&topic=9271&subtopic=9279.

63. See Chapter 1.

64. *Red Lion,* 395 U.S. at 390.

65. *C.B.S. v. F.C.C.,* 453 U.S. at 396.

66. *Id.* at 397.

Conclusion

1. Remarks of Michael J. Copps, FCC Commissioner, "The Beginning of the End of the Internet? Discrimination, Closed Networks, and the Future of Cyberspace," New America Foundation, Washington, D.C., Oct. 9, 2003.

2. 520 U.S. at 226–27 (Breyer, J., concurring).

3. *Schneider v. State,* 308 U.S. at 163.

4. 201 F. Supp. 2d at 410.

5. 929 F. Supp. at 844.

Index

Inner City Press, 13

Intel v. Hamidi, 94, 102–3. *See also* State action doctrine: in cyberspace

International Corporation for Assigned Names and Numbers (ICANN), 99, 100, 114, 155, censorship, 105–10. See also State action doctrine: in cyberspace

International Society for Krishna Consciousness (ISKCON) v. Lee, 73–75. *See also* Public forum doctrine

Internet: content discrimination, 21–23; data transmission fundamentals, 19–21; generally, 19–21. *See also* Censorship

Kennedy, Justice Anthony, 64, 71, 74–75, 76, 84

Kreimer, Seth, 6, 143

Langdon, Christopher, 16, 110

Lebron v. National Railroad Passenger Corp., 49. *See also* State action doctrine

Lessig, Lawrence, 22

Lloyd v. Tanner, 88–90, 93, 95, 101. *See also* State action doctrine

Madison River Communications: Voice over IP censorship, 9

Marsh v. Alabama, 36–39, 48–54, 88, 95–96, 141. *See also* State action doctrine

McNeil v. Verisign, 108. *See also* ICANN: censorship

Meiklejohn, Alexander, 30. *See also* First Amendment: affirmative conception

Miami Herald v. Tornillo, 62, 138–39

Mill, John Stuart, 25. *See also* First Amendment: negative conception

Milton, John, 25. *See also* First Amendment: negative conception

Must carry obligations, 60–65. *See also* Cable Television Consumer Protection and Competition Act of 1992

MySpace, 10

NARAL Pro-Choice America, 8, 131, 144

National Do Not Call Registry, 144

National Science Foundation (NSF), 20, 99, 106

National Technical Systems v. Schoneman, 86. *See also* Public forum doctrine

Network Neutrality: bills introduced, 131–33; proposed regulation, 136–49. *See also* Federal Communications Commission: Broadband Policy Statement; Broadband Service Providers: regulation of

Network Solutions, Inc.: domain name censorship, 8. *See also* ICANN: censorship

New Media Journal, 13

Nickolas v. Fletcher, 83. *See also* Public forum doctrine

O'Neill, Onora 38

Packet switching, 19

Pasquale, Frank, 150

Perr, John, 15–16

Posner, Richard, 46

Pruneyard Shopping Center v. Robins, 93–97. *See also* State action doctrine

Public forum doctrine, contraction in cyberspace, 77–87; contraction in real space, 72–77; generally, 42–48; state responses, 85–86; restoring values of, 84–87. *See also* Children's Internet Protection Act; *American Library Association v. United States*

Red Lion Broadcasting v. F.C.C., 56–61, 138, 141. *See also* Fairness doctrine

Made in the USA
Middletown, DE
18 January 2018